Drawn to Landscape

Kirbild, 1934. From the Collection of F. Douglas Adams and used by permission.

Drawn to Landscape

The Pioneering Work of J. B. Jackson

Edited by Janet Mendelsohn and Chris Wilson

Drawings, Watercolors, and Photographs
by J. B. Jackson

with contributions from
Miguel Gandert,
F. Douglas Adams, Bob Calo,
Timothy Davis, Peter Goin,
Paul Groth, Helen Lefkowitz Horowitz,
and Paul F. Starrs

George F. Thompson Publishing
in association with
the University of New Mexico,
Hubbard Foundation,
Foundation for Landscape Studies,
and Albuquerque Community Foundation

J. Wood

~~Hho Max.~~

Personal History of David
Copperfield

The Monsoon
_____

This book is dedicated to

Marc Levitt,
for love and support through the years.

Joanne Hauser Wilson and
the memory of Martin Wilson,
for starting me on the path of history.

The memory of John B. Jackson,
for his friendship and encouragement.

Whenever we go, whatever the nature of our work,
we adorn the face of the earth with a living design
which changes and is eventually replaced by that of
a future generation. How can one tire of looking
at this variety, or of marveling at the forces within
man and nature that brought it about? . . . A rich
and beautiful book is always open before us.
We have but to learn to read it.

—J. B. JACKSON,
FROM THE INAUGURAL ISSUE OF
LANDSCAPE (SPRING 1951)

Contents

Near San Isidro, Aug 22, 220

Introduction

Landscape Legacy

CHRIS WILSON
AND JANET MENDELSOHN

The commonplace aspects of the world could teach us
a great deal not only about American history and society
but about ourselves. It is a matter of learning how to see.

—JOHN BRINCKERHOFF JACKSON (1984) [1]

We only see what we look at. . . . The way we see things
is affected by what we know or what we believe. . . .
To look is an act of choice.

—JOHN BERGER (1972) [2]

This book and the DVD that accompanies the limited hardcover edition highlight the work of John Brinckerhoff (J. B.) Jackson (1909–1996), historian of the American cultural landscape. J. B. Jackson re-defined *landscape* not as scenery but as the record of human interactions with nature. He came to see this landscape as an invaluable historical document, created largely by ordinary people going about their day-to-day lives.

Jackson often said that his goal was to teach people *how to see*. But the choices he made about *what to look at* set him apart and often placed him in opposition to conventional wisdom. Jackson made the choice to look at things and spaces where he had no business, yet he made them his business, and then it was his purpose to teach, entice, and provoke the rest of us into understanding the history and meaning of our surroundings. Jackson began this effort during the early 1950s when, without professional credentials or a university affiliation, he founded *Landscape*, a magazine he edited, self-published, and mailed to a list he had compiled of graduate schools and design professionals. Both the tone and the substance of *Landscape* caught people's attention. It wasn't a scholarly journal; it was aimed at general readers. It was fresh and insightful, literate and humorous. And it took as its subject ordinary places, the kind of places most people drive through to get to some place else.

OPPOSITE:
Near San Isidro, New Mexico, August 22, 1990. From the J. B. Jackson Pictorial Materials Collection, Center for Southwest Research and the School of Architecture and Planning, University of New Mexico, Albuquerque, and used by permission.

The things Jackson chose to look at were so taken-for-granted that they were often invisible to Americans or, if noticed, vilified as nuisances and public eyesores. During the 1950s and 60s, Jackson wrote with interest and enthusiasm about billboards, strip malls, and parking lots—the new roadside architecture created by the automobile. This put him at odds with professional landscape architects and regional planners who were concerned about urban sprawl and critical of what they saw as the unregulated hodgepodge of the roadside strip. These designers pointed to Europe's planned, orderly, and contained spaces as models for what America should emulate. But Jackson celebrated the culture of the automobile. He saw the road as an unregulated space shared by all Americans. For Jackson, the road was evidence of American vitality, openness, and equality of opportunity.

If the first task Jackson set for himself was to get people to look at the entire everyday landscape, later, during the 1970s and 80s, he shifted his emphasis and increasingly drew attention to what he saw as a more stratified America. In particular, he drew a distinction between *establishment* landscapes that are often designed to keep people out and *vernacular* spaces—unregulated, egalitarian, and often improvised and temporary. He wrote about the day-to-day struggles of the poor and working class. When he looked at a front yard with three or four rusted cars up on cement blocks, he saw not the eyesores that a civic reformer might but rather how they were used as spare parts to keep the family car running. He delivered lectures to students of architecture in defense of mobile homes and trailer parks, arguing that they provided inexpensive housing complete with modern utilities and conveniences to people who might otherwise be living in rundown places they could not afford to maintain. Increasingly, he tried to engage our sense of fairness and to expand our awareness of and concern for one another. His later work celebrated community, compassion, and respect for ordinary human struggle. When his utilitarian perspective put him at odds with the people he called "beautificationists," that was just fine with Jackson. He loved a good tussle.

With the exception of an acclaimed novel, *Saints in Summertime* (1938), and a well-regarded book of non-fiction, *American Space: The Centennial Years, 1865–1876* (1972), Jackson wrote essays.[3] The short form seemed to suit him. Essays allowed him to suggest the deep meanings of a topic without exhausting it, and then he could leave the details and nuances to scholars and move on to another subject. The essay form also accommodated, what Paul Groth calls, Jackson's "very flexible sense of order."[4] Any readers could open up a collection of Jackson's essays and, like a sequence of photographs, start anywhere. Each one was its own trip—its purpose being gained on the journey, not at the destination.

In this respect, the DVD that accompanies the limited hardcover edition of this book (and is available separately) is a fitting way not only to present J. B. Jackson to a new generation of readers, but also a terrific introduction to the concept of the cultural landscape to a new generation of students and teachers. The DVD (Appendix A) includes the two original documentaries made, respectively, by Bob Calo (1989) and Janet Mendelsohn and Claire Marino (1988), about Jackson late in his life; a new segment of interviews with six esteemed geographers, historians, writers, and photographers about how they discovered and were influenced by Jackson's ideas, about his impact on their field, and his continuing relevance today; and portfolios of Jackson's drawings, watercolors, and teaching slides that complement Portfolios A and C in this book. The DVD's Menu allows one to choose where to start and skip around. Like Jackson's essays, the DVD is a collection of different ways to spend time with the man, with each chapter providing a glimpse of a different aspect of his method, his preoccupations, and his legacy.

The seven essays in this volume, likewise, offer multiple perspectives on Jackson's life and ideas while also outlining the direction of contemporary landscape studies. Historian Chris Wilson's elegiac reminiscence (Chapter 1), written soon after Jackson's death and revised here, provides an overview of Jackson's life and career. Architect F. Douglas Adams (Chapter 2 and Portfolio A) leavens his discussion of Jackson's drawings and watercolors with anecdotes from the annual drawing road trips the two took together. Geographer Paul F. Starrs and photographer Peter Goin (Chapter 3 and Portfolio B) survey the history of *Landscape* magazine, emphasizing Jackson's role as the founding editor and publisher from 1951 to 1968. Jackson's subsequent turn to teaching at Harvard University during the fall semester and at the University of California, Berkeley during the spring semester is the focus of geographer and architectural historian Paul Groth's discussion (Chapter 4 and Portfolio C), in particular what his system for organizing his collection of teaching slides suggests about his conceptual landscape categories. Historian Helen Lefkowitz Horowitz (Chapter 5) uses a comparison of the Mendelsohn and Kalo films as a background to her own interactions with Jackson as the editor of the last collection of his essays, published posthumously as *Landscape in Sight: Looking at America* (1997).[5] Janet Mendelsohn's conversation with Bob Calo (Chapter 6 and the DVD), each of whom made seminal documentaries, respectively in 1988 and 1989, about Jackson late in his career, suggests something of Jackson's changing personas. And historian Timothy Davis's erudite survey of landscape studies (Chapter 7) encompasses not only Jackson's work and other classics in the field, but also the post-Jackson scholarship, artistry, and activity that demonstrate the ongoing vitality of the original concept of cultural landscape studies in a dizzying range of disciplines: American Studies, Architecture, Art History, Cultural and Human Geography, Environmental History, Gender and Sexuality, Historic Preservation, Landscape Architecture, Photography, Popular Landscape Interpretation, Race and Ethnicity, Sense of Place Epistemology, and Vernacular Architecture Studies, among others.

Davis helps us address the often-asked question, "How do we gauge the significance of Jackson's contribution?" Beyond an immense body of scholarship, we can point to changes in the ways that architects, planners, and landscape architects think about the spaces they design, in how historians, geographers, and anthropologists study physical settings of human interactions, and in how artists and writers interpret the everyday landscape. Furthermore, Jackson's work has helped convince architects to consider the everyday along with aesthetics in their designs. In urban planning, there is new interest in creating spaces that adapt to people's needs, spaces that celebrate the human presence and welcome improvised uses. In academia, Jackson's notions of the cultural landscape and of the vernacular have become commonplace in departments of American studies, anthropology, art, geography, history, and regional studies and in schools of architecture, landscape architecture, and planning. His work has helped expand the notion of what constitutes a valid *text* for study. And his methods have attracted interest in direct observation of the entire built environment and in the use of nontraditional sources such as oral histories, maps, aerial photographs, and the sort of informal yet informed field interview at which he excelled.

Though Jackson always insisted that he was an outsider, in time he fostered a community of like-minded design professionals, geographers, historians, artists, and writers who went on to import his ideas into their own fields. In the years since his death in 1996, many of these scholars and practitioners have written about Jackson's legacy, his life, and his method.[6] Recalling Jackson, those who knew him well talk about his kaleidoscopic personality and the ways he remained elusive, revealing different parts of himself to different people. He was a man of many personas: Writer (under his own name and multiple pseudonyms), rancher, artist, aristocrat, day laborer, teacher, devout Christian, outsider, good neighbor, and generous benefactor. He was unforgettable.

In this book and in the DVD, we offer our own kaleidoscope of archival evidence, impressions, interpretations, and remembrances. It is our hope that Jackson's vision and legacy will endure for generations to come, as the changing landscape continues to offer insights into who we are as a people.

Cattle ranch in northern New Mexico, 1952. From the Collection of Helen Lefkowitz Horowitz and used by permission.

Drawn to Landscape

Mark Twain remembered, in his youthful memoir, *Life on the Mississippi* (1883), how beautiful his first sunsets were, reflected golden and metallic off the river.[1] But, after he had learned his long, hard lessons at the wheel under veteran riverboat pilots and had himself risen from cub to captain, those sunsets lost their benign glow. In every ripple of the water's surface, in every eddy and swirl, Twain could now read a submerged wreck, a new sandbar that had grown since the last passage, or a hidden log waiting to snag his boat.

The writings and teachings of J. B. Jackson have been like the lessons of an old riverboat pilot for three generations of students of the American landscape—geographers and historians, architects and planners, landscape designers and photographers, journalists and social commentators. Jackson, like Twain, taught us to read things previously unseen below the surface, but, unlike Twain, what Jackson revealed were not signs of danger and dread but, instead, the manifestations of human aspiration and perseverance. Before one encountered Jackson in person or on the page, the everyday world that surrounds us seemed ordinary and unimportant—if we saw it at all. After exposure to Jackson's writings and ideas, every building and road, every fence line and front yard became a conscious sign of human ingenuity and striving. Before Jackson, *landscape* was a genre of painting or a designed garden; after him, *landscape* encompassed the entire range of human interactions with the natural world.

Born to a wealthy American family in Dinard, France, on September 25, 1909, John Brinckerhoff Jackson was educated in private schools in the eastern U.S. and in Europe. His parents divorced when he was four, and all his life he had a close relationship with his mother, who lived modestly and worked as a buyer for Bonwit Teller department store in New York City. He had only slight contact with his wealthy but distant father. His strongest male influence came from his father's brother, his Uncle Percy, a Wall Street lawyer. The young Jackson first came to the West in 1926, when he summered at his uncle's ranch near Wagon Mound, of largely Hispanic Mora County in northeastern New Mexico. There, he learned to ride and rope cattle but also spoke French as required on Sundays.[2] As the treasurer and a fundraiser for the School of Amer-

OPPOSITE:
Fig. 1.1. "J. B. Jackson, cultural geographer, 1983." Photograph by Anne Noggle and used by permission of Martha A. Strawn and the Estate of Anne Noggle. Originally appeared in John Brinckerhoff Jackson, *The Essential Landscape: The New Mexico Photographic Survey*, edited by Steven A. Yates (Albuquerque: University of New Mexico Press, 1985), 50.

ican Research and as the chief legal advisor to Edgar Lee Hewitt, the director of the Museum of New Mexico, both in Santa Fe, Uncle Percy and his teenaged nephew had entre to the inner circles of cultural workers who were defining the Santa Fe Style and remaking the city into a tourist mecca and romantic art colony.[3]

During that first summer in New Mexico, Jackson and his uncle were houseguests of the White sisters, themselves transplants from New York and leading local patrons of the arts. This was the summer the Whites dedicated their new swimming pool with a mock Mayan rite staged by archeologist Sylvanus Morley and lyric poet Witter Bynner, which culminated with the sacrifice of an Indian maiden into the pool. During another summer, Jackson and his uncle visited Morley's Mayan excavation site. At his camp in the Central American jungle, they dined from china and crystal with the Morley family at the high table, while the other archaeologists and staff supped nearby on more modest fare. When he grew bored with this scene, Jackson struck out alone on a journey by tramp steamer along the tropical coast.

Jackson spent much of his childhood at boarding schools. He was sent to Le Rosey, one of the world's most elite and prestigious schools near Rolle, Switzerland, where, being small, he was the target of nasty bullying and where, being nearly the only American, he was intensely lonely. One of his few happy memories, which he later recalled to F. Douglas Adams with amusement, was teaching his younger classmate, the future Persian Prince Aga Khan, to ice skate.[4] After further schooling at the Choate School (now Choate Rosemary Hall) in Wallingford, Connecticut, in 1923 and graduation from Deerfield Academy in Deerfield, Massachusetts, in 1928, he spent his first year of college (1928–1929) at the University of Wisconsin-Madison's Experimental College, then transferred to Harvard College, where he wrote and edited for the *Harvard Advocate*, the undergraduate literary magazine.

After receiving a bachelor's degree in history and literature from Harvard in 1932 and after brief graduate work studying architecture at M.I.T., Jackson studied drawing in Vienna and traveled throughout Europe by motorcycle for two years. A first novel, *Saints in Summertime* (1938), landed him on the cover of *The Saturday Review of Literature*, a premier venue at the time, and he published two articles about Europe in the thrall of fascism before enlisting in the U.S. Army in 1940. The discipline and anonymity of life as an enlisted man at Fort Bliss near El Paso, Texas, satisfied him, but then someone read his personnel file and saw the Harvard degree and fluency in several languages. Made an officer and assigned to intelligence, Jackson scanned Mexican newspapers for information on Partido Acción Nacional (National Action Party or P.A.N.), the right wing political party which was suspected of hidden ties to the Nazis.

While in France during the war, Captain Jackson made daily rounds of the company's intelligence officers under his command. When the time came to assimilate their information and find a place to spend the night, he would direct his driver back to one of the chateaus they had passed that day. For the chateaus' owners, who were members of the landed gentry and suspected of collaboration with the Nazis almost by definition, the presence of this American officer at their door at dusk on the day of liberation was a matter of some apprehension. But, when they heard his cultivated French accent, they visibly relaxed.

As the best wine and food appeared from the cellar, the conversation often turned to common acquaintances they might have from Jackson's boarding school days at Le Rosey. His hosts could often provide useful information about likely conditions on the German side of the front lines. In their libraries, Jackson found thick volumes on regional folklore, vernacular architecture, and agricultural practices, which helped him discern if a German tank might be hidden in a local barn or which of the roads ahead might be well enough drained to carry an army truck at this time of year. Like many other veterans, Jackson looked back on this time as the most electrifying and fulfilling of his life.

After World War II, he tried the life of a cowboy on his uncle's ranch but was thrown from a horse and spent a year in hospital convalescing from his injuries. Then during the spring of 1951, from his home in Santa Fe at the age of forty-one and having seen more of the world than most of us would see in two lifetimes, Jackson founded the small magazine with the simple name that would make him famous: *Landscape*. Here is how he concluded his statement of intentions:

> Whenever we go, whatever the nature of our work, we adorn the face of the earth with a living design which changes and is eventually replaced by that of a future generation. How can one tire of looking at this variety, or of marveling at the forces within man and nature that brought it about?
>
> The city is an essential part of this shifting and growing design, but only a part of it. Beyond the last street light, out where the familiar asphalt ends, a whole country waits to be discovered: villages, farmsteads and highways, half-hidden valleys of irrigated gardens, and wide landscapes reaching to the horizon. A rich and beautiful book is always open before us. We have but to learn to read it.[5]

Writing in longhand with a fountain pen on blank sheets of paper, Jackson would discard sheet after sheet of false starts until he found the right opening and the right tone for a topic—writing passages over and over until he had a polished essay ready for his typist. His voice and his concerns are there from the first: The conversational and confiding manner in his use of the inclusive "we," an ability to perceive the heroic, and nearly biblical quality to be found in our seemingly mundane works—"we adorn the face of the earth with a living design"—and the marvel of discovering such "a rich and beautiful book always open before us."

Although the peak circulation of *Landscape* under Jackson never exceeded 3,000, it was read worldwide by leading figures in numerous fields and by students who would emerge as scholars, writers, and designers in their own right. Articles on vernacular architecture, cultural geography, ecology, historic preservation, landscape and architectural design, urban planning, tourism, and even body language and the anthropology of space (some translated by Jackson from European and Latin American sources) were leavened by an extensive book review section and often spirited exchanges on the ideas surfacing in the journal. The writers Jackson published ranged from his own predecessors to colleagues, friends, and promising students— from Fred Kniffen, Siegfried Giedion, Lewis Mumford, and Carl O. Sauer to Reyner Banham, Grady Clay, Garret Eckbo, and Edward T. Hall, from Herbert Gans, Lawrence Halprin, Kevin Lynch, and Amos Rapoport to Christopher Alexander, David Lowenthal, Denise Scott Brown, and Yi-Fu Tuan.

Jackson's own essays, published at a rate of two or three per year, were equally wide ranging and anything but antiquarian. In one 1956 article, for instance, Jackson cajoled architects and planners to abandon their elitist denigration of the automobile strip and, instead, appreciate and engage its raw commercial vitality. Appearing sixteen years before Venturi, Scott Brown, and Izenor published their classic book, *Learning from Las Vegas* (1972), passages such as this came as something of a revelation:

> Neon lights, floodlights, fluorescent lights, spotlights, moving and changing lights of every strength and color—these constitute one of the most original and potentially creative elements. . . . It would be hard to find a better formula for obliterating the workaday world and substituting that of the holiday than this: nighttime and a garden of moving colored lights. It is perhaps too much to say that the neon light is one of the great artistic innovations of our age, but one wonders what a Gothic or a Baroque architect would have done to exploit its theatrical and illusionist possibilities, its capacity to transform not only a building but its immediate environment. The contemporary architect will have none of it. . . . A prejudice against any taint of commercialism in decoration is so strong in a segment of the public that one of the chief targets of civic reform groups is usually the local display of neon lights. And yet one would have to be blind indeed not to respond to the fantastic beauty of any neon lighted strip after dark.[6]

Jackson opens an essay from the following year, "The Stranger's Path," by admitting that he is "one who is by way of being a professional tourist with a certain painfully acquired knowledge of how to appraise strange cities."[7] He knows the route taken by single, often working-class men throughout nineteenth- and early-twentieth-century American cities. This route generally starts at the train or bus depot and runs away from the fashionable parts of town along a path lined by pawn shops, employment agencies, greasy spoons and taverns, boardinghouses, rescue mis-

Fig. 1.2. The Strip, Signs. (Las Vegas, Nevada), April 1970. 3-G-05. From the J. B. Jackson
Pictorial Materials Collection (Wilson Collection), Center for Southwest Research and the School
of Architecture and Planning, University of New Mexico, Albuquerque, and used by permission.

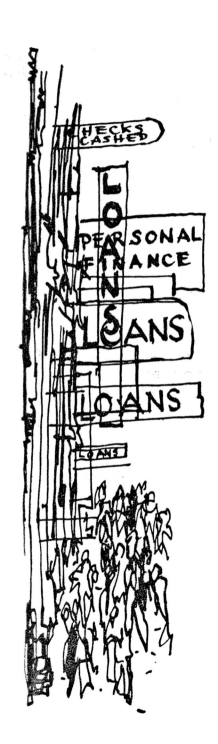

Fig. 1.3. Drawing by J. B. Jackson from his essay, "The Stranger's Path," *Landscape*, Vol. 7, No. 1 (Autumn 1957): 13. Used by permission of Peter Goin and Paul F. Starrs, Black Rock Institute, Reno, Nevada.

sions, cheap hotels, and whorehouses—in short, skid row. "I have derived much pleasure from exploring the Path and learning a few of its landmarks," Jackson confides, "hours in unknown cities that might otherwise have been dull thereby became enjoyable. We are welcomed to the city by a smiling landscape of parking lots, warehouses, pot-holed and weedgrown streets where isolated filling stations and quick lunch counters are scattered among cinders like survivals of a bombing raid."[8] Here is found some of the rough and tumble vitality that staid communities need to survive. But the civic reformers are as uncomfortable with this district as they are with the automobile strip. In fact, they would obliterate it from city after city only a decade later under the benevolent auspices of the Urban Renewal Agency. (To see the remains of "The Stranger's Path" in American cities at the time of Jackson's death in 1996, one went in search of vast parking lots and street corner clumps of homeless men. Today, in 2015, these sites cleared by Urban Renewal are increasingly occupied by the mixed use infill buildings that are signatures of the contemporary reurbanization of our cities.)

The city planner of 1957 instead held up the ideal of "the pedestrian traffic-free center, with frequent references to the Piazza San Marco in Venice." But, insisted Jackson, that great plaza's "animation comes not from the art monuments that surround it; on the contrary, it is enclosed on three sides by a maze of streets and alleys whose function is almost exactly that of the Path." He likens this flow of humanity to "a river, a stream; a powerful, muddy, untidy but immensely fertile stream. . . . The Stranger's Path exists in one form or another in every large community, either (as in most American cities) ignored, or, as in the case of Marseilles and Barcelona and many other cities in the Old World, preserved and cherished. . . . If we seek to dam or bury this ancient river, we will live to regret it."[9]

Jackson lived alone in a flat-roofed adobe villa that he designed and built during the mid-1960s at La Cienega, a time-worn Mexican-American village ten miles south of Santa Fe. After he passed his magazine on to a younger editor, Blair Boyd, of Berkeley, in 1968, he began making a solo journey around the country each year on his motorcycle. A leisurely ride across the South or Midwest brought him to Harvard University each fall to teach, then quickly west to the University of California, Berkeley for the spring term, and finally another exploration south along the Pacific Coast or through the Rockies home for the summer. Observations and insights from his travels—often captured as slides taken for teaching—course through his essays.

After his ankle was crushed in an accident with a car during the early 1980s, Jackson gave up his cycle and his solo tours. The odd jobs he began to take at this time kept him out and in touch with local people. An early riser, he would set off in his small Toyota pickup truck, fitted out with a tool rack, six days a week to clean up and haul trash for a transmission shop, a private post office, and a series of builders and landscapers. But he always returned home by early afternoon to write. It was not uncommon for him to be paying someone in need of a job to keep up

Fig. 1.4. J. B. Jackson's home in La Cienega, New Mexico, late 1960s. Photograph likely by Jackson. From the J. B. Jackson Pictorial Materials Collection (Wilson Collection), Center for Southwest Research and the School of Architecture and Planning, University of New Mexico, Albuquerque, and used by permission.

his grounds while he was away on his own rounds of work. In the final few years of his life, each time he emerged weak and shrunken from an ordeal in the hospital, he would throw himself back into this work the next day, and each time he regained most of his weight and vitality.

A patrician by birth and education, Jackson paradoxically devoted his career to deciphering and exulting in works of popular taste and common people. While he could dismiss a waiter advancing on the table with a curt flick of his hand, he also derived profound personal satisfaction from menial labor, from taking orders, and from doing a good, thorough job. "It is a blessing to be of service," he explained simply.[10]

To pass a late Saturday or Sunday afternoon at his kitchen table during the 1980s and early 1990s meant being interrupted by phone calls from opposite coasts and the visit of a neighbor or two in need of help or advice or just coming to pay their respects. Not infrequently, a young person was there, too, or their visit expected the following week. They had been started on their own cross-country explorations by Jackson's writings and had come now to put a face to the voice who had spoken from the page and to receive some quiet words of encouragement. Next to coffee cups and a plate of crackers and Camembert sat stacks of books—two or three of them recently arrived and inscribed by former students or people Jackson had never met but who had been inspired by his essays and magazine.

A sociable conversationalist and animated raconteur, Jackson nevertheless was a private man who showed different faces to his many friends. To *The New York Times,* to friends in academia, and to those of his generation and class in Santa Fe, he was Brinck. To the succession of Black fundamentalist and hard-scrabble, Texan born-again congregations he joined, he was Brother Jackson. But to his Hispanic neighbors and the village priest, to a young generation of followers, and to those he met on the Stranger's Path, he was simply John.

When I asked him once, "Whatever had happened to some of the first authors to appear in *Landscape?*" (some of whom I suspected were pseudonyms), he was evasive but allowed that Edgar Anderson, the historical ecologist, was the first person to submit work to the magazine. That Anderson only appears in its third year of publication suggests that not only the pieces signed by J. B. Jackson and Ajax, but also those by S. C. Babb, Robert Capot-Rey, A. C. Conway, David Bixby Hawk, and H. G. West—indeed the entire contents of the early issues—were the sole work of the magazine's founding editor and publisher. Each pseudonym had a different set of interests and expertise and, to an extent, a different writing style. After contributions from outside authors began to appear in the magazine, these pseudonyms ceased contributing essays but continued to write book reviews in their areas of expertise.

Whether Jackson was striding the dark, paneled halls of Harvard in his motorcycle jacket or exploring the landscape cross-country on his black BMW R-60, he cut a romantic and mythic figure for architects, designers, and academics burdened by the demands of professional practices and departmental politics. When mutual friends swapped stories about Jackson and compared details they had learned of his life, they found that they sometimes didn't match. Jackson's distaste for the personal and the biographical, it seems to me, led him to practice sly deceptions: No one would know the entire story. Once, when I complimented him on a profile that had run in *The New York Times*, he told me that he had grown so annoyed at the reporter's "impertinent questions" that, when asked his birthday, he gave the wrong date by two days.[11]

Perhaps my reminiscence dwells too long on the personal and not enough on the man's ideas, but Jackson's essays speak eloquently for themselves and remain widely available. Early articles from *Landscape* magazine on Southwestern borderlands are collected in *The Essential Landscape: The New Mexico Photographic Survey* (1985) and those on general American topics in *Landscapes: Selected Writings of J. B. Jackson* (1970). In his one book of nonfiction, *American Space: The Centennial Years, 1865–1876* (1972), he examines the shaping of the continent during the century following Independence, while, in *The Necessity for Ruins: And Other Topics* (1980), he brings together the best pieces written during his years at Harvard and Berkeley. After retiring from teaching in 1978, Jackson wrote *Discovering the Vernacular Landscape* (1984) and *A Sense of Place, a Sense of Time,* which won the 1995 PEN International award for the best collection of essays. A selection of his best essays, along with an excellent biographical essay by historian Helen Lefkowitz Horowitz, can be found in *Landscape in Sight* (1997), which provides the best introduction to his work.[12]

On a last field trip by car into northern Mexico in 1988, Jackson, then in his late seventies, retained the demeanor and habits of a mind acquired nearly a half century earlier as a field intelligence officer during World War II. He already knew historic travel accounts and geographies of the region. After breakfast, he would scan two or three local newspapers. Then, over coffee and an unfiltered Camel cigarette, he would report, "Indians marched into the Ignacio Zaragoza plaza yesterday to protest the construction of a private dam above their *ejido*," or continue bemused, "Señora María Josefa Terazzas entertained her friends with a tea yesterday afternoon at her home on the Avenida Zarco." Familiar with the landscape and communities of the region for more than fifty years, he chose to circle the raw, developing fringes of Cuidad Chihuahua, Cuauhtemoc, and Delicias, where he might talk to people. At neighborhood groceries, plazas, parks, and, above all, construction sites, he had his driver stop.

Dressed in stub-toed motorcycle boots, blue jeans, and a black leather jacket purchased during a stay at the American Academy in Rome—a jacket with stiff, padded shoulders befitting his erect carriage—Jackson strode directly up to the construction workers who were building a new public-housing complex of reinforced concrete and soft-fired brick. After exchanging pleasantries and an easy bit of self-deprecating humor, he launched directly into a courteous but

Fig. 1.5. J. B. Jackson in San Jose, New Mexico, during the shooting of Bob Calo's documentary film, *J. B. Jackson and the Love of Everyday Places* (1989). Photograph by Associate Producer John Lovell, March 1987, and used by permission.

firm interrogation: "Who is paying to have these apartments built?" "Who will live here?" "How do they make their living?" "From this far out, how will they get to work?" "How many square meters?" "How many bedrooms?" "Will there be many grandparents living in?" "Where will the children play?" "Where will the women wash their clothes and the men work on their cars?"

Behind such mundane questions were his efforts to find meaning in contemporary social, political, and economic realities. In his later years, he asked not only how do we read the signs of human efforts on the landscape, but also—in this world increasingly regimented by government and corporations, this world where the old spatial hierarchies have been dissipated by the automobile, television, and globalization—where do we find social vitality and where can we glimpse the vernacular ingenuities of common people?

J. B. Jackson's ashes lie buried beneath a white military headstone in a corner of the San Jose Cemetery (Figs.1.6 and 1.7) at La Cienega, his home for four decades. Set on the dry shoulder of a rocky, red hill—surrounded on two sides by a barbed-wire fence, on one side by a stone retaining wall, and on the fourth side, facing the old adobe chapel, by chainlink and a galvanized farm gate—it is a final resting place most people from his social background would find exceedingly humble. But for those who have learned to read that rich and beautiful book that is always open before us, the hand-crafted headstones and wrought-iron grave cribs, the mobile home peeking around the brow of a nearby hill, the fresh stucco and shiny aluminum-frame windows of the chapel, and the majestic cottonwoods planted a century ago along the irrigation ditch in the valley below are all outward signs of something more, something noble, something even of potential comfort to mortal beings. Jackson may have said it best when he wrote: "The beauty that we see in the vernacular landscape is the image of our common humanity: hard work, stubborn hope and mutual forbearance striving to be love."[13]

Figs. 1.6. and 1.7. J. B. Jackson's headstone (left) in the San Jose Cemetery (right), La Cienega, New Mexico, December 16, 2014. Photographs by George F. Thompson and used by permission.

Chapter 2

J. B. Jackson:
Drawn to Intelligence

F. DOUGLAS ADAMS

During his years of teaching at Harvard University, John Brinckerhoff Jackson (known to me as "Brinck") had two curious distinctions. First, his class on the American landscape, listed in the course catalogue as *VES 127: Studies of the Man-made American Environment since the Civil War* but popularly known as "Gas Stations," had the largest enrollment of any course in the university. Second, he was one of a handful of faculty members who only had an undergraduate degree. He described himself simply as "Mr. Jackson."

In his opening lecture, Jackson was both formal and gracious, a style that seemed slightly incongruous with the commonplace elements of landscape that he promised to discuss. From each student, he required one long paper about landscape, preferably on a topic drawn from direct experience, and each student had a personal interview with him about the assignment. After three years, as the course's enrollment increased from sixty to more than 300 students, this seemingly casual task grew into a massive commitment of Brinck's time. But he did not pull back. He always insisted on meeting personally with every student.

At some level, I believe he thought of himself as the commanding officer of a motley army of inexperienced field investigators. A personal meeting was an opportunity to size up each of his troops as well as to impress on every one of them the essential seriousness of the task. While Jackson's approach to these interviews was, intentionally, conversational and informal, his underlying message was the importance of developing an arsenal of good questions and doing thorough research to prepare for what one might encounter in the field. He wanted his students to pay attention to every detail, for everything about a place can be a possible clue to its understanding and meaning. Speculation should never cease, and initial questions should become stimuli for new ones, prompted by the actual encounter with a site.

I was Brinck's student long before I became his teaching fellow and friend, and I vividly recall my first face-to-face meeting with him more than forty years ago. With his short, powerful physique and his brush-cut military hairstyle, he didn't look like a typical professor. His manner was something different as well. I was struck by his verbal directness, utterly devoid of academic

OPPOSITE:
Fig. 2.1. Some of J. B. Jackson's drawings pinned up in the pantry of his house in La Cienega, New Mexico, ca. 1990. Photograph by F. Douglas Adams and used by permission.

jargon, and by his insistence that he was not an expert but simply a dedicated amateur. He was, he maintained, just like his students, and he invited us to become his companions on the quest to discover patterns in the everyday landscape and to speculate on their meaning. We would, he promised, find much that was surprising; we would even find beauty, though it sounds paradoxical, in the very banality and tedium of endlessly repeated landscape forms. We were to be fellow explorers, making our way, whether from a New England village or across the gridded landscape of the American Heartland, whether traveling on farm roads or highways, driving past strip malls, or grabbing coffee at truck stops. Amidst the social upheavals of the 1960s, "Mr. Jackson," at Harvard, seemed like an adventurous outlaw with a Western spirit, a motorcyclist and wanderer upon the open road. At the same time, he was steeped in and alert to the proprieties and beauties of high culture. He invited us all to bridge apparent divides and to read the past that is always embedded in the contemporary human-made landscape.

Brinck and I gradually moved from being teacher and student to becoming friends. In looking back, I now recognize that our mutual love of drawing played an important role in this transition. In my first interview with him, when I was an undergraduate at Harvard, I commented that it was thrilling to hear someone speak about the architecture of the everyday, which happened to be a subject I liked to draw. We then chatted about my research topic—the history of Mobil gas stations and their Modernist redesign by Eliot Noyes (1910–1977), the Harvard-trained architect and industrial designer. As we wrapped up, he invited me to meet again and added, "Would you bring your sketchbook?" Not long afterward, we had lunch, and I showed him my sketches of H. H. Richardson's magnificent Sever Hall (1878) on the Harvard campus, which he examined with great interest.

Our friendship deepened when I took a year off from graduate school and my wife and I became VISTA volunteers in El Paso, Texas, about 320 interstate miles south of where Brinck lived. He had just designed and built a large, traditional adobe house in La Cienega (Fig. 1.4), ten miles south of Santa Fe, and during our VISTA year we were able to spend occasional weekends as his guest and go off on sketching expeditions with him. For the remainder of his life, I set aside a few days each of the next twenty-eight years to join him on a sketching trip. A few years before his death, he gave me many of the drawings that he had made over the course of his lifetime.

During the period when I traveled with Brinck around the Southwest, he seemed ambivalent about his sketches and treated them with apparent disregard. He often used poor-quality paper, and he was careless with the completed sketches, often losing part of an image as he ripped a sheet from his sketchpad. After returning from a trip, he would pin them near the back door in his kitchen, but sometimes I'd find sketches on the floor (Fig. 2.1). Only in the mid-1980s, after we had by then shared more than ten years of annual motorcycle trips, did I learn that he had kept many of his early drawings, including drawings dating back to his school days and sketches he

Fig. 2.2. J. B. Jackson and Doug Adams outside Brinck's home in La Cienega, ca. 1992. Photograph by F. Douglas Adams and used by permission.

made during World War II. The fact that he kept these pieces surely indicates that he was deeply attached to this visual record of his field observations. When I first saw the collection of Brinck's war sketches in 1982 and heard him describe them, I began to feel that his probing mind and powerful aesthetic had largely been formed when he was an intelligence officer during World War II. And it is in that spirit that I share that military story.

Brinck enlisted in the U.S. Army in 1940. He first joined the New Mexico cavalry but was selected for Officer Candidate School shortly after enlisting. He was trained at Camp Richie in Washington County, Maryland, for six months and then joined the G-12 Intelligence Section in North Africa. His primary service in World War II was as a military intelligence officer, for which two particular aspects of his early life had prepared him well: As a child and adolescent, he had traveled and lived in Europe, mastering French and German, and, later, he was often in the position of being a watchful and respected outsider.

Jackson's independent temperament made him an unlikely success in the military. He was at first as surprised as his superiors by his ability to do intelligence work, but the war experience steadied him, turning a privileged and sometimes indulged individual into a trained instrument for both field observation and judgment. During World War II, he served with the 9th Infantry and saw a great deal of military action. He participated in three amphibious invasions: first in Africa, then in the Italian campaign (where he was badly wounded, almost losing his right arm), and finally as part of the invasion of Normandy, landing at Omaha Beach two days after D-Day. While dangerous, the intelligence work he did must have suited his restless energy.

During the summer of 1944, Brinck was billeted in a Norman estate with a sizeable library devoted to the surrounding bocage country, and it was here where Brinck first discovered and read the work of European geographers about the European landscape in their native languages. Later in the fall of 1944, during the lull before the Battle of the Bulge when Brinck was stationed at Command Post 39 in a country house near Malmedy, Belgium (Fig. A.8), he again studied that bocage landscape in the apparent lull before the assault on the Ardennes Forest.

His research was not abstract but practical, and he came to understand how landscape had been used over time—where roads had been carved, how forests and hedgerows had grown or fields had been harvested, where rivers had been bridged, and, of critical importance, how weather and terrain can impact strategy and impact an outcome.[1] Such things play a crucial role in the strategy of war: A bridge whose span is broken, a road that can be easily blocked, and a building that offers a sniper's post onto a street can decide the fate of a battle. Brinck concluded that war favors those who see the landscape realistically, who discover what is actually there rather than what they hope or expect should be there.

As a field officer in the war, he learned to be attentive to even the slightest details of the human-made landscape and also to glean information about it from even the briefest encounter.

The development of these intellectual powers, while within the discipline of the military influenced his subsequent thinking about the importance of geography. For example, "Landscape as Seen by the Military," an essay in *Discovering the Vernacular Landscape* (1984), he ascribes the Allies' unsuccessful attempt to invade Germany in the fall of 1944 to their limited maps, the failure to prepare properly for a fierce winter for troops billeted outdoors, and a lack of familiarity with the terrain.[2]

Beyond learning about the landscape and making sketches, Brinck's wartime experience taught him a new way to connect with strangers. It was then, I believe, that he discovered that the key to interrogating an enemy soldier is to befriend him, to establish a fraternal bond, to find some element of shared experience or outlook on life that can create empathy and even an emotional kinship. As anyone who studied under or taught with Brinck soon discovered, he had a remarkable gift for honing in on some seemingly casual remark. The answer to one of Jackson's questions—such as "Where are you from?"—might generate the response, "Oh, I remember that town . . . with the war memorial below the square," and this, in turn, might start a conversation about what had changed since Brinck had been there, or what streets the interlocutor used to walk on, or what their condition was, or the reason why this travel had been undertaken. The *landscape* became a starting point for human bonding, and discussion of *landscape* became the first step in creating a sense of community. Brinck's experience as an army interrogator made him recognize that landscape is not just the shape and form of nature, but also an interior psychic and social place that affects an individual's character, demeanor, and outlook.

Brinck once spoke of his interrogations of captured German troops engaged in the Battle of the Bulge, the largest land battle in the history of the U.S. Army. He recalled that many of the prisoners were seventeen-to-twenty-year-old boys, just conscripted from school. It was not too hard to get the youths to talk. Unlike their combat-hardened officers, they were horrified and traumatized by the brutality of battle and the slaughter of those who surrendered. They were each ordered to keep a daily journal, a *Soldbuch*, though their writing was of little intelligence value; it normally described little more than a boy's confusion and fear at a time when he was lost in the dense woods and, ignorant of strategy, did not understand the shape of the battle.

The officers were a marked contrast. Most of them were survivors of the terrible Russian campaign. They had no qualms about killing, and at the Battle of the Bulge they were equipped with sixty of the best tanks in the war, the lethal Tigers that could destroy the less-sophisticated American machinery. Hardened fighters, they were keenly aware of strategy but wouldn't open up under normal techniques. It took ingenuity to get them to talk.

One such German officer, a veteran of both the African and Russian campaigns, was a particularly hard nut to crack. Brinck unfolded an imperfect map of the Ardennes Forest, the best the Allies possessed, but the prisoner remained sullenly silent, unwilling to give anything away.

Fig. 2.3. J. B. Jackson with drawing pad in northern New Mexico,
ca. 1992. Photograph by F. Douglas Adams and used by permission.

Then, rather casually, Brinck spoke of how different the open desert of Africa was from that dense forest. Suddenly, the prisoner became animated, voluble, and fiercely critical of the German High Command. The High Command had planned the route badly, he fumed, missing important road connections and causing the tanks and other vehicles to run out of gasoline only sixty kilometers (37.3 miles) from the Allied fuel depots in the Netherlands, their tactical objective. In his eagerness to convince Brinck that he was a fierce combatant, that his failure was due to others' mistakes, the officer lost his defensiveness and became completely open about discussing strategic information he had guarded fiercely only a moment before.

This strategic view of the landscape entered into Brinck's later sketches. Like a military strategist's diagram, they are quick, energetic, and to the point. They are never edited for picturesque effect; rather, they acknowledge and delight in what is actually there, the very expression (and even intrusions) of human use that some artists might reject as unsightly. Brinck imposed a curious discipline on our drawing sorties. One of his favorite regimens when on the road was to insist that we stop for an allotted time, say fifteen minutes, and draw the view—whatever it might be. This seemed thoroughly arbitrary to me. And, of course, that was the point: It forced us to observe what was there, rather than to fall back on some preconceived notion of what makes a picturesque landscape.

Brinck treated our sketching trips like reconnaissance missions. He immediately made contact with local people by leading with some telling observation—such as "When did the old downtown hotel close? It was excellent! I stopped there perhaps eight years ago."—and off he and his new comrades would go with an extended conversation. Even before hitting the road, he made sure to inform himself, to scan the local newspaper for notices of auctions and other events. He took note of, and sought explanations for, change and transformation—a new building going up along the highway or signs of decay in an old downtown. Finally, Brinck was always gracious. "That pie on the counter looks delicious. Is it homemade?" And he was unfailingly courteous, sometimes offering, "Look me up, if you're ever passing through Santa Fe."

There is no way to know how many artworks Jackson made during his lifetime. He practiced drawing and, to a lesser extent, watercolor from 1931 until his death in 1996 as an aid to his field observations while traveling in the United States, Latin America, Europe, and Africa. Youthful watercolors and travel drawings led to hasty field sketches during World War II. During his years as editor and publisher of *Landscape* magazine from 1951 to 1968, he drew primarily to create illustrations for the magazine (Figs. 1.3, 3.2, 3.5, and 3.6). Later, during his years of intensive teaching at Harvard and UC, Berkeley, in the late 1960s and 1970s, the camera largely replaced the sketch pad, as he took slides for use in the classroom. Following his retirement from teaching, drawing in the field again became a major pleasure, especially on trips to Europe and on the annual sketching road trips in the Southwest with me.

It is likely that the 260 drawings given to me by Brinck represent the majority of the existing artwork. Helen Lefkowitz Horowitz's collection, also given to her by "Mr. Jackson," as she knew him, comprises fifty-five additional drawings. It is interesting to take note of the dates and subject matter of these two collections. There are many sketches from the war years and from 1979 onward. With the exception of the sketches he made during a long trip to Europe in 1957, there are relatively few drawings from 1950 through the mid-1970s. Perhaps Brinck had little time for drawing during these years, since he was fully occupied with *Landscape* magazine until 1968, and then he taught full time at Harvard and Berkeley for more than a decade. Also, as Paul Groth writes (Chapter 4), Jackson built a substantial archive of teaching slides during these teaching years, so perhaps he was occupied more with making photographs of the landscape than with making sketches. Another explanation may be that Brinck, who was so cavalier about his drawings, may simply have lost or destroyed any others.

Of the approximately 315 drawings in the two collections, the largest number were done in Europe, and of those the largest groups are from World War II, from 1957, when he traveled in eastern and western Europe, and from 1983–1984, when he spent a year as a resident scholar at the American Academy in Rome. Another substantial group of drawings are of American landscapes, almost all of which were done in the Southwest, mostly after 1975. This work focuses on natural elements—trees, mountains, and scrubland—but sometimes the drawings contain suggestions of humanmade elements, such as cultivated fields, roads, and small settlements. Jackson also made a practice of drawing examples of highly visible and iconographic structures within the American landscape, such as chapels, courthouses, grain elevators, railroad stations, and occasional residences. Surprisingly, there are few sketches of the subject matter that dominated his teaching and writing: The American vernacular landscape, the highway, and the strip. And, in his American drawings, there are no people.

What to make of this? A possible explanation is that, for Brinck, drawing was playful and largely a private pleasure and not always about field observation. And it appears that he took the most pleasure from the New Mexican desert and the picturesque towns and grand architecture of Europe.

J. B. Jackson was gifted in many ways—as an observer, draftsman, writer, public speaker, teacher, and figure with a very special talent for connecting one-to-one with other human beings. Thus, being drawn to his intelligence has multiple meanings: There are the drawings as a record of Brinck's life in G-12 in World War II, the observational intelligence to study and speculate about the everyday humanmade landscape, and the passion to read in this physical space the markers to the cultural distinctions of its making. The genius and intelligence of his writings also live in his vibrant drawings.

Portfolio A

Drawings and Watercolors
by J. B. Jackson, 1931–1994

FROM THE COLLECTIONS OF
F. DOUGLAS ADAMS,
HELEN LEFKOWITZ HOROWITZ,
AND CHRIS WILSON

Fig. A.1. Dunster House at Harvard
University in Cambridge, Massachusetts,
1931. From the Collection of Helen Lefkowitz
Horiwitz and used by permission.

Chichen-Itzá
1936

Fig. A.2. Mayan ruin at Chichén Itzá, Yucatán, Mexico, 1936. From the Collection of Helen Lefkowitz Horowitz and used by permission.

Dakar

1942

Fig. A.3. Two views of a tree and landscape in Dakar, Senegal, 1942. From
the Collection of F. Douglas Adams
and used by permission.

view from
Chilbolton Ave

Fig. A.4. View from Chilbolton Avenue
in Winchester, England, Winter 1943.
From the Collection of F. Douglas
Adams and used by permission.

Fig. A.5. Residence in Sicily, Italy,
1944. From the Collection of F. Douglas Adams and used by permission.

Fig. A.6. Park in Luxembourg or, possibly, Jardin du Luxembourg in Paris, 1944. From the Collection of F. Douglas Adams and used by permission.

Fig. A.7. Church Saint-Laurent on Place de la Madeleine in Verneuil-sur-Avre, France, June 1944. From the Collection of F. Douglas Adams and used by permission.

Fig. A.8. Command Post 39 with Jeep, near Malmedy, Belgium, before the Battle of the Bulge, Autumn 1944. From the Collection of F. Douglas Adams and used by permission.

Fig. A.9. Field reconnaissance, Höfen
an der Enz, Germany, Autumn 1944.
From the Collection of F. Douglas
Adams and used by permission.

Fig. A.10. Field reconnaissance, Höfen an der Enz, Germany, Autumn 1944. From the Collection of F. Douglas Adams and used by permission.

Fig. A.11. Tank barrier in the
Ardennes Forest near Wallonia,
Belgium, December 1944. From the
Collection of F. Douglas Adams and
used by permission.

Fig. A.12. Ludendorff Bridge over the Rhine River at Remagen, Germany, March 1945. From the Collection of F. Douglas Adams and used by permission.

TOUR D'ALGUE 1945, JKA

Fig. A.13. Tours D'Algue, France,
May 8, 1945. From the Collection
of F. Douglas Adams and used
by permission.

HETTANGE, AUGUST 8

Fig. A.14. Railroad siding in Hettange, France, August 8, 1945. From the Collection of F. Douglas Adams and used by permission.

Fig. A.15. Telephone poles, road,
and railroad in the American Southwest, 1947. From the Collection of
Helen Lefkowitz Horowitz and used
by permission.

Fig. A.16. View of FDR Drive, East River, and New York City, New York, August ca. 1950s. From the Collection of F. Douglas Adams and used by permission.

Fig. A.17. Institut de France along
the Seine River in Paris, 1957. From
the Collection of F. Douglas Adams
and used by permission.

Fig. A.18. View of Pleven and the
Danube River, Bulgaria, 1957. From
the Collection of F. Douglas Adams
and used by permission.

Fig. A.19. Skyscraper in Düsseldorf, Germany, 1957. From the Collection of F. Douglas Adams and used by permission.

Fig. A.20. Railroad compartment in Düsseldorf, Germany, ca. 1984. From the Collection of F. Douglas Adams and used by permission.

Bitonto

Fig. A.21. Town square in
Bitonto, Italy, 1983. From the
Collection of F. Douglas Adams
and used by permission.

Fig. A.22. Urban living in Rome, Italy, 1984. From the Collection of F. Douglas Adams and used by permission.

Fig. A.23. Castel Sant' Angelo (Mausoleum of Hadrian), Lungotevere Castello, Rome, Italy, 1984. From the Collection of F. Douglas Adams and used by permission.

archives, Rome

Fig. A.24. The Archives in Rome, Italy, ca. 1984. From the Collection of Chris Wilson and used by permission.

1975
Pueblo. Colo

Fig. A.25. The Union Depot, Victoria Avenue, and B Street in Pueblo, Colorado, 1975. From the Collection of F. Douglas Adams and used by permission.

HOOPER, COLO
AUG 24 1984

Fig. A.26. False-front facades in
Hooper, Colorado, August 24, 1984.
From the Collection of Helen Lefkow-
itz Horowitz and used by permission.

near Stuttgart, Arkansas
1987

Fig. A.27. Grain elevators near
Stuttgart, Arkansas, "Rice and Duck
Capital of the World," 1987. From the
Collection of F. Douglas Adams and
used by permission.

Fig. A.28. Back porch in Seattle, Washington, 1989. From the Collection of F. Douglas Adams and used by permission.

navaho hogan
1980

Fig. A.29. Navajo hogan in northwestern New Mexico, 1980. From the Collection of Helen Lefkowitz Horowitz and used by permission.

Fig. A.30. Pruned cottonwood trees in the forecourt of J. B. Jackson's house in La Cienega, New Mexico, 1984. From the Collection of F. Douglas Adams and used by permission.

Fig. A.31. Parked car at neighbor's
house in La Cienega, New Mexico,
1965. From the Collection of F. Douglas
Adams and used by permission.

La Cienega
Chapel of San Antonio
1982

Fig. A.32. Chapel of San Antonio
de Cieneguilla in La Cienega,
New Mexico, 1982. From the
Collection of Helen Lefkowitz
Horowitz and used by permission.

Fig. A.33. Landscape along Route
66 in Tucumcari, New Mexico, 1982.
From the Collection of F. Douglas
Adams and used by permission.

OCT. 28, 1994

Fig. A.34. Roadside landscape in northern New Mexico, October 28, 1994. From the Collection of Helen Lefkowitz Horowitz and used by permission.

CANYON DE
CHELLY, NOV 2
1991

JPW

Fig. A.35. Parking lot at Canyon de
Chelly, New Mexico, November 2,
1991. From the Collection of F. Douglas Adams and used by permission.

1993

Fig. A.36. Bridge over Interstate 25 near La Cienega, New Mexico, 1993. From the Collection of Helen Lefkowitz Horowitz and used by permission.

Fig. A.37. Road to West Blue
Mountain in Socorro County, New
Mexico, August 22, 1986. From the
Collection of F. Douglas Adams and
used by permission.

Fig. A.38. Woods near Santa Fe, New Mexico, 1982. From the Collection of F. Douglas Adams and used by permission.

Fig. A.39. Trees at Mesa Verde, Colorado, September 14, 1992. From the Collection of F. Douglas Adams and used by permission.

My criteria for selecting the thirty-nine drawings and watercolors in Portfolio A were completely personal. During the last few years of our travels together, Brinck, after a sketching trip, would often open a folio of his earlier work and tell stories that the drawings evoked for him. The images that appear in Portfolio A and the stories that follow come from those shared moments with Brinck. Indeed, when Brinck told me he had dedicated *Discovering the Vernacular Landscape* to me, he spoke of how his drawings and watercolors brought alive these vibrant visual chronicles of events in his experience of landscape.

Early Drawings (Figs. A.1 and A.2)

The first drawing in Portfolio A (Fig. A.1) depicts Dunster House, one of two new dormitories at Harvard University completed under President Abbott Lowell's "House Plan." The plan called for seven houses (dormitories) to be built near and along the Charles river "to separate upperclassmen from freshmen, who would remain in Harvard Yard."[3] Dunster House was named in honor of Henry Dunster, "who became the first President of Harvard College at the age of thirty-one, immediately after his arrival in the Colony of Massachusetts Bay in 1640."[4] Brink's rendering of this new architectural marvel reflects the building's strength and character. Its impressive tower resembles the Tom Tower of Christ Church in Oxford, England.

The second drawing (Fig. A.2), of a distinguished Mayan ruin at Chichén Itzá in the Yucatán peninsula of Mexico, is drawn in ink with remarkable confidence and skill. Of all the surviving early sketches, this one best prefigures Brinck's later energetic style of drawing. Jackson's mastery of perspective and form are evident in the shading of the curved turret of the temple and its separation from the lower plinth. The subject is, in some sense, conventional. This drawing was made on a trip with his uncle, Percy Jackson.

World War II (Figs. A.3–A.14)

There exist some forty sketches made during World War II. Brinck first showed them to me when he was in his eighties, after one of our yearly sketching trips, which, by then, had become a ritual we had enjoyed for almost twenty-eight years. The care with which he had preserved these wartime drawings, along with the GI helmet he kept in his bedroom, suggest that they were important documentation of both his personal odyssey and the development of his observational skills.

The majority of Brinck's wartime sketches were made in France and Germany, although he also made drawings and sketches in Belgium, England, Italy, Luxembourg, North Africa, and Sicily. The sketches he made as part of his intelligence work taught him to render topography with impressive economy, as seen in his two views of a tree and landscape in Dakar, Senegal (Fig. A.3). There are also many drawings that appear to be made only for himself, such as his watercolor of a residence in Sicily (Fig. A.5) and his drawing of a park in Luxembourg (Fig. A.6). Both are expressive of *peace*, and one can see an emerging style that, at times, is reminiscent of Théodore Rousseau (1812–1867), a preeminent master of the Barbizon School. These drawings depict ordinary scenes with deep appreciation, and they seem to express a profound yearning for some viable order. Perhaps the act of making drawings helped him to see past the savagery of war and maintain his ability to take pleasure in the everyday world.

By the time his sketch of a verdant English landscape (Fig. A.4) was made in the winter of 1943, Brinck had fought in North Africa and in the invasion of Sicily, where he was so badly wounded that his right arm was at risk of amputation. This drawing in Winchester seems both leisurely and calm, loosely rendered in quick, linear strokes with a soft pencil, the space balanced across the whole composition. It reveals Brinck's training in drawing, from his year of post-graduate study architecture at M.I.T. and his continued study of graphic design in Vienna in 1933.

Brinck was scheduled to land at Normandy on the first day of the invasion, but his boat (a British trawler) went astray in the fog as it headed towards the port of Le Havre, France. He arrived at Omaha Beach two days after D-Day. In his quickly-made sketch of a Catholic church in a small town in Houte-Normandie (Fig. A.7), he captures the scale of the building and the depth of the facade in striking light, more evidence of Jackson's technical competence as a draftsman. This sketch was made just after the Allies' breakthrough out of Normandy, which had been a German stronghold and where Brinck's unit had experienced heavy casualties. One can see in this sketch a celebration of survival and the joy of being alive. Perhaps it was this drawing that led me to ask Brinck about his most powerful memory of the invasion. After some consideration he said, "French bread and vichyssoise!"

The view of a gambrel-roofed villa (Fig. A.8) is one of the many command posts where Jackson was quartered during the fall of 1944. The war seemed to be almost won. This villa appears to be in a Belgium town near Malmedy, and the drawing was made before the time of the German counterattack that winter through the Huertgen Forest. In his essay, "Landscape as Seen by the Military," Brinck wrote that his interest in geography—first sparked after D-Day in the Norman bocage country—was again engaged during the winter of 1944 when, in such a command post, he found a popular German book about Frederick the Great: "What impressed me was the description of Frederick as an old man [after a war] . . . traveling about his impoverished and ruined country . . . stopping to talk to villagers and farmers. 'How much do you pay for bread' 'What rent do you pay?' 'What crop are you planting? . . . What he was collecting was intelligence of an almost Classical sort: What men *did* was what mattered…what the countryside provided in the way of food and shelter was what interested him. . . ."[5] Thus, a depiction of a defining moment in the formation of Jackson's vision; how like him to capture both the incidental goose and the Jeep.

Two sketches (Figs. A.9 and A.10) were executed during the period when Brinck served as an intelligence officer for General George S. Patton. These sketches of Höfen are the result of on-the-ground reconnaissance; as in several other contemporaneous intelligence sketches, the letters (B and A in Fig. A.9 and K and L in Fig. A.10) indicate the location of enemy troops. It was Brinck's habit, after a night of interrogating prisoners, to commandeer a Jeep and driver in the early dawn and reconnoiter behind enemy lines to see if he could better understand the terrain and incorporate what he had learned from the interrogation sessions. These drawings reminded him that his drivers were so nervous that they'd give him less than a minute to complete each sketch. "That," he told me, "was a great incentive to develop a precise high-speed technique!"

There are many ghosts hovering behind Brinck's hasty sketch of a tank barrier (Fig. A.11). This three-by-six-inch pencil drawing was made during the Battle of the Bulge, when heavily supplied German tanks made a surprise attack against the inadequately equipped Allied troops. Command communication had broken down, and Jackson's job was to make contact with the troops who were lost in the dense forest without winter clothing. The sketch records a makeshift Allied wooden barrier across a poorly defended roadway.

One drawing from March 1945 (Fig. A.12) depicts the famous Ludendorff Bridge at Remagen, Germany, a huge railroad bridge built across the Rhine River in 1917 as the major German supply route to the Western Front. During World War II, the bridge became the first Allied crossing point on the Rhine River on March 7; and, for five crucial days after the retreating German Army partially destroyed it, it remained a viable crossing point for the Allies. Men and vehicles crossed on wooden boards placed across the railroad tracks before the structure collapsed. There is a story that Colonel William Westmoreland (of Vietnam repute) crossed one night by lying on the hood of his Jeep, directing his driver with hand signals to avoid the shell holes in the temporary surface.

The sketch of Tours D'Algue (Fig. A.13) was made around VE (Victory in Europe) Day, May 8, 1945. I believe it may be one of the first of Jackson's drawings to focus on a vernacular subject—an ordinary street scene—and it is a marvelous record of the everyday. Though the view offers the same kind of direct observation Brinck used in his intelligence sketches, it is clearly less hurried. He seems most interested in the broken forms of the local architecture, apparently at a road intersection, and there is a very crisp rendering that evokes the light of a more southern landscape. The stippling in the drawing defines the stone edges of the buildings and emphasizes the complex geometry of the forms.

The image of a railroad siding in Hettange (Fig. A.14), on the border between France and Luxembourg, may appear innocent, but, for Brinck, it had profound meaning. The war in Europe had ended in May, and the drawing was made on August 8, the day that Brinck learned of Hiroshima and the probable end of World War II in the Pacific. This was the first moment since September 1939 when he might look forward to a world not engaged in war, and, after more than five years of military service, he must have wondered about his future. Now he had time for a moment of reflection, time to make a visual record of the permanence of the simplest things. Perhaps this view simply shows the things immediately before him, but I like to see the landscape elements as treasured essentials: There is the receding line of the railway tracks; the railroad siding with its semaphore light; a slight rise and edge of habitation in the near distance; and an isolated house on a ridge above a gentle field. We feel the solace of the familiar and the everyday, even with foreground intrusion of lamppost and wires. It is a private moment experienced in a public space in which some order is seen to prevail after many years of destruction. One does not see signs of war here.

Post-World War II Years (Figs. A.15 and A.16)

Jackson spoke of his drawing of a railroad, highway, and telephone poles (Fig. A.15) as part of the chronicle of his return to civilian life during 1947, when he drove his army surplus Jeep cross-country, heading "home" for New Mexico to try ranching. He knew the Southwest from his childhood experiences on his Uncle Percy's ranch near Wagon Mound in northern New Mexico, and he was drawn to New Mexico's beautiful desert, its ancient history of native Pueblo and Spanish settlements, its outsider artistic community, and its isolation from mainstream America. It was only after a horse rolled over on him and he suffered a badly broken leg that he decided to abandon ranching. He spent some months writing small highway travel guides, then went on to found *Landscape* magazine during the spring of 1951.

This drawing captures the simplicity and allure of the American rail-and-road corridor before the Interstate Highway System was established in 1956. These early cross-country routes were often identified by distinctive markings on the telephone poles at the road's edge. The straight alignment of the road usually paralleled railroad tracks, but most were poorly paved at the time, so travel was tedious and uncomfortable. It appears that Brinck pulled over to the shoulder and chose an oblique view that captured the roadbed running parallel to the railroad's embankment. The drawing emphasizes the rhythmic, recessional cadence of the telephone poles, road, and train tracks. It is a glimpse of the vastness of space that is uniquely American but not unique in itself. Brinck often spoke of the tediousness of this kind of repetitive space, but he also saw in it a certain admirable order and a governing geometry that he likened to the gridded landscape imposed west of the Appalachian Mountains by Thomas Jefferson and rendered as law in the Northwest Ordinance of 1787.

But Brinck was just as interested in the urban vernacular as he was in the rural vernacular. One of his more intriguing views is of New York City, circa 1950s (Fig. A.16), in which Brinck provides a memorable scene of the FDR Drive and East River, looking south toward the emerging modern skyline of America's largest city. Here Brinck reveals a complete urban mosaic with an emphasis on simplifying the complicated with distinctive lines and scale.

The European Trip of 1957 (Figs. A.17–A.19)

Throughout the 1950s, Brinck devoted most of his time to *Landscape* magazine. For the first few issues, when the magazine focused on the cultural history of the Southwest, he was the magazine's editor, publisher, distributor, illustrator, and sole writer. Later, as the magazine's reputation grew and its scope expanded to include other regions of the U.S. and even the European landscape, it attracted a roster of important writers and scholars. *Landscape* was also able to publish major European geographers, with Jackson serving as the translator of works originally written in French and German.

Brinck took at least one extended vacation from *Landscape* to travel in Europe during 1957, his first visit there since the war. There are some fifteen drawings in the collection that appear to have been made on this trip. Curiously, they are all incorrectly dated 1959; this is probably due to the fact that they were originally undated, and he tried to date them from memory during the early 1990s.[6]

When Jackson made his drawing of the Institut de France (Fig. A.17) and its famous centerpiece, the dome of the Académie Française, he was well aware of the exalted role of the Académie in French culture. When he talked with me about this drawing, he laughed about what he saw as the self-importance of the members of the Académie (known as "immortals"). He liked to imagine them valiantly defending the French language from the insidious corruptions of vernacular slang and the influx of English terms. This view of the Institut, pictured largely in shadow, evokes the French love of order in the building's neo-classic architecture with its centering dome. The repeating vertical lines reiterate its architectural harmony, while the looser rendering of the River Seine and the horizontals of the barges provide a counterpoint.

Looking at this drawing, Brinck recalled that, two days after the liberation of Paris on August 25, 1944, General Patton sent him on a hunt for up-to-date maps of possible routes from France, Belgium, and Luxembourg toward the Rhine. The retreating Germans had removed all records, but Jackson discovered that, during the Nazi occupation, the geographers at the Institut Géographique Nationale (IGN) in France had secretly copied the German maps. Brinck relished the fact that the German command had been outsmarted by the French bureaucrats.

In addition to visiting several western European cities, Brinck spent time in eastern Europe. This was at the height of the Cold War, and he wanted to see what he could of Communist urban planning. There are at least fifteen sketches dating from this trip. Brinck made several ink drawings of the hillside city of Pleven, Bulgaria. The view of the terraced massing of structures overlooking a bend in the Danube River (Fig. A.18) has a marvelous cryptic energy. He also traveled to Germany where, impressed by the success of post-war reconstruction, he drew an admiring sketch of a glass skyscraper in Dusseldorf (Fig. A.19). The lustrous blue of the drawing darkens as a strong vertical line emphasizes the impressive height of the building and marks the shadow it casts on the buildings beyond.

The American Academy in Rome, 1983–1984 (Figs. A.20–A.24)

During the early1980s, Brinck withdrew from active teaching. He claimed he wished to be a recluse, but he was privately thrilled to be invited as a resident scholar to the American Academy in Rome in 1984 and to be pursued for numerous speaking engagements. His writing also flourished during his last decade, and he produced carefully crafted essays, most of which comprised his two final books, *Discovering the Vernacular Landscape* (1984) and *A Sense of Place, a Sense of Time* (1994).[7]

Brinck's rendering of a railroad compartment of a train in Dusseldorf (Fig. A.20) expands a tightly confined actual space into a cozy retreat. He did several sketches of these interiors while he traveled. These drawings have a great spontaneity while still being detailed, and they invite an affection for how we settle into places that we inhabit temporarily, to make them briefly our own. This drawing exults in the generous upholstery of the carriage and the large luggage rack, suggestive of an earlier period of travel and of long journeys with much luggage.

One of the many street scenes that Brinck drew during his year at the Academy includes a town square in the southern Italian town of Bitonto (Fig. A.21), which is empty of people at what appears to be midday in the heat of summer. There is a wonderful stage-set luminosity to the drawing, as the blue sky and shadows vibrate with the yellow walls. A narrow Roman street (Fig. A.22) is captivating in its colors and the profusion of clues to the human presence, especially the houseplants on a roof, the varying angles of the shutters, and the red car just inserting itself down the narrow shaft of the street.

Jackson's use of color changed during his year in Italy, and in many subsequent drawings he continued to use these brilliant, almost garish hues. There is also a sense of ease, the pleasure of being in the moment, in Brinck's drawings from his year at the American Academy. He delighted in a Europe now prosperous and intact, so changed from his childhood and from the devastating war years.

Brinck drew the Castel Sant'Angelo (Fig. A.23) several times during his year in Rome. In this sketch, his use of perspective and shading captures the structure's striking sculptural form. The parked cars and a vendor's umbrella, though roughly drawn, provide a deft suggestion of present use. In addition to its powerful curved form, the structure's complex architectural accretions and changes of use were of great interest to Jackson. Built in CE 123 to house the emperor Hadrian's ashes, it was transformed during the Middle Ages into a military fortress. Reduced in size during 1889–1906 to accommodate new traffic patterns, it is now used as a museum. Brinck often wrote about changing uses of buildings and how those changes reflect economic pressures and cultural shifts. He was fascinated to see banks become restaurants or clothing stores, gas stations become churches, and movie theaters become supermarkets. He was also equally pleased to see buildings where classic form suggests a grandeur befitting a building's contents. Such is the case with Brinck's effective rendering of the Archives in Rome (Fig. A.24).

American Road Trips (Figs. A.25–A.28)

The 1970s and early 1980s were the years when Brinck and I started to travel together by motorcycle on our annual "drawing trips." He loved the sensations of motorcycle travel and even prized its discomfort, since it encouraged frequent stops and serendipitous encounters. During a motorcycle trip in 1975, Brinck and I passed through Pueblo, Colorado, where we stopped at Pueblo's renowned Union Depot train station. Built in 1889, this handsome, Richardsonian-Romanesque structure (Fig. A.25) represents the apotheosis of a period when train travel was grand and luxurious. In its heyday, this station had separate waiting rooms for ladies and gentleman, a first-class restaurant, a laundry service, and even a barbershop. When Brinck and I visited, the building was partly abandoned and in disrepair.

The false-front facades of Hooper, Colorado (Fig. A.26), recall pre-World War II village society, now largely forgotten, when families who lived on isolated, outlying farms took Saturday or Sunday rides to town to buy supplies, socialize, and attend church. When Brinck recounted memories of his childhood visits to his Uncle Percy's ranch near Wagon Mound, some 150 miles northeast of Santa Fe in Mora County, he described the formality of the Sunday luncheon table (where only French was spoken) and his relief when he was finally sent to the stable to tell the foreman to hitch up the wagon for the trip to town. Years later, when we returned to Wagon Mound, he was deeply saddened by its dereliction and abandonment.

In Brinck's quick sketch of grain elevators (Fig. A.27), he emphasizes the dramatic and singular monumentality of these concrete cylinders. Jackson may have had in mind Le Corbusier's modernist manifesto, *Vers une Architecture* (1923), in which Corbu celebrates the repetitive purity of form that modernists admired about industrial structures.[8] But here the focus is not on cubic form alone: Brinck's sketch also includes a road and a receding railroad. More importantly, it is located in one of America's vast agricultural landscapes, of which Stuttgart, Arkansas, is a major regional player in the production of rice. Visually, the verticals with which the blue sky is rendered further anchor the structure to the ground, while the angle of recession invites the viewer into the vastness of American space, what photographer Frank Gohlke later called "the measure of emptiness."[9]

The sketch of a home in Seattle (Fig. A.28) illustrates a mass-produced back porch design. Built of stick-framed construction that is common all across North America, the house demonstrates how ordinary materials can be assembled to define private spaces for domestic rituals. The drawing focuses on the technology of the building elements: We observe the slightness of the stick framing and the minimal porch and stair, invoking a culture of ad-hoc informal sociability. For those who heard Brinck lecture, this sketch also reminds us of his descriptions of its opposite—the formal front porch graced with a swing seat, cushioned chairs, wicker table, and the attraction of iced drinks and leisurely company on a hot day.

Closer to Home (Figs. A.29–A.39)

Brinck wrote frequently about the house/home as a physical and social realm. Often, his writing is concerned with the mobile or impermanent temporary structure, but three sketches—the one of Seattle (Fig. A.28), one of a vernacular hogan (Fig. A.29), and another of his own classic adobe hacienda (Fig. A.30)—show permanent domestic structures. Brinck's home was of his own design, a sprawling building on a terraced hillside, with a library and bedroom wing on the western side and a trellised sitting area to the southwest. An imposing northern portico faced a graveled forecourt, shaded by rows of cottonwoods pruned in a European style. Channeled hillside springs kept these and other plantings green most of the year. While the original design from 1966 included a wing for his mother, she died before the project was completed. Once, when questioned about the forecourt's formality, he explained that the space was intended for get-togethers with his motorcycle club, although there is photographic evidence that at least one wedding was held in that same courtyard.

The hogan is a traditional Southwestern structure associated most closely with the Navajo (*Diné*) people. Brinck's observation was that utility was foremost in native Indian domestic design; the surrounding landscape was not tended, not picturesque. A hogan might have a garden at some remove, but it never had surrounding plantings, which would allow the truck shown at the right to be conveniently drawn up to the entry. Though they seem dissimilar, both the hogan and Brinck's house are traditional vernacular structures, handcrafted from local materials, regional in character and construction. So, too, are other structures that Brinck drew in La Cienega, including a neighbor's house (Fig. A.31) and the Chapel of San Antonio (Fig. A.32). In fact, Brinck's drawing of a car parked in a neighbor's driveway (Fig. A.31) is one of several drawings and photographs he made in contemplation of working people's reliance on their automobiles. In his later years, as he considered the economic struggles of working people, he observed front yards filled with cars in various states of repair and remarked on not only the ingenuity it took to keep at least one old car running, but also the ways in which economic opportunity relies on mobility in our society.

His drawing of the landscape along Route 66 near Tucumcari (Fig. A.33) shows one of the aspects of New Mexico that Jackson most loved—the high desert made verdant by traditional communal irrigation practices. I remember the day we crested a ridge and pulled over to sketch this oasis from the viewpoint of the road's edge. Brinck recorded the scene with cheap colored crayons he had purchased the previous day in a five-and-dime store. The drawing counterpoints the emerald green of the irrigated fields with the yellower green of the fertile margin, adding the grazing livestock—those marvelous cryptic marks of brown—on the left side of the page. The picture is framed by a burnt sienna butte, light brown foothills, and, beyond, a purple line of distant mountains. Soft gray clouds float in a wispy pale-blue sky.

In the sketch made just two years before his death (Fig. A.34), Brinck records with vigor and sharpness of line the elements of the arid New Mexico roadscape. The road fits into the terrain and becomes a part of the landscape as a sinuous ribbon of maintained surface. This is *not* a modern road designed on an engineered gradient to facilitate the flow of traffic; it is a more wavering space within the natural contours of the landscape. Recession and depth are conveyed by the confidence and spontaneity of Brinck's line and by the stacked layers of the composition. There is also a playful quality to this drawing, particularly evident in Jackson's choice of color— the bright pink of the road and the even more vivid pink of a distant mountain. I have a strong attachment to the sketch of Canyon de Chelly (Fig. A.35), for it was made when Brinck and I arrived at the scenic site after a long car trip. Before us was the modest motel and, beyond, the dramatic canyon oasis we would tour the following day. Brinck's first instinct was to draw the parking lot. This is a brilliant example of his way of observing the landscape and *not* editing out the essential human elements. While he takes delight in the varying shades of green in the trees, he also captures the slate-gray parking lot and the vivid red and yellow cars. The landscape of the modest little car park interested Brinck as much as the massive canyon to which it granted access. The vibrant color palette seen in this drawing shows that his enthusiasm for brilliant color persisted long past his year in Rome.

Jackson had a passion for etymology. He delighted in obscure terms such as bustrophodonic (the meander pattern of an ox-plowed field), and he poured over arcane journals about supermarket layouts and cross-country trucking logbooks to find new words. Odology was Brinck's term for both the space of the road and the chronicle and experience of the traveler—the trajectory of an odyssey, the urge to go forward, to seek, to discover the realm ahead. For Brinck, there was always some journey ahead. While the road is a frequent subject of his drawings, it is interesting that Brinck, who became celebrated for his 'discovery" of the roadside strip and other "vernacular" environments, made few sketches of these landscape elements.

The image of an interstate highway's bridge and landscape near his home (Fig. A.36) was made late in his life. The Interstate Highway System, begun in 1956 by the Eisenhower Administration, was a major new environment developed during Brinck's lifetime. Brinck dubbed the interstate highway a "synthetic space," because, like the German autobahn on which the American interstate was based, it created a uniquely controlled and engineered environment. Unlike the fit of road and land seen in rural settings (Fig. A.34), natural contours were restructured into controlled gradients to facilitate the constant speed and flow of the most economically critical American vehicle—not the passenger car but the eighteen-wheeler truck. In this engineered environment, all local distinction was overruled, and new domains such as the cloverleaf intersection were introduced. Jackson's drawing calls attention to the modern-looking nature of this new design, even as our imagination may wander back to Roman aqueducts. Here, the slight arc of the horizontal line acts like a lintel and emphasizes the long span of the highway bridge, while the strong verticals act like posts and call attention to the columnar, open-median exterior buttresses. Earlier parkway bridges, with their central abutments that visually narrowed the road, caused vehicles to slow down and resulted in a high rate of accidents. So here we see a bridge span designed, at substantial cost, to influence the driver's unconscious reactions and keep traffic moving at a constant speed.

In the sketch of the road to West Blue Mountain (Fig. A.37), the roadway is seen to be seeking a direct route, which then gains beauty and distinction as it undulates across the slope of the landscape and terrain toward the impressive mountain in the background. This road has the look of an inviting, well-worn path that subtly integrates into the larger landscape, a far cry from an all-purpose-built transit route. This road is what Brinck called a "social road," one that passes through hamlets and villages and links towns, ranches and farms, and other outposts as much for sociability as for commerce. The road becomes a place of potential encounter, where neighbors can catch up on news and the biker can stop to ask the way or pull over at will. For Brinck, frequently a stranger in motion, the social road was also space for a community of travelers.

In Jackson's oeuvre, there are several images of woods and many depictions of solitary trees. One wonders if they comment on society and on Brinck himself, always a private, shielded individual. Near the end of Jackson's life, he was reinventing himself, preparing for another final trip, becoming more deeply religious, wondering how the spirit lives on.

His rendering of a dense copse of woods near Santa Fe (Fig. A.38), perhaps near Aspen Vista, is a stunning drawing of a family of form. If asked, this is probably my favorite of Brinck's drawings, for here he challenges us to see the individual characteristics of the various tree trunks as well as the pattern of similar forms that create the grove. This is a moment rendered dynamic and brought alive by a sharp contrast between light and shadow and by the raw, vibrant, active lines. I see this as a depiction of the group, the collective, balanced against the merits of the individual. In opposition, another drawing shows a solitary cottonwood at Mesa Verde (Fig. A.39), resplendent in fall foliage, with a strong presence yet quite alone. Brinck made several drawings of single trees, drawn as if each had a unique spirit. Many of these, in autumn gold, suggest to me meditations on old age and the challenges and rewards of being, ultimately, a solitary figure grounded in his home place in La Cienega.

Brinck, then eighty-three, had retired from active lecturing and was flattered to find not a declining but a broadening recognition for his writing, the occupation in which he took greatest pride. It was only then, for the first time, that he considered authorizing an exhibition of his sketches. In March 1996, five months before he died, the Municipal Art Society of New York staged an exhibition of Jackson's drawings. Herbert Muschamp, the architecture critic for *The New York Times*, wrote in appreciation, "No one familiar with the writings needs further proof that Jackson has an eye. But like Ruskin's drawings, Jackson's graphic work shows that the man has a hand as well."[10]

LANDSCAPE

Human Geography of the Southwest

VOLUME 1

NUMBER 1

SPRING 1951

Fifty Cents a Copy

Chapter 3

In the Beginning Was *Landscape*

PAUL F. STARRS AND PETER GOIN

A reflective pilgrim on the road to Santiago always
makes a double journey back when he tries to recollect
his memories—the backward journey through Time and
the forward journey through Space.

—WALTER STARKIE (1957)[1]

In 1951, following distinguished service in World War II, a gnomish and deliberate man took a hard look at the field of human geography and saw ample room for change. He took insights from earlier authors and artists, geographers and naturalists—among them George Perkins Marsh, Nathaniel Southgate Shaler, William Henry Jackson, George R. Stewart, and Carl O. Sauer—and recast their practical visions of landscape.[2] Today, this instigator and interloper's name is hardly a secret: For decades, John Brinckerhoff Jackson would pen scholarly discussions of the German, French, and English origins of the term landscape and eventually craft essays sufficient to fill a half-dozen anthologies.[3] But Jackson's greatest contribution, for those who have followed in his footsteps, was his role as tutor and propagator. Later on and nearing sixty, he would become a lecturer of renown at Harvard University and the University of California, Berkeley and a generous mentor for those drawn to his ideas. His early platform was a magazine, *Landscape*, from which he projected insights into a dozen scholarly and professional fields. As the magazine's founder, publisher, and editor, Jackson produced an initial issue in the spring of 1951 (Fig. 3.1), from his home base in La Cienega, near Santa Fe, New Mexico.

With nifty sleuthing, Helen Lefkowitz Horowitz, editor of *Landscape in Sight* (1997), the most thorough collection of Jackson's work, established that Jackson not only conceived of the magazine, but he wrote nearly everything in the first issues.[4] Essays delivered under pseudonyms complemented Jackson's signed articles and were rounded out by Jackson's translations of small yet pointed pieces he gleaned from foreign-language sources.[5] "When Jackson began to publish his

OPPOSITE:
Figure 3.1: Front cover of *Landscape*, Vol. 1, No. 1 (Spring 1951). Used by permission of Peter Goin and Paul F. Starrs, Black Rock Institute, Reno, Nevada.

writings and drawings in *Landscape*," recounts Horowitz, "he brought talents that had been carefully nurtured in his youth and broadened in the 1930s and 1940s by travel, drawing, and writing in Europe, ranching in New Mexico, and military service in World War II."[6] While Jackson in 1951 already had to his name several articles and an acclaimed novel published, his magazine was something else again: It was a means of controlling everything in the publication process—the text, photographs, and sketches used; the layout and design; the paper and typefaces; and, once the circle widened, who he would invite to share and become allies to his vision. *Landscape* was social media easily a half-century ahead of its time, and the links listed, ideas iterated, theories presented, and philosophies tied in were acts of a mind filled with marvels.

Curiosity about the everyday helped propel Jackson into publishing. A deep interest in ordinary landscapes could not be foretold by his prep years attending one of the world's most elite private schools, Le Rosey, near Rolle, Switzerland, and New England's prestigious Choate School and Deerfield Academy. After a year at the University of Wisconsin-Madison, Jackson moved on to Harvard and studied there with F. O. Matthiessen, a pioneering teacher and author who argued that novels and literary non-fiction of what he called the American Renaissance were distinctly new forms of expression—a view Jackson relished. Jackson's interest in the vernacular grew during his European travels in 1934 and 1935 and crystalized during his tenure as a ranch hand in northeastern New Mexico after World War II. Later in life, Jackson told Horowitz "that he responded as he did to ranch life not because he was tolerant but because he had in him a streak of commonness."[7]

The initial print run of *Landscape* was 150 copies, Jackson recalled, with just twenty paid subscriptions, which goes miles toward suggesting why early issues are hard to find in libraries.[8] He shared copies with friends and mailed them to people he had never met but whom he believed might appreciate its look and themes. *Landscape* clearly was not about library subscriptions; instead, it was concerned with a certain modulated kind of preaching. To this impulsive start, Paul Groth and Todd Bressi trace a whole new form of study: "the organized twentieth-century project of taking the ordinary American cultural environment seriously can reasonably be said to have begun [with Jackson] in 1951."[9]

The only article for which Jackson took credit in the initial issue of *Landscape* was cryptically titled "Chihuahua; As We Might Have Been." It began with an echoing thunderclap: "There have not been many frontiers like this one, I imagine. An abstraction, a Euclidean line drawn across the desert, has created two distinct human landscapes where there was only one before . . . Line and river, idea and unifying force, they have been made to divide an entity which the earth created and men accepted for some three hundred years—the Spanish Southwest."[10] So many elements in that opening salvo are perfectly Jacksonian, starting with a semicolon in the title that built a meditative separation between people and place. The "I imagine" is all at once personal and assertive and resolute, each a quintessentially Jackson attribute. His discussion of the sundering of space by human superposition revisited the whole concept of the borderlands and drew attention to the distinctions of the American imposition (if it can be called that) upon the Spanish-Mexican-Indigenous cultures of northern Mexico.[11] Jackson's acknowledgment of past cultural-historical geographies, presented as a matter of plain fact of resounding importance, offered a programmatic statement that *Landscape* would carry forward through his editorship (Fig. 3.2).

Landscape, the magazine—a more appropriate term, somehow, than calling Jackson's creation an academic journal or weighing it down as a scholarly publication—was distinctive. Fully formed it was not, and on the title page Jackson telegraphed regular course corrections. The first (Fig. 3.1) and second issues bore a masthead, *Landscape: Human Geography of the Southwest*, which seemed to promise a constrained regional view. But, by the third issue, the areal scope broadened with Jackson's clarifying rider: "Human geography is the study of how man modifies the face of the earth as he works and moves about and provides himself with shelter."[12] Two numbers later, he adjusted the title, distilled by then to *Landscape: Magazine of Human Geography* (Fig. 3.3), with a didactic explanation: "Human Geography is the Study of Man the Inhabitant."[13] At the end of the magazine's fifth year, an identity was more or less firmly in place.[14] There were nudges toward

Fig. 3.2. Private chapel and portion of a fortified plaza in Chimayo, New Mexico, from J. B. Jackson, "First Comes the House," *Landscape*, Vol. 9, No. 2 , Winter 1959–1960: 31. Used by permission of Peter Goin and Paul F. Starrs, Black Rock Institute, Reno, Nevada.

nostalgia, however. For the Tenth Anniversary Issue in 1960 (Fig. 3.4), Jackson would insert a small note that read, in part, "'The Human Geography of the Southwest'—such was the original subtitle of *Landscape*. We have rarely left the region for long, and never willingly."[15]

Jackson's goal of expanding the visual appetite of readers was apparent from the initial issue, which opened with not one but two views from on high: A cover photograph by Laura Gilpin of a high Colorado mountain valley (Fig. 3.1) and, facing the table of contents, a Soil Conservation Service photograph of a New Mexico scene somewhat cryptically captioned, "Seen from the air the difference between the two landscapes is most marked." But Jackson moved immediately to clarify the caption, nailing down his point in "The Need of Being Versed in Country Things," an essay that followed the photographs: "It is from the air that the true relationship between the natural and the human landscape is first clearly revealed."[16] Two landscapes, indeed.

From 1951–1955, an invitation beckoned on or near the magazine's title page: "*Landscape* is interested in original articles dealing with aspects of human geography, particularly in those suited to illustration by aerial photographs." Given a strong visual focus, Jackson illustrated articles with available drawings, engravings, maps, site and floor plans, and, above all, bird's-eye views, plans, and aerial photographs. Taking pleasure in oblique or aerial views was not exactly revolutionary. Nadar (Gaspard-Félix Tournachon) ascended in hot air balloons to photograph Paris in the late nineteenth century, while aerial surveys funded by the American Geographical Society beginning in the 1910s pushed to the remote edges of the world.[17] But Jackson was not too much interested in the exotic and the hard to reach; he wanted his audience to consider a larger view that was pushed with clean writing in a clear style, presented in a magazine that featured interesting photographs of knowable spots. The aerial view, however, offered more than a well-gained perspective; it was a search for understanding that has been echoed by photographer-authors since the 1930s.[18]

As innovative as was Jackson's devotion to photographs, maps, and drawings, what particularly distinguished *Landscape* was his prose—plain spoken yet eloquent, precise, and sometimes slightly caustic. Unencumbered by a scholarly apparatus of footnotes and bibliographies, he crafted essays in the tradition of the renowned essayist Michel de Montaigne (1533–1592). This, in turn, attracted scholars who intended to write well. The botanist Edgar Anderson later remembered that an approving review of his book, *Plants, Landscapes, and Life in Landscape*, "led me to J. B. Jackson, the able editor of that remarkable publication. With a piquant combination of sharp criticism and flattering appreciation, he charmed out of me a series of short essays."[19] Nearly Jackson's equal as a literary stylist, with the botanist's observant eye for the everyday, Anderson would publish sixteen essays in the magazine, more than anyone except Jackson himself. "When he commented on writing style and audience," reported Paul Groth and Todd Bressi, "Jackson despaired at the 'totally academic style—dry, without color or detail, stifled by

OPPOSITE:
Fig. 3.3. Front cover of *Landscape*, Vol. 4, No. 2 (Winter 1954–1955). Used by permission of Peter Goin and Paul F. Starrs, Black Rock Institute, Reno, Nevada.

LANDSCAPE

MAGAZINE OF HUMAN GEOGRAPHY

VOL. 4. NO. 2.   WINTER 1954-55   SEVENTY-FIVE CENTS

LANDSCAPE

MAGAZINE OF HUMAN GEOGRAPHY

FALL, 1960

VOL. **10** NO. **1**

PHOTO CREDITS: Page 11: N.M. Dept. of Development; Page 16: Annual Report BAE 1895-96; "The Navaho," Harvard Univ. Press; N.M. Dept. of Development; Page 17: Edwin N. Wilmsen drawings; Page 21: Standard Oil (N.J.); Page 27: N.M. Dept. of Development; Page 30: U.S. Dept. of Interior; Page 32: J. B. Jackson; Pages 33 and 35: Arthur H. Doerr, John W. Morris, J. B. Jackson; Pages 38-39: Philip L. Wagner, Aerial view—Cia. Mexicana Aerofoto, S.A.; Pages 46-47: Philip L. Wagner.

footnotes—written only for a small public of scholars who may (or more likely may not) see the work's landscape potential.'"[20]

The Tenth Anniversary issue of *Landscape* (Fig. 3.4) occasioned a well-deserved bout of self-promotion. Testimonials flooded in from contributing writers, leaders in the field, and well-wishers: Ansel Adams, Edgar Anderson, Grady Clay, Pierre Deffontaines, Fred Kniffen, John Leighly, David Lowenthal, Ian McHarg, Lewis Mumford, Erwin Raisz, Carl Sauer, Christopher Tunnard, former U.S. Secretary of Agriculture Henry Wallace, and the estimable Gilbert White. They constituted a virtual "Who's Who" of landscape-scale scholarship, innovation, and professional vision.[21] Jackson would write for the occasion, "Many of the notions we held about the relation between man and his environment, rural or otherwise, have gone by the board; but to our credit it must be said we never urged a return to country living, much less a return to nature; we never wittingly minimized the role of the city in our culture, nor doubted the value of the new landscape evolving around us."[22] Yet he'd claim, "All that the magazine wanted to do—and in our inexperience it seemed feasible enough—was to revive in another form the kinship man had once felt for the living world, the sense of belonging to it; to remind our readers that the natural environment can satisfy our spiritual as well as our material wants."[23]

Jackson hoped not only for writers to *Landscape* who were capable of such things, but also readers able to bend their minds around the everyday places and spaces that surround them (and us). It was a shout-out for the vernacular, the ordinary, and the common landscape. And Jackson proved, in his magazine, an adage so widely used by teachers that the origin has long ago disappeared into uncertainty, although geographer Peirce Lewis rephrased it among his "Axioms for Reading the *Landscape*": "The more you know, the more you see."[24] That argument was singularly appropriate for someone who was, as Helen Lefkowitz Horowitz put it, "an artist as well as a writer" and one who could demonstrate "how landscape makes manifest our strivings, how the basic human motive for creating landscapes, especially the domestic landscape, is 'the recreation of heaven on earth.'"[25]

In 1979, historical geographer D. W. Meinig offered an evaluation of what Jackson had accomplished in his seventy years: "Jackson points the way in his insistence on looking the modern scene squarely in the face; and his admonition is not simply for us to be comprehensive and tolerant, but to see the ordinary landscapes of the automobile, mobile home, supermarket, and shopping center as legitimately 'vernacular'—that is, native to the area, but an area now defined more at the national than the local scale."[26] The exhortation worked on students, colleagues, and professionals in architecture, design, and a dozen additional fields. As Berkeley geographer James J. Parsons put it simply when interviewed in 1987, "We were smitten."[27]

While many jumped onto the Jackson bandwagon, a substrate of academicians who prided themselves on theoretical acumen shied away from Jackson's work, treating it as a superficial

OPPOSITE:
Fig. 3.4. The contents page on the inside front cover of the Tenth Anniversary issue of *Landscape*, Vol. 10, No. 1 (Fall 1960). Used by permission of Peter Goin and Paul F. Starrs, Black Rock Institute, Reno, Nevada.

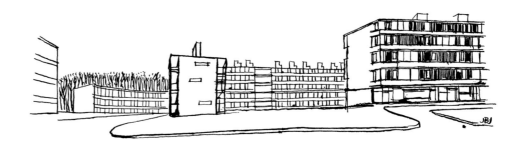

[top] Fig. 3.5. Drawing from "Cumbernauld, The New Town," *Landscape*, Vol. 12, No. 3 [Spring 1963]:19. Used by permission of Peter Goin and Paul F. Starrs, Black Rock Institute, Reno, Nevada.

[bottom] Fig. 3.6. Drawing from "The Almost Perfect Town," *Landscape*, Vol. 2, No. 1 [Spring 1952]: 2. Used by permission of Peter Goin and Paul F. Starrs, Black Rock Institute, Reno, Nevada.

and cultural geography-lite. To say that everyday landscapes were credible and useful was to the ears of these detractors, something scary, subversive, unacceptable, and even reprehensible.[28] To them, the everyday landscape was unappealing—and particularly so the inhabitants thereof. In the view of deniers, a landscape-based approach grounded in fieldwork lacked that defensible space sealed by a macadam of chic social theory. The dense jargon that the hegemons of critical theory considered essential for the academics, and whose goal was a chokehold on that-which-should-be-studied, was not for Jackson and his successor publisher-editors at *Landscape*.

Jackson's goal was anything but modest, and his success was substantial, which irritated the theorists even more. While he was given to bemoaning a lack of influence, that was, in large part, sheer theater. The architecture critic and author Jane Holtz Kay put the matter accurately in a review published in 1989 in *The New York Times:* "Mr. Jackson's utterances and personal environment speak of judgments, of a refined ease with esthetics. The artworks, Oriental rugs and antiques, the portico and spaces of the handsome adobe house he designed, attest to a keen sensibility. Outside, the Jackson-made surroundings merge the native cottonwood and Eastern import grass with the same breaking down of boundaries as his work."[29] Such notices in the *Times* do not speak to an absence of authority or the want of an audience.

J. B. Jackson was editor and publisher of *Landscape* for more than fifteen years when calls to teach at Berkeley and Harvard, and solicitations from other editors seeking his essays, consumed so much of his time that he elected to turn the reins over to someone else. His point was made. In 1968, Jackson sold all rights to *Landscape* to Blair Boyd, of Berkeley, California, for one dollar, with an understanding that the magazine would continue under the new publisher-editor.

Blair Boyd had grown up in Ohio, attended boarding school in New Mexico and, like Jackson, graduated from Harvard with a major in English and history, though Boyd's college years were interrupted by a stint in the U.S. Navy. With a background in New England progressive theater, Boyd migrated further west, taking on a stretch in editing at the University of New Mexico Press. After a few years in Albuquerque, he shifted to the Pacific Slope during the early 1960s to begin graduate work in geography at UC, Berkeley. Drawn toward the Free Speech Movement there and its activist ferment, Boyd turned back from conventional graduate work to filmmaking and the development of business interests. He had studied with Jackson and knew him well, and they enjoyed similar ideas and ambitions in publishing. Presented with the rare opportunity to acquire a magazine that was the talk of his Berkeley teachers, Boyd jumped at the chance and, as a result, would publish the magazine from 1969 to 1994, editing it himself during many of those twenty-five years, exercising throughout an exquisite taste in language and design.[30]

Landscape reached a firmer scholarly footing right away: In 1969, Boyd appended a bibliography of "Further Readings" to all articles, and, in 1970, he established an editorial board for the first time. The editorial board conducted enthusiastic, family-scale deliberations in Boyd's living room, with Jean Vance, Clare Cooper Marcus, and Roger Barnett as long-term board members and Barbara Wilms, Michael Laurie, Paul Groth, Peter Dodge, Roland Dickey, James Davis, and Stan Anderson on and off the board at various points. While Boyd listed himself as the editor of *Landscape* for more than fifteen years, Bonnie Loyd, of San Francisco, took over as the managing editor in 1979 and from 1985–1992 served as the overall editor of *Landscape*, with Boyd retreating to the role of publisher while remaining the magazine's gray eminence. Reading those late-life *Landscape* issues shows that adding the title of editor to Bonnie's portfolio was a wise choice. During the late 1970s, she had to her credit a distinguished masters thesis in geography written at Syracuse University and significant experience in editing and book publishing; most of all, she shared Boyd's enthusiasm for producing a class-act magazine.[31]

Readers—and authors—developed a taste for the *Landscape* style. Some, such as landscape historian Robert Riley—billed for a time as Associate Editor—and Dan Luten, a retired research chemist and a leading environmental author and development skeptic, contributed regular columns during the Blair Boyd *Landscape* era. Luten's essays, in particular, were masterpieces of concision and data. Among Jackson's bequests to Boyd was an enduring interest in eloquent essays about place that maintained a literary style. Bret Wallach, a 1960s product of Berkeley's Department of Geography, for instance, published essays in *Landscape* of such eloquence that they helped spade the ground for his recognition in 1984 as a MacArthur "genius" awardee.[32] If anything, the quality and range of submitted articles picked up, as Bonnie Loyd increasingly shepherd the day-to-day details of managing a magazine. Furthermore, the layout and design improved with a rising professionalism in production (see pages 116–19), reaching a new generation of readers, scholars, and artists.

After Jackson stepped down as editor and publisher, he contributed an additional half-dozen articles to *Landscape*, essays that reflected roving new interests. The magazine evolved, as might be expected with its shift from northern New Mexico to the burgeoning university setting of Berkeley. The greatest improvement, though, came from a dissemination of Jackson's way of seeing and understanding landscape. Many a photographer, artist, architect, philosopher, and writer, in the U.S. and internationally, made a mark by appearing in the pages of *Landscape*.

After twenty-five years under Blair Boyd and Bonnie Loyd, publication of the magazine slowly wound down, easing in 1992 and finally ending in 1994, as Boyd's business interests changed and he decided to stem an outgoing financial tide. In 2005, geographer Paul F. Starrs and photographer Peter Goin acquired *Landscape* from Boyd with a commitment to safeguard its legacy, hopeful at some future date to restart publication.[33] The two University of Nevada professors chartered the nonprofit Black Rock Institute in 2005 in part as a vehicle to support *Landscape*, publish books, and foster educational outreach. A massive survey in 2010 to see which

Landscape essays the magazine's fans considered most significant or important led to the idea of creating an anthology of the best of *Landscape*.[34]

Now, more than six decades after Jackson initiated *Landscape* magazine, scholars and practitioners see landscape history and cultural landscape studies as a coherent unit of analysis. If a landscape is not so militantly bounded as a watershed or so allusive as a bioregion, it is a flexible and useful concept precisely because it includes humans and their activities as an evolving element on the land. Despite Jackson's patrician roots, he was very much a student of the commonplace, of the vernacular landscape and its people. As Jackson declares at the end of Robert Calo's 1989 documentary, *J. B. Jackson and the Love of Everyday Places*, "I'm always impressed with the fact that the prayer that we all give is: 'Give us this day our daily bread.' It is not: 'Give us a supply of bread for ten years.' It is daily. It is on this small, intimate, neighborhood scale that we should live or that we do live."[35] John R. Stilgoe, a teaching assistant of Jackson's at Harvard during the 1970s who went on there to a distinguished scholarly and writing career, wrote in 1998 about the shift in perception begun by Jackson: "Ordinary American landscape strikes almost no one as photogenic. . . . Most Americans simply cannot imagine why anyone would scrutinize what they themselves ignore. Deep down, at the very core of the American psyche, they know too that they are unable to make sense of the landscape around them, that someday a stranger may come and see the jewel they missed, and after seeing it, take it away."[36] Throughout its history, *Landscape* exhorted us all to take a second look at the conventional and to find in it lessons about what we want, what we have been, and—even—what we are becoming.

If *Landscape* magazine changed significantly through time—both under and after Jackson—it came to the scene as a curious invention: It was a small magazine, published and edited by someone who believed in a message worth passing along, one that found a following among practitioners and scholars ready for fresh ideas and a more direct, less jargon-choked style. *Landscape* owed its beginnings and inspiration to J. B. Jackson. That spirit continued after Jackson entrusted it to the care of Blair Boyd and then Bonnie Loyd, as *Landscape* continued to make its mark among generations of sophisticated devotees, representing a cross-section of interests. As the magazine matured, it acquired increasing luster as a destination for intelligent essays and place-based art. *Landscape* had a life of its own; the influence of Jackson's work as editor and author played forward through the later *Landscape* years, developing into a particularly western U.S. school devoted to people and their works—to landscape, in all its essentials. "*Landscape*, in this sense, was not a painting, a vista, or a garden," argue Groth and Bressi, "but rather a particular area shaped by a cultural group and strongly influenced by the limits of soil, climate, and plant life. [Carl O.] Sauer and the so-called Berkeley School of cultural geography shifted the sense of landscape back from a composed image to the place itself."[37]

The run of *Landscape* magazine presents an evolving treasure trove of information, technique, and ideas. No other single archive equals its depth of understanding and affection for the built environment and for the ideologies and knowledge that are poured into our surroundings. The magazine was more than photographs, maps, drawings, philosophy, and ably marshaled ideas. For better than forty years, *Landscape* offered a blueprint for how to understand the world around us.

Portfolio B

Front Covers of *Landscape*, 1952–1991

An enduring magazine of place, space, and time, *Landscape* began in 1951 and ceased publication in 1994. J. B. Jackson served as the founder, editor, and publisher until he sold all rights in 1968 to the magazine to Blair Boyd, of Berkeley, California. Boyd served as editor until 1985 and publisher until 1994. He was joined in 1979 by Bonnie Loyd, of San Francisco, who took over as the managing editor and subsequently served as the overall editor from 1985 to 1992. The magazine was acquired in 2005 by Paul F. Starrs and Peter Goin, with all rights to the name, past issues, and ownership of all material under copyright. Under the direction of Starrs and Goin, the rich heritage of *Landscape* will generate new pathways into further understanding the land upon which we all live and depend. All front covers are used by permission of Peter Goin and Paul F. Starrs, Black Rock Institute, Reno, Nevada.

LANDSCAPE

VOL. 2, NO. 1   SPRING 1952   FIFTY CENTS

LANDSCAPE

VOL. 2, NO. 2   AUTUMN 1952   FIFTY CENTS

LANDSCAPE

VOL. 4, NO. 1   SUMMER 1954   FIFTY CENTS

LANDSCAPE

MAGAZINE OF HUMAN GEOGRAPHY

LANDSCAPE

WINTER 1956-57   75 CENTS

LANDSCAPE

THE URBAN SCENE

WINTER 1958-59 $1.00

LANDSCAPE

VOL. XI   NO. 3

Spring   1962

$1.00

Tourism

and

Mobility

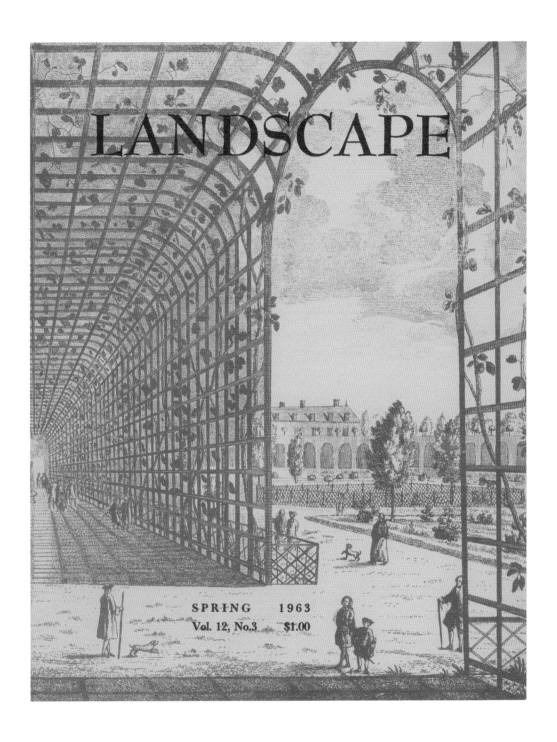

LANDSCAPE

SPRING   1963

Vol. 12, No.3 $1.00

LANDSCAPE

SPRING 1964
Volume 13, No. 3 $1.00

SPACE AND BEHAVIOR • BIOCLIMATOLOGY • INDIAN LANDSCAPES • MOBILE

ARCHITECTURE • EDUCATION FOR LANDSCAPE ARCHITECTURE

PHENOMENOLOGY OF THE DWELLING • BOOK REVIEWS

LANDSCAPE

FOUR ENVIRONMENTS • URBAN SEMANTICS • ENVIRONMENTAL
BEAUTY • BRIDGES • AREQUIPA • FULFILLMENT AREAS
BOOK REVIEWS

VOL. 16, NO. 2   WINTER 1966-67 $1.00

20th Anniversary Issue

Landscape

Spring 1976   Volume 20, Number 3

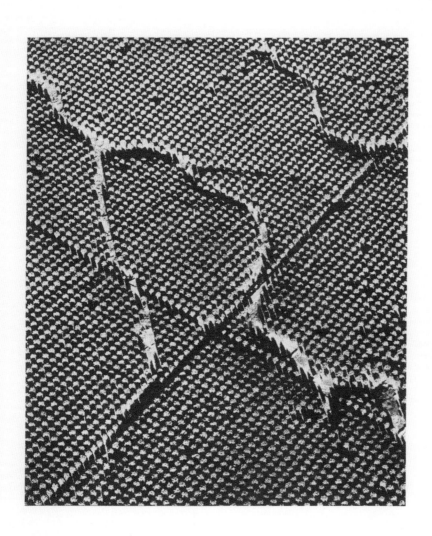

Landscape

1981   Volume 25, Number 2

Landscape

VOL. 28, NO. 2, 1985 $6.95

Landscape

Volume 31, Number 1 Spring 1991

$6.95

Chapter 4:
J. B. Jackson's Slides

Landscape Categories for Thinking and Learning

PAUL GROTH

John Brinckerhoff Jackson's 35-millimeter color slides—and the systematic but idiosyncratic ways in which he organized them—are vivid windows into how Jackson thought about American landscapes and what he looked for as he traveled around the country. Jackson seems to have been a reluctant photographer. For most of his life he had actively used drawings, not photographs, to study cultural landscapes. Yet photos were there, too, in his methods. We know he learned to study aerial photography and maps during World War II. In his seventeen years of publishing *Landscape* magazine he encouraged authors to illustrate their articles with photographs, and, on his page layouts, he often added the photographs of others and his own drawings (but not his photos). He began to take and use a few of his own slides during the 1960s, when he was in his fifties, and took slides in quantity starting in 1970.

So why, in 1970, do we see Jackson's sudden change of heart about taking photographs? The major push came from the demands of teaching and lecturing. The earliest slides, from 1963, coincide with the year that Jackson began teaching a graduate seminar in the Department of Landscape Architecture at the University of California, Berkeley. By 1967 and 1968, respectively, Jackson's courses at Berkeley and at Harvard University had moved from seminar-sized enterprises to lecture classes for 200 to 300 students. He also was being asked more frequently to give public lectures. In short, the challenges of addressing hundreds of listeners greatly increased his personal use of a camera. Later, he began to use his slides as visual notes, as sets of ideas that he stored away as he studied new landscape elements and prepared essays about them.

For effectiveness with a large crowd, Jackson's slides score high points. They are taken in excellent light conditions, always have a tight frame around his subjects (although his subjects might be unusual), and they tell a story. Consider, for instance, a photograph that shows virtually all the parts of an Idaho farmstead and farm—in fact, all the parts of the Western American farm after 1870—in one image (Fig. C.3). The buildings all date from the early 1900s; the white two-story house, in late afternoon light, stands in its own fenced yard; the barn and outbuildings define a former work yard, now unused and covered in grass; an old windmill and a tall evergreen tree slant at almost the same angle; in the background is a huge hillside field, freshly plowed. In a surprisingly large proportion of the foreground is the straight, graveled, section-line road of the U.S. rural grid, an important aspect of rural American life. Jackson has walked across the road in order to include it.

Even when Jackson used slides to illustrate his lectures, he did not do so in the manner of art and architectural historians, who most often lecture with two paired images on the screen. Instead, Jackson would typically lecture without slides for thirty-five to forty minutes, forcing his audience to conjure mental images of their own, from their own experience. Then, at the end of his talk, Jackson would show five to seven images that highlighted and reviewed his points. Talking first, then showing slides, was a brilliantly circuitous way to teach designers and geographers. Jackson suggested, first, how to think and, then, how to connect the eyes to the brain.

To arrive at those few most telling photographs, Jackson eventually assembled a collection of close to 5,000 slides, about a tenth of which were copies of images from books and magazines or images given to him by students and colleagues. Many of the slides of New England could have been taken on day trips out of Cambridge, Massachusetts, during the years Jackson taught at Harvard. When he traveled with others, they made a point to give him copies of their best photographs. We know that, in 1985 and 1986, Jackson, impressed by the work of the Albuquerque photographer Miguel Gandert, hired him to take slides of the vernacular economy and everyday lives of people in the Southwest for lectures that Jackson was to be giving at Rice University (Gandert's images appear in Figs. C.43, C.59, 7.6, and 7.7).

Jackson and Gandert traveled together in and around Santa Fe and Albuquerque for a week, Jackson pointing out what he wanted and Gandert adding his own ideas. Jackson eventually selected about 100 slides (out the more than 1,000 photos that Gandert shot) and included them in his home slide collection. On one later occasion, when Janet Mendelsohn's film crew from Harvard was shooting with Jackson, he arranged for Gandert to accompany them, saying to the crew, "Go with Miguel. He knows what I see."

Cross-country trips, usually taken alone, were the source of most of Jackson's slides. With some interpolation using automatic slide dates on the cardboard mounts, one can piece together routes Jackson traveled between Harvard and Berkeley and back to Santa Fe. And, for the Southwest and Mexico, it is clear that Jackson carried a camera along on many short trips, carefully piecing together his visual thoughts of those close-to-home areas.

In order to move the slides with him from Harvard to Berkeley each year, Jackson stored his collection on transparent sheets the size of a piece of paper, with twenty slides per sheet. The sheets were three-hole punched, and kept in a series of eighteen three-ring binders. Some of the binders were very thick, holding a dozen of more pages of slides; other binders were thin, with only four or five pages. On the spine and front of each binder, Jackson wrote a few summary terms to help him find the more specific topics on the sheets inside.

When Jackson retired from teaching at Harvard, he gave some of his teaching collection slides to his successor there, John R. Stilgoe. A few years later, at Berkeley, he gave another large share of his slides to me, along with his lecture notes and a photocopy of the bibliographic cards he used in his lectures and research. What struck me most at seeing Jackson's slides was the way in which he organized them. They were not kept in the order he used them in his lectures. Instead, Jackson stored his slides in ninety-six categories of landscape elements, often with several sheets under any one category; that is, a sheet labeled *churches I* would be followed by *churches II* and *churches III*. The front-of-binder headings were typically more general. In one binder, which he labeled MAPS, PLANS, AND AIR VIEWS, he included sheets with titles such as *local maps (USA)* and *the grid*. The binder labeled THE STRIP included not only categories one would expect such as *traffic*, *motels*, and *gas stations*, but also other transportation systems such as *vehicles*, *ships*, *harbors*, *canals*, and *airports*. Jackson clearly saw all types of regional connections as related ideas. A separate binder, labeled ROADS AND HIGHWAYS, had sheets with eleven other roadside elements such as *truck stops*, *road construction*, *official signs*, and *highway ecology*. Oddly (although perhaps not so oddly, since strict hierarchy and logic were not characteristics that Jackson valued), the actual sets of pages about the strip were in a different fat cloth-bound binder whose spine, after some editing, was eventually labeled STRIP, COMMERCIAL SIGNS, SMALL TOWNS, STRIP SIGNS, RURAL CENTERS, and SPORTS.

Before I began actively using Jackson's slides in my course lectures, I invented a system of numbers and letters based on Jackson's binders and catalogued each of the slides. For instance, the slide 2-D-18 is from the second binder, the fourth page, and number 18 in the location on that page. With these added location tags, Jackson's slides remained in his order, even when I was using them every week.

Over time, Jackson had moved some categories around. The binder heading MOBILE HOMES was crossed out on the SMALL TOWNS binder. Jackson had moved the several sheets labeled *mobile homes* to the binders labeled DOMESTIC ARCHITECTURE—a change that tracked Jackson's thinking and writing. He initially saw and wrote about trailers as an exceptional symbol of mobility but later came to see their meaning not as an exception but as an intertwining part of the centuries-long history of a great many kinds of temporary dwellings in Europe and early America.

No matter what the category in which he eventually filed his slides, Jackson the artist also worked as Jackson the documentary photographer and teacher. His slides are often arresting and provide riveting views, but he rarely kept an image that might be seen as merely picturesque. Jackson may not always have completely stopped his black BMW motorcycle to take a slide, and his camera focus was not always sharp, but each slide is a lesson in how to see the landscape. See, for instance, his 1987 photograph of a small village church near Santa Fe (Fig. C.56). Jackson includes the dramatically backlit, traditional adobe church with its three spires and crosses and separate bell tower behind the churchyard wall, yet he frames the view with thoroughly modern elements. Dominating the foreground is a large satellite dish, protected by a chain-link fence; on the other side is part of a pickup truck. The steeples and satellite dish all point to the sky as past and present connections to the cosmos. The gravel plaza shines in the sun; for all we know, the plaza may have been what caught Jackson's eye. Jackson classified this image not under *church* or *TV* but under *New Mexico*; all these elements together spoke to him about key elements of New Mexican village life as he found it in 1987.

In a 1971 photograph of an L-shaped apartment building in Holyoke, Massachusetts, with a fairly imposing brick facade, Jackson takes his view from the side to reveal wooden rear stairs and laundry lines; his category is *tenement houses* (Fig. C.14). As he does with so many of his urban views, Jackson's 1984 photo of downtown Boston (Fig. C.11), classified under *city views*, includes the juxtapositions one sees in everyday life. He prominently foregrounds a red pickup truck with a white camper van top, and a woman in a green raincoat. Jackson often kept vehicles, streets, parking lots, and passers-by in the forefront of his slides.

The open spaces of America—located in the binder FIELDS, LAWNS, PARKS, LANDSCAPING—were important to Jackson, and this binder held a high number of slides compared to the others. In addition to the cover categories, inside Jackson placed *streets, street life, shopping centers*, and *vendors*. An unlabeled binder held another set of categories close to Jackson's heart: sheets about rural social institutions such as *camp meetings, churches, forests, pastures*, and *schools*. Why was the binder unlabeled? Perhaps it was the first of the binders, and hence needed no label.

As was true in his writing, Jackson enjoyed humor and irony. He might simply record jokes that people added to the landscape, as with the highway-strip Dairy Queen managers in 1971 who added to their corporate sign the message, "Stop now. The next five restaurants are mirages" (Fig. C.30). Or consider the irony of United Farm Workers of America protestors in front of a gourmet food store (Fig. C.20) or of an early 1900s small-town bank with an exquisite Greek Revival style cast iron facade, which in 1977 Jackson found in use as a Honda motorcycle shop. Jackson filed that slide under *monuments.*

When I first received and studied the slide collection in 1978, the eighty slides in four pages of slides labeled *monuments* were a puzzle. Jackson had not yet written or lectured about this topic. A year later, he returned to the UC, Berkeley campus to give an evening lecture, which he later published as "The Necessity for Ruins." The lecture made clear his interest in monuments of all types, although his end-of-talk slides were entirely different from the slides then stored in my office. This was, for me, the first proof that, by this time in his career, Jackson was using his slides (as many scholars of the built environment do) as visual notes and research tools. It also suggested that he still had a substantial number of slides at home and was still adding to his collection.

Many times in his teaching and writing, Jackson returned to the topic of the single-family house. By far, houses made up the largest number of slides in any single category. About a sixth of Jackson's images were in two fat binders labeled DOMESTIC ARCHITECTURE I AND II; inside these binders were only three subsidiary categories of their own: *mobile homes*, as noted above; *porches*; and *roofs*. The rest of the pages simply collected single-family houses under *domestic architecture,* in chronological order. In those slides, Jackson often records the dignity and pride shown by individual home owners. In an undated photograph, labeled merely *technostyle* (one of his two lecture categories for middle-class houses), he shows an early 1900s cubic house in the late fall, with an ample porch with pairs of columns and an immaculately maintained front yard (Fig. C.16).

In a category separate from *domestic architecture*, Jackson placed a large number of slides under *vernacular houses*. These were usually very small, blue-collar homes either self-built or minimally provided by mining, factory, or ranch owners for their employees. But Jackson's eye was not only on the simplicity or smallness or meanness of one-room or two-room dwellings; he was also usually documenting some local, individual addition to the scene. In his 1971 photograph of two miners' shacks in Globe, Arizona (Fig. C.46), the minimal wooden dwellings are flanked closely by other structures. In the immediate background is a steep, eroded hill—probably a slag heap or the edge of a tailings pond, since a smelter smokestack towers in the distance. But, within this otherwise grim scene, the residents of one of the houses valiantly have planted a small palm tree in the yard, included to the left of the photo. Frequently, Jackson looked for traces like these of individual actions played out within broader economic and social forces.

Another way Jackson used the term "vernacular" in his writing was in regard to the informal, temporary ways that people used and claimed space for their own purposes. The examples might be a garden, people parking various vehicles in unusual places, youths playing stickball in a city street, people selling things at a swap meet in the corner of a parking lot, or children doing acrobatics on a front yard.

Although a substantial share of Jackson's survey courses addressed twentieth-century American cities and the houses in them (especially in the suburbs), his slide categories for other aspects of the city—especially the central business district—were much more tentative than other parts of his system. No binder collected most of the urban landscape elements. Highway strips, factories, and public gathering places each had their own slim notebook of slide sleeves. Jackson scattered the rest of the history of the twentieth-century city in many different volumes. One unlabeled binder held slide sleeves with the categories of *lodges, clubs, fraternal, etc.*; *banks*; *stores*; *office buildings*; *warehouses*; and *parking*. Inexplicably, this binder also had a sheet of slides labeled *light and color. New Deal projects*, *streetcars*, and *urban transportation* were in a different binder. On the basis of this evidence, at least, it is safe to say that the central sections of American cities, with their more corporate and congregate landowners and builders, did not interest Jackson nearly as much as the outlying areas of cities, where he could observe the impact of individual investors and occupants.

For his bibliography cards, Jackson used almost exactly the same system of ninety-plus categories he used for his slides. There is nothing magical about Jackson's categories, but they do show him at work, teaching himself how and what to see. His lectures and essays, usually published without notes, made his site knowledge seem easily acquired, but his expertise and vision were constructed, hard-won skills.

The slides and their categories also display the ease with which Jackson moved between, on the one hand, literally hundreds of local, individual examples of a building or sign or open space and, on the other hand, much more generic and abstract landscape types. Jackson hand-labeled almost every slide with some locational clue—the city or state, perhaps the region. He did not care about when he took the slide or on which of his many trips across the country. But the abstract landscape types seem to have meant much to him; Jackson wrote, revised, and re-wrote the categories for a great many slides. Jackson first labeled a 1965 slide of a small, informal valley town (Fig. C.47) as "Tennessee"; then later as "south, cities"; and finally "village," filed on the slide page *towns*. The ways he thought about a particular scene, and then sought to classify it, record the tensions and interplay between the idiosyncratic and the generic.

Jackson was also reflexive, often keeping in view part of the rear-view mirror of his motorcycle, or the windshield column of his car (Fig. C.33), to record himself as the conscious observer and editor of the scene in front of him. For instance, in a slide showing what he called the "roadside ecology" of plants, which received more water by the side of the highway than plants further away, he is careful to include the rear-view mirror of his pickup truck (Fig. C.5).

Two years after he gave me his slides so I could continue teaching his subjects at Berkeley, Jackson asked for the slides to be returned, on loan, because he was reprising his survey courses as a visiting lecturer at the University of Texas in Austin. The following year, Jackson sent his slides back to me but not in their sleeves. He stacked the empty sleeves at the bottom of a large box and used the slides themselves as excelsior-style packing around two nineteenth-century books on agriculture that he had borrowed from the Berkeley campus libraries. Jackson didn't seem to put a particularly high value on his life's photographic output, or, perhaps, he was commenting wryly that I was taking his slides too seriously.

That year's back-and-forth exchange of Jackson's slides also made clear that he needed some of his slides for the thinking and writing that he was still intending to do—and which he did do, in more of his published collections of essays. When I began to return the slides to new, archival-quality sleeves, I found that Jackson had sent me an overlapping but different and larger set of slides than in his first gift. The first set included roughly 1,800 slides; this second shipment was about 2,100 slides. Many pages were partly empty, even though they earlier had been full with slides; I knew, because of the catalogue numbers I had added to each image. And Jackson had sent 300 additional slides, although in no new categories. I could easily add new pages using the old headings.

In 1995, Jackson gave another large set of 1,800 slides to Chris Wilson at the University of New Mexico. Once again, they were loose slides, and Wilson remembers that they arrived in a Labatt's Beer box. About half of the slides had my cataloging system labels—so they had been part of Jackson's initial gift to me. Wilson surmises that, like my set, these were primarily teaching slides.

About that same time, a year prior to his death, Jackson forwarded to me a final set of about 1,000 slides, all still filed in their categories and transparent sleeves. When the boxes arrived, I opened them carefully, knowing they would be a rare glimpse into that very private life of Jackson's office at his house. What had he kept near his desk, as visual notes for present and future essays? A series of sheets of slides about different American regions. Excellent slides, many copied from books, in the categories of *farmsteads*, *fields*, *plantations*, and *sharecroppers*. More than 100 slides of his drawings and watercolors. At least sixty more slides of *street life* and another sixty slides he labeled simply as *urbanism*—here were notes for what he was thinking about the center city. Several more sheets of *vernacular houses* but no more of the *domestic architecture* slides he had collected during his teaching years. One hundred slides were labeled *southwest* and its *pueblos*. But, most of all, he had saved almost 200 slides of New Mexico, the region that had first inspired him to start his *Landscape* magazine and that continued to fascinate him. Many of these were images taken by Miguel Gandert.

The scattered fractions of Jackson's slides are currently being collected in one place: The Jackson Collection at the Center for Southwest Research in the Zimmerman Library at the University of New Mexico in Albuquerque. With the assistance of Audra Bellmore, Curator of the Jackson Collection, and Jason Miller, Librarian of the Visual Resources Center of the College of Environmental Design at the University of California, Berkeley, Jackson's slides are also being digitized. When cataloging is complete, the goal is for the complete collection of slides to be accessible through Websites connected to both libraries.

If there is a single theme that ties together all of Jackson's slides, it is his classic geographical fascination with the hand of humans on Earth. Even in those moments when he is photographing a scene simply because of its beauty of light, color, and the composition of visual elements, as he does in a 1971 slide of a highway, clouds, and sunlit landforms in the High Plains of New Mexico (Fig. C.6), there is always a human element. The simple farmhouse to the left visually ties together trees along a stream and the gravel section-line road—all of which balance the dominant elements of the highway paralleled by power lines.

Again and again in J. B. Jackson's life work, one sees that his thinking and writing went together with looking and seeing. His photographs and their categories are a partial but important record of the process all students of the landscape hope for—to learn from what we can see.

J. B. Jackson meeting informally
with graduate students following a
lecture at the University of California,
Berkeley, 1981. Photograph by Jennifer Williams and used by permission.

Portfolio C

Teaching Slides by J. B. Jackson, 1963–1987

J. B. Jackson took color slides most intensively during his teaching years at Harvard University and the University of California, Berkeley during the late 1960s and 1970s. The captions accompanying this portfolio record all available information provided by J. B. Jackson for each slide, organized in three clusters. First, the general file name is given; then, following a semicolon, the name of the plastic filing sleeve in which the slide is housed. Capitalization has been edited for consistency. Second, all additional information that appears on the slide mounts is presented, with brackets indicating new material inserted for greater clarification. (The name of the slide sleeve is often written on the slide mount but not repeated here to avoid repetition.) Recorded last is the three-digit number of the filing system developed by Paul Groth and based on Jackson's filing system, which is now used to organize the slides in the J. B. Jackson Pictorial Materials Collection at the University of New Mexico in Albuquerque.

Fig. C.1. Farms, General; Fields VI. Field Patterns, Eroded Fields, Missouri, Nineteenth Century, no date. 7-F(4)-03. From the J. B. Jackson Pictorial Materials Collection (Groth Collection), Center for Southwest Research and the School of Architecture and Planning, University of New Mexico, Albuquerque, and used by permission.

Fig. C.2. Farms, General; Farmsteads II. American River Valley, [California], April 1970. 7-M(2)-08. From the J. B. Jackson Pictorial Materials Collection (Groth Collection), Center for Southwest Research and the School of Architecture and Planning, University of New Mexico, Albuquerque, and used by permission.

Fig. C.3. Farms, General; Farmsteads. Ash, Idaho, no date. 7-M-12. From the J. B. Jackson Pictorial Materials Collection (Groth Collection), Center for Southwest Research and the School of Architecture and Planning, University of New Mexico, Albuquerque, and used by permission.

Fig. C.4. Farms, General; Fields I. Palouse, January 1974. 7-D-15. From the J. B. Jackson Pictorial Materials Collection (Groth Collection), Center for Southwest Research and the School of Architecture and Planning, University of New Mexico, Albuquerque, and used by permission.

Fig. C.5. Connections (all transportation except the strip); Country Roads, Paved II [Possibly NM41 in the Galisteo Basin], New Mexico, no date. 2-E-02. From the J. B. Jackson Pictorial Materials Collection (Groth Collection), Center for Southwest Research and the School of Architecture and Planning, University of New Mexico, Albuquerque, and used by permission.

Fig. C.6. Connections (all transportation except the strip); Highway Ecology, Eco-Highway, no date. 2-G-11. From the J. B. Jackson Pictorial Materials Collection (Groth Collection), Center for Southwest Research and the School of Architecture and Planning, University of New Mexico, Albuquerque, and used by permission.

Fig. C.7. Connections (all transportation except the strip); Interstate, Roads, and Structures, April 1975. 2-H-05. From the J. B. Jackson Pictorial Materials Collection (Groth Collection), Center for Southwest Research and the School of Architecture and Planning, University of New Mexico, Albuquerque, and used by permission.

Fig. C.8. Connections (all transportation except the strip); Interstate, Roads, and Structures, March 1971. 2-H-04. From the J. B. Jackson Pictorial Materials Collection (Wilson Collection), Center for Southwest Research and the School of Architecture and Planning, University of New Mexico, Albuquerque, and used by permission.

Fig. C.9. Connections (all transportation except the strip), Parking II. Austin, [Texas], April 1980. 2-I (2)-03. From the J. B. Jackson Pictorial Materials Collection (Groth Collection), Center for Southwest Research and the School of Architecture and Planning, University of New Mexico, Albuquerque, and used by permission.

Fig. C.10. Cities, General; City Views I. San Francisco, September 1975. 4-D-15. From the J. B. Jackson Pictorial Materials Collection (Groth Collection), Center for Southwest Research and the School of Architecture and Planning, University of New Mexico, Albuquerque, and used by permission.

Fig. C.11. Cities, General; City Views IV, November 1984. 4-F(2)-02. From the J. B. Jackson Pictorial Materials Collection (Groth Collection), Center for Southwest Research and the School of Architecture and Planning, University of New Mexico, Albuquerque, and used by permission.

Fig. C.12. Cities, General; Streets I. City Views, Streets, [Boston], no date. 4-P-06. From the J. B. Jackson Pictorial Materials Collection (Groth Collection), Center for Southwest Research and the School of Architecture and Planning, University of New Mexico, Albuquerque, and used by permission.

Fig. C.13. City Institutions, City Centers, and Urban Workplaces; Office Buildings I. Montreal, [Canada], October 1970. 5-M-09. From the J. B. Jackson Pictorial Materials Collection (Groth Collection), Center for Southwest Research and the School of Architecture and Planning, University of New Mexico, Albuquerque, and used by permission.

Fig. C.14. Dwellings; Tenement Houses. Holyoke, Massachusetts, September 1971. 6-U-07. From the J. B. Jackson Pictorial Materials Collection (Groth Collection), Center for Southwest Research and the School of Architecture and Planning, University of New Mexico, Albuquerque, and used by permission.

Fig. C.15. Dwellings; Mass Housing. Stanton Hill War Housing, Washington, DC, January 1971. 6-V-05. From the J. B. Jackson Pictorial Materials Collection (Groth Collection), Center for Southwest Research and the School of Architecture and Planning, University of New Mexico, Albuquerque, and used by permission.

Fig. C.16. Dwellings; Domestic Architecture Post-1890s (technostyle). Tech., 1900–1925, no date. 6-L-05. From the J. B. Jackson Pictorial Materials Collection (Groth Collection), Center for Southwest Research and the School of Architecture and Planning, University of New Mexico, Albuquerque, and used by permission.

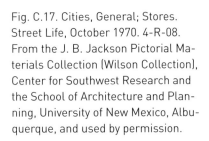

Fig. C.17. Cities, General; Stores. Street Life, October 1970. 4-R-08. From the J. B. Jackson Pictorial Materials Collection (Wilson Collection), Center for Southwest Research and the School of Architecture and Planning, University of New Mexico, Albuquerque, and used by permission.

Fig. C.18. City Institutions, City Centers, and Urban Workplaces; Office Buildings I. Fall River, [Massachusetts], no date. 5-M-14. From the J. B. Jackson Pictorial Materials Collection (Wilson Collection), Center for Southwest Research and the School of Architecture and Planning, University of New Mexico, Albuquerque, and used by permission.

Fig. C.19. Fremont Theater, S. Chas. Lee, San Luis Obispo, [California], November 1972. From the J. B. Jackson Pictorial Materials Collection (Wilson Collection), Center for Southwest Research and the School of Architecture and Planning, University of New Mexico, Albuquerque, and used by permission.

Fig. C.20. City Institutions, City Centers, and Urban Workplaces. Stores, January-February [no year]. 5-T-03. From the J. B. Jackson Pictorial Materials Collection (Wilson Collection), Center for Southwest Research and the School of Architecture and Planning, University of New Mexico, Albuquerque, and used by permission.

Fig. C.21. City Institutions, City Centers, and Urban Workplaces; Shopping centers, pedestrian malls. San Bruno, [California], February 1971. 5-P-16. From the J. B. Jackson Pictorial Materials Collection (Wilson Collection), Center for Southwest Research and the School of Architecture and Planning, University of New Mexico, Albuquerque, and used by permission.

Fig. C.22. Connections (all transportation except the strip); Country Roads, Paved III, no date. 2-E(4)-18. From the J. B. Jackson Pictorial Materials Collection (Groth Collection), Center for Southwest Research and the School of Architecture and Planning, University of New Mexico, Albuquerque, and used by permission.

Fig. C.23. Rural Institutions and Small Towns; Small Town III. Hand Houses, Texas, May 1980. 8-V(2)-11. From the J. B. Jackson Pictorial Materials Collection (Groth Collection), Center for Southwest Research and the School of Architecture and Planning, University of New Mexico, Albuquerque, and used by permission.

Fig. C.24. Cities, General; Street Life V, September 1989. 4-R(5)-06. From the J. B. Jackson Pictorial Materials Collection (Groth Collection), Center for Southwest Research and the School of Architecture and Planning, University of New Mexico, Albuquerque, and used by permission.

Fig. C.25. Farms, General; New Deal
I, Disruption, Mobility. TVA, Wheeler
Dam, Alabama, May 1975. 7-I-14.
From the J. B. Jackson Pictorial Materials Collection (Groth Collection),
Center for Southwest Research and
the School of Architecture and Planning, University of New Mexico, Albuquerque, and used by permission.

Fig. C.26. Recreation and Sports;
Lawns, April 1971. 9-D-13. From the
J. B. Jackson Pictorial Materials Collection (Groth Collection), Center for
Southwest Research and the School
of Architecture and Planning, University of New Mexico, Albuquerque, and
used by permission.

Fig. C.27. City Institutions, City Centers, and Urban Workplaces; Warehouse, September 1985. 5-U-15. From the J. B. Jackson Pictorial Materials Collection (Groth Collection), Center for Southwest Research and the School of Architecture and Planning, University of New Mexico, Albuquerque, and used by permission.

Fig. C.28. City Institutions, City Centers, and Urban Workplaces; Courthouses. Santa Rosa, [California], March 1970. 5-D-12. From the J. B. Jackson Pictorial Materials Collection (Groth Collection), Center for Southwest Research and the School of Architecture and Planning, University of New Mexico, Albuquerque, and used by permission.

Fig. C.29. The Strip, Signs; Commercial I, March 1972. 3-G-18. From the J. B. Jackson Pictorial Materials Collection (Wilson Collection), Center for Southwest Research and the School of Architecture and Planning, University of New Mexico, Albuquerque, and used by permission.

Fig. C.30. The Strip. Signs; Commercial I. Albuquerque, June 1971. 3-G-07. From the J. B. Jackson Pictorial Materials Collection (Groth Collection), Center for Southwest Research and the School of Architecture and Planning, University of New Mexico, Albuquerque, and used by permission.

Fig. C.31. The Strip; Strip II, '50s. Strip. Decorations, Illegible Blvd., no date. 3-E-10. From the J. B. Jackson Pictorial Materials Collection (Groth Collection), Center for Southwest Research and the School of Architecture and Planning, University of New Mexico, Albuquerque, and used by permission.

Fig. C.32. The Strip; Gas Stations. Country Store, [Garfield, Texas], April 1980. 3-A-15. From the J. B. Jackson Pictorial Materials Collection (Groth Collection), Center for Southwest Research and the School of Architecture and Planning, University of New Mexico, Albuquerque, and used by permission.

Fig. C.33. [No title], October 1983. [No slide number.] From the J. B. Jackson Pictorial Materials Collection (Wilson Collection), Center for Southwest Research and the School of Architecture and Planning, University of New Mexico, Albuquerque, and used by permission.

Fig. C.34. House, Black Dallas, [Texas], March 1987. [No slide number.] From the J. B. Jackson Pictorial Materials Collection (Wilson Collection), Center for Southwest Research and the School of Architecture and Planning, University of New Mexico, Albuquerque, and used by permission.

Fig. C.35. Dwellings; Mobile Homes IV. Trailer Court, Fairfield, California, March 1971. 6-P(3)-05. From the J. B. Jackson Pictorial Materials Collection (Groth Collection), Center for Southwest Research and the School of Architecture and Planning, University of New Mexico, Albuquerque, and used by permission.

Fig. C.36. Dwellings, April 1975. 6-A-09. From the J. B. Jackson Pictorial Materials Collection (Wilson Collection), Center for Southwest Research and the School of Architecture and Planning, University of New Mexico, Albuquerque, and used by permission.

Fig. C.37. New Mexico and Pueblo
Indian; New Mexico V, no date.
10-E-9. From the J. B. Jackson
Pictorial Materials Collection (Groth
Collection), Center for Southwest
Research and the School of Archi-
tecture and Planning, University of
New Mexico, Albuquerque, and used
by permission.

Fig. C.38. Rural Institutions and
Small Towns; Celebrations. Sayre,
Oklahoma, May 1976. 8-E-09. From
the J. B. Jackson Pictorial Materials
Collection (Groth Collection), Cen-
ter for Southwest Research and the
School of Architecture and Planning,
University of New Mexico, Albuquer-
que, and used by permission.

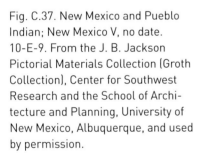

Fig. C.39. Recreation and Sports; Parks, Commons, Gardens. Parks, February 1972. 9-E-09. From the J. B. Jackson Pictorial Materials Collection (Groth Collection), Center for Southwest Research and the School of Architecture and Planning, University of New Mexico, Albuquerque, and used by permission.

Fig. C.40. Recreation and Sports; Aleatory Sports. Lawn, April 1975. 9-B-09. From the J. B. Jackson Pictorial Materials Collection (Groth Collection), Center for Southwest Research and the School of Architecture and Planning, University of New Mexico, Albuquerque, and used by permission.

Fig. C.41. Rural Institutions and Small Towns; Rural centers II. Auction, South Dakota, May 1976. 8-D-05. From the J. B. Jackson Pictorial Materials Collection (Groth Collection), Center for Southwest Research and the School of Architecture and Planning, University of New Mexico, Albuquerque, and used by permission.

Fig. C.42. Land Division; Maps and Miscellaneous. People, April 1975. 1-U-01. From the J. B. Jackson Pictorial Materials Collection (Groth Collection), Center for Southwest Research and the School of Architecture and Planning, University of New Mexico, Albuquerque, and used by permission.

Fig. C.43. City Institutions, City Centers, and Urban Workplaces; Street Life VI. Photograph by Miguel Gandert, October 1985. 4-R(6)-05. From the J. B. Jackson Pictorial Materials Collection (Groth Collection), Center for Southwest Research and the School of Architecture and Planning, University of New Mexico, Albuquerque, and used by permission.

Fig. C.44. Recreation and Sports; Park, Commons, Gardens III, July 1985. 9-E(3)-18. From the J. B. Jackson Pictorial Materials Collection (Groth Collection), Center for Southwest Research and the School of Architecture and Planning, University of New Mexico, Albuquerque, and used by permission.

Fig. C.45. City Institutions, City Centers, and Urban Workplaces; Stores, June 1973. 5-R-08. From the J. B. Jackson Pictorial Materials Collection (Wilson Collection), Center for Southwest Research and the School of Architecture and Planning, University of New Mexico, Albuquerque, and used by permission.

Fig. C.46. Dwellings; Vernacular Houses V. Globe, Arizona, April 1971. 6-A5-1. From the J. B. Jackson Pictorial Materials Collection (Groth Collection), Center for Southwest Research and the School of Architecture and Planning, University of New Mexico, Albuquerque, and used by permission.

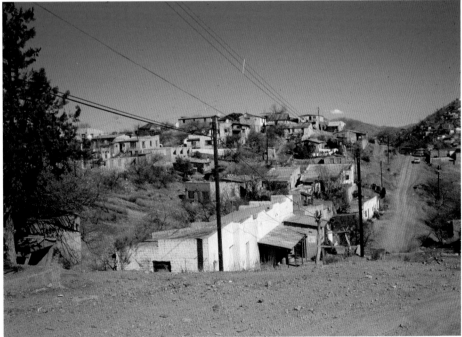

Fig. C.47. Rural Institutions and Small Towns; Small Town III. South, Cities, Tennessee Village, J. B. Jackson, December 1965. 8-V(2)-02. From the J. B. Jackson Pictorial Materials Collection (Groth Collection), Center for Southwest Research and the School of Architecture and Planning, University of New Mexico, Albuquerque, and used by permission.

Fig. C.48. [No title], April 1981. [No slide number.] From the J. B. Jackson Pictorial Materials Collection (Wilson Collection), Center for Southwest Research and the School of Architecture and Planning, University of New Mexico, Albuquerque, and used by permission.

Fig. C.49. Dwellings; Mobile Homes I. Trailers-Bus, January 1971. 6-0-01. From the J. B. Jackson Pictorial Materials Collection (Groth Collection), Center for Southwest Research and the School of Architecture and Planning, University of New Mexico, Albuquerque, and used by permission.

Fig. C.50. Connections (all transportation except the strip). Info Signs, August 1973. 2-T-08. From the J. B. Jackson Pictorial Materials Collection (Groth Collection), Center for Southwest Research and the School of Architecture and Planning, University of New Mexico, Albuquerque, and used by permission.

Fig. C.51. Recreation and Sports; Lawns. Gravel Lawn, Sun City, Arizona, 1971. 9-D-11. From the J. B. Jackson Pictorial Materials Collection (Groth Collection), Center for Southwest Research and the School of Architecture and Planning, University of New Mexico, Albuquerque, and used by permission.

Fig. C.52. Rural Institutions and Small Towns; Churches V, October 1980. 8-J(2)-12. From the J. B. Jackson Pictorial Materials Collection (Groth Collection), Center for Southwest Research and the School of Architecture and Planning, University of New Mexico, Albuquerque, and used by permission.

Fig. C.53. Black Church (South), no date. [No slide number.] From the J. B. Jackson Pictorial Materials Collection (Wilson Collection), Center for Southwest Research and the School of Architecture and Planning, University of New Mexico, Albuquerque, and used by permission.

Fig. C.54. Church (S. Antonio), Cienega, [New Mexico], February 1972. [No slide number.] From the J. B. Jackson Pictorial Materials Collection (Wilson Collection), Center for Southwest Research and the School of Architecture and Planning, University of New Mexico, Albuquerque, and used by permission.

Fig. C.55. Rural Institutions and Small Towns; Camp Meetings, Revivals, August 1973. 8-A-12. From the J. B. Jackson Pictorial Materials Collection (Wilson Collection), Center for Southwest Research and the School of Architecture and Planning, University of New Mexico, Albuquerque, and used by permission.

Fig. C.56. New Mexico and Pueblo Indian; New Mexico IV, no date. 10-D-03. From the J. B. Jackson Pictorial Materials Collection (Groth Collection), Center for Southwest Research and the School of Architecture and Planning, University of New Mexico, Albuquerque, and used by permission.

Fig. C.57. Rural Institutions and
Small Towns. Rural Center, Jackson,
Kentucky, May 1976. 8-P-10. From
the J. B. Jackson Pictorial Materials
Collection (Wilson Collection), Center
for Southwest Research and the
School of Architecture and Planning,
University of New Mexico, Albuquer-
que, and used by permission.

Fig. C.58. Farms, General; Farmsteads, Tractors. Cotton Packing,
near Coachella, California, February
1974. 7-L-12. From the J. B. Jackson
Pictorial Materials Collection (Groth
Collection), Center for Southwest
Research and the School of Architecture and Planning, University of
New Mexico, Albuquerque, and used
by permission.

Fig. C.59. Cities, General; Street Life II [New Mexico]. Photograph by Miguel Gandert, October 1985. 4-R2-12. From the J. B. Jackson Pictorial Materials Collection (Groth Collection), Center for Southwest Research and the School of Architecture and Planning, University of New Mexico, Albuquerque, and used by permission.

Fig. C.60. Farms, General; Agribusiness. Migrant Labor, California, April 1976. 7-A-11. From the J. B. Jackson Pictorial Materials Collection (Groth Collection), Center for Southwest Research and the School of Architecture and Planning, University of New Mexico, Albuquerque, and used by permission.

Fig. C.61. Farms, General; Farmsteads. Colorado, April 1967. 7-M-03. From the J. B. Jackson Pictorial Materials Collection (Groth Collection), Center for Southwest Research and the School of Architecture and Planning, University of New Mexico, Albuquerque, and used by permission.

Fig. C.62. Signs and West Grid, near Burlington, Colorado, no date. [No slide number.] From the J. B. Jackson Pictorial Materials Collection (Wilson Collection), Center for Southwest Research and the School of Architecture and Planning, University of New Mexico, Albuquerque, and used by permission.

Chapter 5

Mr. Jackson: Establishment Man, Vernacular Man, Protean Man

HELEN LEFKOWITZ HOROWITZ

I

Who was J. B. Jackson, and what does he have to teach us? *Figure in a Landscape: A Conversation with J. B. Jackson* and *J. B. Jackson and the Love of Everyday Places*, two films made during the last decade of his life, offer key answers.[1] Jackson was a fresh and original thinker with an extraordinary eye. He was a writer, artist, and photographer with the gift of enabling us to see anew the physical world around us. Jackson gave us images and patterns that allow us to make sense of common things and to delve into uncommon ones. To me, he was a beloved friend. Many years after his death, J. B. Jackson remains alive in these films, a great and quirky man with brilliant insights on the landscape.

Janet Mendelsohn and Claire Marino present an excellent overview of "Mr. Jackson" (as I, tongue in cheek, often called him) and his ideas in their aptly titled documentary, *Figure in a Landscape* (1988). The film appropriately begins with Jackson giving his definition of landscape as not scenery but the organization of human-made space. After a clear, brief statement of Jackson's intellectual achievement, the film moves briskly through his life, illustrated by photographs: His birth in France to American parents, early travels in Europe, studies at Harvard, and military service in World War II. The camera offers us pastoral scenes of Jackson sketching and pruning trees. We watch him give a lecture and greet former students over cocktails.

The heart of the film is the illumination of Jackson's ideas about landscape. With a beautiful touch and superb use of aerial films, Mendelsohn and Marino give us delightful images and Jackson's voice describing the New England village, the grid, the small town and the house, the front yard, the road and the strip, autonomous spaces, and the vernacular landscape. There is a fine sense of progression. To hear Jackson speaking in voice-over about the American landscapes presented on the screen both demonstrates and dramatizes his ideas.

The photography is handsome, and the illustrative matter is rich in historic footage, old photographs, postcards, and commercial film. Elegantly produced, the film has a luminous quality.

In many ways, it is the American equivalent of William Hoskins's BBC television series, "The Making of the English Landscape" (1972).[2] When I first saw *Figure in a Landscape*, I dreamed that it might grow into a comparable series of twelve films.

The man presented here is an *homme juste*, a man of balance and serenity. There is a unity not only about the America he has studied, but about the man himself. This is a face he often presented to the public, especially when he was speaking to a new audience hearing his ideas for the first time.

A quite different J. B. Jackson appears in Bob Calo's film, *J. B. Jackson and the Love of Everyday Places* (1989). Calo focuses on one of Jackson's myriad themes and sets it in his life in the West. After an introduction in which Jackson speaks of the central thrust of his writing and a chorus of admirers reflects on his importance, Calo takes Jackson on the road in New Mexico and Colorado. As they venture first through the Pueblo ruins of Chaco Canyon, then through a deserted agricultural village, a thriving hamlet, a struggling small city that has lost its industrial base, a wealthy neighborhood in Colorado Springs, and Denver's downtown, Jackson comments on what he sees. We look with him at particulars of the landscape, an unoccupied New Mexican house from the nineteenth century, a decaying Main Street, and a family kitchen. We have the pleasure of Jackson's immediate, spontaneous reactions, his grimaces at the noise of a truck, his warm response to a couple hoping to open a country store, his enjoyment as he listens to a man sing. The central idea that Jackson focuses on here was very much on his mind during the 1980s, the contrast between the ordered environments of the Establishment striving for permanency and the local, temporary environments of the Vernacular.

The road trip is interrupted by World War II artillery, and viewers are introduced to Jackson's biography, especially his intelligence work in the European theater. After a brief stint as a regular soldier, Jackson's full command of French and German enabled him to enter military intelligence. To prepare for the advance of Allied troops, one of his tasks was to understand the terrain lying immediately ahead of him without seeing it at firsthand. To do this he examined aerial photographs, maps, guidebooks, and local studies in the libraries of houses where he was billeted. His curiosity and broad-ranging interests led him to the work of French geographers. After the war, when a fall from a horse forced him into physical inactivity, Jackson single-handedly founded, edited, and published *Landscape*, a magazine devoted to human geography to which he contributed many of its most noteworthy essays.

The trip resumes: New Mexican poverty and plenty, a lot for selling agricultural machinery. We pause for an excursion into medieval history and the role of the street. The pieces begin to come together. The producer suggests a relationship between the conflicts Jackson sees between the Establishment versus the Vernacular and his own life as a gentleman-scholar in love with ordinary things. In Denver, Jackson offers a fascinating analysis of the changing street as it has responded to motorized transport, with honey-combed structures to accommodate parking, and he criticizes contemporary urban planning that emphasizes pedestrian leisure instead of work.

The camera gives us images of the man himself around his house, writing in his study, greeting a visiting writer who has made a pilgrimage to see him. We learn that Jackson works as a day laborer, his vocation as a writer unknown to his neighbors, and that he is a devout Christian. A commentator tells us to look at his house and his choices. Finally, Jackson closes the documentary, teasingly suggesting parting shots to the producer: the man walking his dog, getting into his truck, or going into the sunset. This is a Jackson charmingly aware of the genre in which he is being encased.

These two documentaries offer very different portraits of the man and his ideas. Both make clear that much of Jackson's importance lay in his university teaching. For the decade ending in 1978, he split the academic year between Harvard in the fall and Berkeley in the spring. In the Berkeley-centered video by Calo, Jackson is presented as a man of the Southwest who dresses informally, meets his neighbors, punctuates his sentences with a cigarette, and spices his comments with vivid language. He is the Vernacular Man. The Harvard-centered film by Mendelsohn and Marino captures his image in more formal moments, and he speaks the elegant cadences of his written prose. The Establishment claims him. As an Easterner who made a conscious decision to move to the West during the late 1930s, Jackson himself knew how to project these two differing documentary conceptions of him. Both are J. B. Jackson, and both are quite conscious self-presentations. But, of course, Jackson was more—an immensely gifted and complex man who wrote and taught on a wide ranges of subjects.

There is a remarkable sequence at the end of Calo's video in which Jackson is interviewed by a young student. Jackson responds by asking the boy what *he* thinks. Embarrassed, the young fellow says his assignment is to get Jackson's ideas. Jackson responds that his ideas are not important compared with the boy's own. The exchange captures the side of Jackson that refuses to play oracle and insists on being a prod, helping others to think. I like this particular moment for the way it captures Jackson's essential kindness, tough though it sometimes was, the kindness of a teacher and ever-curious friend.

Many elements in both films help us understand how J. B. Jackson could become an original thinker, how he found words to change the way we see the world. Both films dramatize certain of his key insights and offer meaningful frameworks to help viewers appreciate them. Each focuses on a major aspect of the man and his many contributions, emphasizing sources and context in ways that enrich our understanding. While the two films convey a sense of Jackson's complexity, he remains beyond both. He offered himself up sequentially as a Vernacular Man and an Establishment Man, dressing the parts and speaking the words. He did not lie. He was both—to a degree. But, of course, he was more. His life and his work cannot be contained by either persona. He was complex, variable, subtle, elusive, and astonishing.

Fig. 5.1. New Mexico and Pueblo
Indian; New Mexico I. Houses, Albuquerque, Alameda, New Mexico [with
J. B. Jackson's BMW motorcycle],
no date. 10-A-15. From the J. B.
Jackson Pictorial Materials Collection (Groth Collection), Center for
Southwest Research and the School
of Architecture and Planning, University of New Mexico, Albuquerque, and
used by permission.

II

A few years after the two documentaries were made by Janet Mendelsohn/Claire Marino and Bob Calo, I decided that certain of Jackson's key essays needed to be gathered in one place. With his assistance and the advice of many scholars and admirers, I put together *Landscape in Sight: Looking at America* (1997), an anthology of his key writings on the American landscape that also included a full bibliography of his work and a generous selection of his drawings and photographs.[3] In the process I learned a great deal about Jackson that I had not known.

I wrote two introductions for the book, one on his life and the other on his opposition to Modernism. At that point, we had known each other for more than two decades. We sustained a Victorian correspondence, full and rich, a source of continual inspiration and delight to me. With my family, I enjoyed long and repeated visits at his home in La Cienega, south of Santa Fe. In the mid-1990s, he agreed to talk with me on tape, conversations that consisted mainly of his recollections. He let me know that he was the sole author of the entire first issues of *Landscape* magazine. I did a great deal of research and gave careful attention to his early writings, including his novel, *Saints in Summertime* (1938). He entrusted many of his written and pictorial materials to my care and designated me his literary executor.

I relished our conversations over the book. One of the many pleasures in Jackson's talk and writing was his irreverence, an irreverence that prods one to think, to feel, to know. He had a devilish side that delighted in overturning assumptions of all kinds, and this flavored his writings, lectures, and conversation.

As I read and reread his essays, I marveled at his imagination and artful prose. Jackson had the ability to enable readers to see the familiar in fresh new ways—how the land looks from a fast-moving motorcycle, what it is like to enter a town at night and walk the traveler's path from the bus station. He explored changes in recreation and taste and how these reshaped the city and gave us the Strip. He made us notice garages and trailer parks. Many of his pieces are both eye-opening and quirky, enlivened by his amusing but utterly serious detail. He loved his BMW motorcycle and appreciated the drive for peak experiences, and these tastes found expression in "The Abstract World of the Hot-rodder" and later essays on sports.[4]

Landscape in Sight focused solely on the American landscape, but Jackson was also an interpreter of the European landscape about whose deep history he had many brilliant things to say. Jackson's pleasure in travel abroad, taste for Baroque architecture, and appreciation of deep historical patterns of living and working on the land fed a major vein in his writing, a hostility to Modernism in its pure architectural incarnations. During the mid-1990s, I read his unpublished manuscript on the European landscape, "The First 1000 Years." Aspects of its origins are unknown at this writing, but I assume Jackson began working on it after the publication of *American Space* (1972) and completed it in the late 1970s. He told me that after W. W. Norton, his publisher up to that time, rejected it, he simply laid it aside. Also in the mid-1990s, I was visiting Jackson at a moment when he—believing his papers were a burden—was energetically tossing them onto a bonfire. I was able to rescue what remained and send these materials and the manuscript to my home in Massachusetts for safe-keeping. After Jackson's death, I gave these papers to the Center for Southwestern Research at the University of New Mexico, where they form an important part of the J. B. Jackson Collection. Some of the chapters of "The First 1000 Years" became essays in *The Necessity for Ruins and Other Topics*, but I continue to hope that the full manuscript will someday find its way into print.[5]

At the end of my work in putting together the anthology of his essays on the American landscape, we sat in his kitchen and went over the planned illustrations. He asked for the first time to read the two introductions I had written. I sent them to him on my return home, and he phoned me after reading them. His voice sputtered with outrage. Somehow in these pieces I had violated his sense of propriety. When pressed for specifics, he objected to my stating that he attended and graduated from Deerfield Academy. I reminded him that this school proudly claimed him as an alumnus and that his attendance and juvenile writings in Deerfield publications were matters of public record. He also pointed to my mention that, as an undergraduate, he had written lyrics for a Hasty Pudding show at Harvard. I answered that this information was easily attained in the Harvard University Archives. Jackson died before we could reach an understanding, but, when the book was in press after his death, I was required by the publisher to delete from the introduction both of these small, but telling, details.

What was really at stake here? I cannot be sure, but my guess is that, at the initial moment when Jackson read my words, he experienced a feeling that he had lost control of his two carefully constructed, albeit contradictory, self-presentations. He never commented on my real detective work: My essay on his opposition to Modernism revealed his many pseudonyms in the early issues of *Landscape* and based its argument on a reading of the articles by those "writers." Nor did he object in the biographical introduction to my reading of his writings of the 1930s and the importance I placed on the way he adapted his fictional voices to his landscape essays. Reading back over my two pieces in the book, I now think that, in both, I suggest protean, fluid possibilities in his nature and something of his trickster quality and that these, not Deerfield or the Hasty Pudding show, were what may have frightened him.

My own insights into Jackson have grown since *Landscape in Sight*. When I first visited him in New Mexico with my husband and children, it initially struck me as charming that this extraordinary man sought to pose as an ordinary one. I gradually came to understand that his vernacular identity had been carefully constructed over many decades. He was a learned man with exquisite taste, and he was very short in stature. In his long adulthood, he had made a series of choices—to ride in rodeos, to try ranching in New Mexico, to travel in Europe and America by motor bike, to enlist in the army in World War II as an ordinary soldier, to get a BMW tattoo on his arm, to drive a pickup truck. Ultimately, it seemed that, although there were psychological sources of his pleasure in ordinariness I could not know, his actions pointed to ways he chose at different periods in his life to define himself as manly.

It was only in one of our last conversations that he enabled me to see that his establishment identity was no simple inheritance but that it, too, had elements of construction. Both of us had traveled to New York City for the presentation to him of the 1995 PEN Award for Art of the Essay. He had bowed out early at his publisher's dinner in his honor after the ceremony, but at the long breakfast the two of us enjoyed the next morning he felt free to talk in an unusually personal way. Some of it was familiar, but a good deal was new. As privileged as had been his childhood and education, financed out of trust funds, his father left the household early in his childhood and spent the rest of his life abroad. In this later angry telling, Jackson expressed his outrage that his father's only communication to him was a single postcard. His mother, a divorcée and a Christian Scientist, was a working woman. Her occupation as a buyer for Bonwit Teller and then an antiques dealer sent them abroad during his childhood and provided the source of many of the beautiful things in his house. At the breakfast, he told me how, during his boyhood, the two of them regularly dropped quarters in a box to save for a long-projected trip to Europe and that, for two years, they poured lovingly over the diagram of cabins in the ocean liner chosen for their voyage across the Atlantic. Thus, although Jackson had many advantages growing up, his childhood life in New York City allowed more observation of the upper class than membership in it. I now believe that elements of both his vernacular *and* his establishment identities were constructed, and, therefore, both were fragile. This may help explain why, in his last decades, he tried out many new selves as a day laborer, an African American (based on no discovered ancestor), an evangelical Christian, and, finally, without any known ceremony of conversion, a Roman Catholic. Ultimately, his simple gravestone at a local churchyard (Figs. 1.6 and 1.7) is marked only by one fixed point in his life, his exemplary military service.

I miss J. B. Jackson terribly. Several days after attending his funeral in New Mexico, a letter from him came in the mail to me in Massachusetts. About a week before his sudden death, rather than continuing to discuss my introduction, I chose to write to him the kind of personal letter that I had normally written—about my family and my thoughts and feelings, hopes and fears. When I traveled to his funeral, I had not known if he ever received this letter. The letter in the mail told me that he had and that he chose to answer in kind, with his usual considerate regard. I treasure that letter as a gift, one that gave me some peace as I faced the loss of this great friend.

I also treasure *Figure in a Landscape* and *J. B. Jackson and the Love of Everyday Places* for evoking his presence once again. They present J. B. Jackson in the two primary ways that he wanted the world to know him. They give us opportunity to hear some of his brilliant ideas and see at play his questioning and searching mind. And they point to some of his most powerful writings, writings that stir admiration and wonder.

Fig. 6.1 [top]. Cover of *Figure in a Landscape: A Conversation with J. B. Jackson*, a film co-directed and co-produced by Janet Mendelsohn and Claire Marino (Santa Monica, CA: Direct Cinema Limited, 1988) and used by permission.

Fig. 6.2 [bottom]. Southwest, 1987. 10-C-11. J. B. Jackson, likely in San Jose, New Mexico, during the shooting of *J. B. Jackson and the Love of Everyday Places* (San Francisco, CA: KQED-TV, 1989). Photograph by Associate Producer, John Lovell, March 1987, and used by permission.

Chapter 6

Shop Talk: A Conversation with the Filmmakers

JANET MENDELSOHN AND BOB CALO

Janet Mendelsohn (with Claire Marino) and Bob Calo each made documentaries about J. B. Jackson, respectively in 1988 and 1989.[1] Mendelsohn's intent was to suggest the broad reach of Jackson's lectures, while Calo's film set out to reproduce the actual experience of being on the road with Jackson. Nearly twenty years later, in the spring of 2007, the two directors got together in Berkeley to talk about their experiences working with Jackson and about different approaches to documentary filmmaking. Editing of that conversation was kept to a minimum, ellipses indicate a pause or interruption, and brackets indicate new material inserted for clarification and when there was laughter.

MENDELSOHN: When Helen Horowitz first reviewed the two documentaries [we made about J. B. Jackson], she said she wished they could be seen back to back.[2] The new DVD [*J. B. Jackson and the American Landscape*] (Fig. 6.5) finally makes that possible. And this is also the first time that you and I have met. So I thought it would be interesting if we could talk about our process and how we came to make such different portraits of him.

CALO: How did you and Jackson meet?

MENDELSOHN: Jackson and I were in the same department at Harvard. He was teaching his big lecture course on the history of the cultural landscape, and I was teaching documentary filmmaking. His course was wildly popular—like there were students from the GSD [Graduate School of Design], and there were people auditing there from all over the university, but it was mostly undergraduates. He had a reputation as an easy grader and probably the entire Harvard football team took his course. But the thing was, at the end of class, they didn't want to leave. They'd cluster around him, these big athletes, and he was a very small man, with a deep voice that carried. And he would be asking *them* questions. "Where are you from?" "Oh yes, I know it. I hope they haven't done anything to that nice courthouse of yours." And this was Harvard University in the early '70s! I remember Jackson talking about this later. He said, "I hate the way that Harvard students come in, and they're immediately made to feel bad and inadequate. Harvard says to them, 'You are empty vessels, and we're going to fill you up with the proper vocabulary and the proper books and so on.'" He said: "I do something different; I say to them, 'You are interesting, and I want to teach you how to value the place you come from.'" And I think the students felt he was really talking to them, and they were also a bit intimidated but fascinated by him.

CALO: I first heard about him in the mid-70's. I was a musician at the time, living in Berkeley. And there was this saxophone player I knew, who still had one foot in the University [of California], and he told me about this guy who gave these great lectures. Since I had a lot of time in those days and a curious mind, I just showed up one day. And there was this dude in a leather jacket and a shaved head, and he had this really great voice, and he was holding forth on what I thought, at first, was this very obscure thing which, in my memory, was something about door frames, Pueblo door frames. And he showed some slides he had taken. And those struck me, too, because there was nothing arty about them; they were very straightforward. But it was just this dazzling performance. And I left feeling expansive and inspired. And then, a few years later, I was getting a masters in broadcast journalism at San Francisco State. I had to write a thesis, and I had intellectual pretensions [LAUGHTER], so I decided to write about video and architecture and place. And I went to see Jackson in his office, and he spilled coffee on the slides, and he was very, very welcoming. He didn't know me from Adam, but it was like, oh, you want to think about this? No problem. So he was incredibly inclusive.

What also blew my mind about Jackson was looking at the original issues of *Landscape* magazine. That, to me, was a revelation, because, first of all, remember, this was the early 70s. There was this whole kind of thing percolating about different ways of publishing and writing . . . small independent magazines, *Radical Software*, *The Whole Earth Catalog*. And here was someone who had done it twenty years earlier, in the '50s. I liked that. I liked the fact that he was an independent operator. I kind of got it. I got it right away. I got that there was this information in the landscape that people always looked *past*, never looked *at*. So I felt like there was a pioneering aspect to it. And then the whole story, the attitude of it; it was irreverent; there was a bit of the trickster about him, you know?

I was at an age when you can still be inspired by a writer. He was a writer that I discovered, the way people discover writers . . . And he joined the other two writers that really kind of made an impression on me, George Orwell and Dashiell Hammett. Jackson was completely different, because he was so optimistic about everything, but these were the three writers I carried around with me. My personal pantheon. It wouldn't have made sense to anyone else; it was a private pleasure. But the subject matter almost didn't matter. The writing was just dazzling. It was just great writing. Somehow, something about the writing I just thought was incredibly lucid and clear.

MENDELSOHN: I came to his writing much later; it was the lectures that pulled me in. I had my own sort of aha moment when he talked about the grid—all those squares and rectangles that you see when you fly over Midwestern farmland. He said people criticize the grid as being

OPPOSITE:
Fig. 6.3. Front cover of *Landscape*, Vol. 9, No. 1 (Autumn 1959). Used by permission of Peter Goin and Paul F. Starrs, Black Rock Institute, Reno, Nevada.

LANDSCAPE

AUTUMN 1959
ONE DOLLAR

Fig. 6.4. J. B. Jackson as a guest lecturer at the University of California, Berkeley, 1981. Photograph by Jennifer Williams and used by permission.

monotonous and not responsive to the topography. And then he talked about the idea behind it: Jefferson's idea that land should be divided to encourage small, individual property ownership, because he believed that owning your own land would make people better citizens. It was a social idea imposed on wilderness. And this was completely new to me. I'd flown across that grid from the time I was four years old, and I'd never thought of it as an idea. But I remembered what I felt as a kid flying over it. I grew up in an apartment building in New York City, and when I saw that grid I noticed that, in a corner of each square, there was a homestead, and I pictured a family down there, very self-contained on their own square of land, all cozy and complete. And that's where I wanted to be . . . I'm sure it had a lot to do with my parents being divorced, but, for me, that grid was an ideal landscape.

And I bet that's how it worked for everyone who heard him lecture. You come to Jackson's work with your own experience. And he framed it in some way, in a historical or theoretical context, and there'd be a collision between what you had seen and this new way of understanding it. And Jackson's brilliance was to make us feel the power of the idea by experiencing it visually as a landscape.

CALO: What made you decide to make a film about him?

MENDELSOHN: I think it was in 1983. Jackson had retired, and Bob Gardner [a filmmaker and the director of Harvard's Film Study Center] got me thinking about making a film, so there'd be a record of that side of Jackson, the spirit of his lecture course, the performance aspect, the way he connected, which we felt was just as important to preserve as his writing. Jackson's lectures had a distinct, conversational tone. He'd say, "I'm not sure I'm right about this, but I like to think such and such . . . But what do *you* think?" You felt you were in on his thought process, but at the same time it was so poised. I loved that tone, his phrasing, the rhythm of his speech. And that's what I wanted for the film. So we worked to get that. And the idea was to find terrific visual material that would illustrate what he was talking about. It's those gathered images that make the film so different from his lectures, because he barely used visuals when he lectured. He'd show five or six slides at the end; that was it. So the film operates very differently; it gives you a feast of images.

How did you come to make your film?

CALO: I had been working at KQED for about eight years. I'd been doing documentaries, mainly current affairs. By then, having had almost a decade's worth of experience as a television producer, I'd figured out that all you needed to make a story work was a great character, and it was so clear to me that Jackson was a great character. So I just thought, "Wow, he'd be great on television." So I wrote him a letter. That was in July of '86. And pretty quickly, about two weeks later, this letter shows up with, you know, the big, beautiful handwriting. And he says, "Well, Dear Mr. Calo, perhaps you'd like to come visit, and we could talk about this."

So I went to visit him. And he just listened and talked and engaged. He was totally present. So we talked for a while, and then he says, "Do you want to take a trip?" He says, "You've got a very nice rental car there; let's go for a ride." So we took this classic trip driving the old road past Chimayo, up toward Taos. And it was sort of like he was offering me an idea of how to do it. And by the end of the trip I felt like, "OK, that's the film I want to make." The film I want to make is what it's like to go on the road with J. B. Jackson. I wanted to try to reproduce the actual experience of traveling with Jackson. It was as simple as that. I always liked the idea of the road trip, the road trip movie. So that became the organizing principle, and we worked to make that the theme and the thread. It required a sense of improvisation and a little faith that "things would happen," unplanned things that would bring warmth and humor and illumination to the subject at hand. And, of course, as I said before, I had a lot of confidence in my main character.

MENDELSOHN: We spent a week or so filming with Brinck [Jackson] in New Mexico and Colorado in June of '86. But when you went to see him later that summer, you had no idea we'd just finished shooting?

CALO: When he told me you'd just finished, that was the first time I heard about it! And I said, "What? Another movie? Oh my gosh, I didn't know that." And he said, "Yeah, they just left here a few weeks ago." And when I first heard that, I figured we couldn't go forward, it wasn't going to happen. I said, "Oh gee, I guess you don't want to do it then?" And he said, "Well, we could do something different." So apparently he saw it as a different opportunity.

MENDELSOHN: I think you called me up and told me what you were doing, and you asked if I could send you a VHS to look at. I was stunned. I couldn't believe he [Brinck] had agreed to make another film. And, you know, I felt like we had made *the* film. How could you? How could he? But then we [Marino and Mendelsohn] had our premieres, and we got a national broadcast on PBS, and I found a distributor and moved on.

Twenty-eight years later, [George F. Thompson, founder of] the Center for American Places, comes up with the idea to reissue the two films together (Fig. 6.5), and I realized I'd never seen your film. So we got a copy and screened it, and I loved it . . . I saw that you were doing something completely different. And the films have a completely different look . . . We shot on film; you were shooting video at a time when it had a rougher look than it does now. So we were using the establishment medium, and we were from the establishment university, and you guys . . .

CALO: That's true; we were the vernacular film crew [LAUGHTER]. It seemed like the right time to do it, because, like you said, it was a picture of where he was at right then. My only worry the

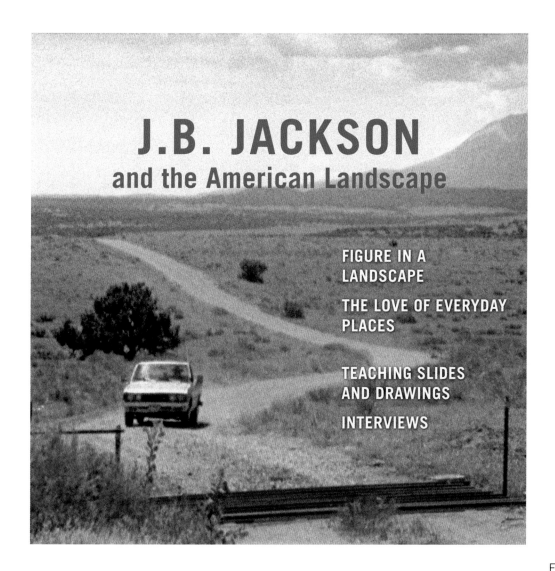

J.B. JACKSON
and the American Landscape

FIGURE IN A
LANDSCAPE

THE LOVE OF EVERYDAY
PLACES

TEACHING SLIDES
AND DRAWINGS

INTERVIEWS

Fig. 6.5. Main menu of *J. B. Jackson and the American Landscape*, a DVD by Janet Mendelsohn (2015) (Appendix A), which includes new material (interviews, artwork, and slides) plus the original documentary films on Jackson produced by Janet Mendelsohn and Claire Marino (1988) and Bob Calo (1989). Used by permission.

whole time was you. That was the only worry. But when I saw your film, it made perfect sense, because your film covered so many subjects and dealt with different parts of the country.

But, with me, it was like he was saying, "I've done that. I've already written that." It's like Miles Davis: "I already did bebop." People said, "Why are you playing this electric music, Miles?" And he said, "Why wouldn't I? Charlie Parker's dead. Why would I play that music again?" The artist is different from the audience.

And that was the other thing that was a great relief for me, because stylistically your film was so different from mine. You know, because my thing was long takes and hanging out. Whereas what you made was more like an introduction to his work in a really richly visual way.

MENDELSOHN: We got a lot of our visual ideas from his essays. The way he used different vantage points/visual perspectives—from the air, walking from the bus station, speeding along a highway. Each one had a device, a conceit, [and] not just an idea but an idea about how to present the idea. The way he could compress his insights into specific examples. We picked that up. We wanted to use a range of visual devices . . . aerial views, tracking shots, time lapse, archival footage, cultural artifacts. So it was conceived as a film with many visual layers.

CALO: That's what I liked about your film. It had a cinematic sensibility. It was clear that you really thought hard about how to visualize the work Jackson had done, like the aerials and that time-lapse thing you did, finding the perfect kind of way of expressing his visual ideas.

MENDELSOHN: Visualizing the patterns Jackson talked about was central to our vision of the film. I knew Robert Fulton, a brilliant filmmaker/cameraman who was known for his aerial work. We needed shots from all over the country, and we couldn't afford to actually hire him to do all that. But Fulton was a fan of Jackson's, so he was willing to work out an arrangement. Whenever he had another aerial assignment, he'd save some film and do a couple of shots for us. We gave him a laundry list, a wish list of shots we wanted. Fulton was a totally unique, creative guy with his own ideas, so I was never sure he was paying attention to what I wanted. But the footage was always spectacular.

CALO: You said it took years to make your film. How did you work?

MENDELSOHN: It was really important to capture his conversational tone, so even though we had to cover a lot of material, we didn't write a verbatim script; the script emerged out of hours of interviews. We went out to Santa Fe and interviewed him for days, drawing him out, getting him to talk about things he'd covered in his course: the house, the front yard, the strip. So we had a structure, but his words weren't pre-packaged. The first time we went there, in 1984, we did mostly sound recording and just a little bit of shooting. This was because I felt we'd get a more relaxed tone if there was no camera. Then we went back to Cambridge and transcribed everything and built the first draft from those interviews. Jackson had already retired [from teaching at Harvard and Berkeley], but, thank God, he got invited to give a lecture at MIT. I think that was in the fall of '85, so we filmed that, and Harvard gave a party for him, and we filmed him in various locations in New England. And then, in 1986, we went out to New Mexico for the major shoot, all the filming in his house, and the trip to Denver, which Claire and I had scouted. But right after that shoot we ran out of money, and we had to write another grant proposal. I went back to Santa Fe on my own in February of 1987 to do the final voice-overs. It went on forever [LAUGHTER].

You said that you and Jackson kind of came up with the idea of structuring the film around a road trip. Did you also decide in advance that he would declare an allegiance to the vernacular landscape, as opposed to the establishment landscape?

CALO: It was totally him; he just went. The first interview he started off by saying, "I'm sorry to disappoint you, but I'm not going to talk about the things that I used to be interested in. My work has taken me in this other direction, kind of an ugly direction. It may not make for a good film." If you look at the transcript, he talked for like forty-five minutes. He just filled up the first tape— and I was like, "Oh, boy" [LAUGHTER]. So I think that was the first time I got the feeling like he took this as an opportunity to think out loud and share it. He said, "I'm really interested in this idea about the Vernacular and the Establishment." [And I asked,] "Which were these two kinds of space?" And he said, "I see it most here in the West, and I think we'll see a lot of this on this trip we're going to take."

MENDELSOHN: He gave you that gift! Paul Groth told me he doesn't think Jackson ever summarized his thinking about the Vernacular as well as he did in that interview. So that's a great moment in your film.

He placed himself so squarely on the side of the underdog. And the way he started your interview—"I'm sorry to disappoint you, but . . . " That grabs your attention, doesn't it?

He did something like that in my film, too. Taking up a surprising position that was counterintuitive or unpopular or wasn't what you'd expect of someone from his background—"You're expecting me to say THIS, so I'll say THAT"—and he liked to set things up like that, as oppositions, and then taking a side.

In my film and in his course, the opposition he set up was between Europe and America. He took up the cause of the U.S., which he saw at the time as more anti-authority, kind of slapped together, unselfconscious. And the way he seemed to portray America as this kind of unified— you know, we all share these experiences. We shared front yards. We shared roads, and we shared looking at it from above. We shared going along the strip. These were shared experiences.

In the 1950s and '60s, Europe was considered a model for planners and architects. So Jackson sees America as the underdog, and he defends the U.S. He says, "Europe is picturesque, it's

Fig. 6.6. J. B. Jackson at the Hilltop Steakhouse in Saugus, Massachusetts, 1987, during the filming of *Figure in the Landscape: A Conversation with J. B. Jackson* (1988). Used by permission of Janet Mendelsohn.

venerable." He says, "I reject that. I like sameness, monotony." Oh [LAUGHTER], you know, and he catches you off guard. And it's complicated, because he had such strong personal ties to Europe; he'd spent so much time there as a kid, and he returned to Europe a lot throughout his life. So I don't think he lost interest in Europe, but he used that way of speaking as a rhetorical device, so it caught your attention. Oh! I always thought Europe was cool, but here's this super cultured guy telling me that the U.S. is really more interesting.

Can you talk about how you got your funding and put together the production?

CALO: Everything went incredibly smoothly. I wrote a one-page proposal to the NEA [National Endowment for the Arts] and just sent it off. And within weeks they said, "OK, here's $10,000." Which is not enough, but I was at a station, and KQED in those days was pretty entrepreneurial, and they found a corporate sponsor, and off we go. It wasn't a big budget. It was like $120,000. And suddenly it was on, and we decided to do it in the spring; I guess it was the spring of '88. We [Calo and Jackson] wrote back and forth a little bit, two or three times, and we hatched this plan. I say 'we' because I don't know if it was him or was it me? I don't know. We were in sync from the beginning.

He chose the locations, starting at Chaco Canyon, stopping in small towns along the way, and ending up in Denver. And I had this improvisational idea, like we'd figure it out as we went along, which, if I were doing it now, I'd be like, "Whoo, you're taking a big risk there, buddy." But I wasn't worried at the time.

And, again, this was all kind of done with this open spirit. If these places are really the way he says they are, we'll find people who embody that. And we did. Like in that town, Villanueva, New Mexico; we just drove into town, and there's this guy, who's the mayor, with his beautiful daughter, and they're up on a ridge, and they're from a land-grant Hispanic family that's been there for 300 years. And we ask them about this obscure stuff, and they just start talking about it right off. Then in another little town, San Jose, there was a guy with a guitar, and suddenly all these drunk guys singing. It was like an acid trip, you know, without the drugs. It was great. So that was the vernacular. And we didn't try to find those people. They found us.

And I think that, also, I was into a non-conventional television style. I've always been trying to find a looser style for television. That's been one of my interests, to be looser and less authoritative. And I'm still doing it now. Basically, my whole career has been based on trying to find this conversational way of doing storytelling in which it's not big a deal, the producer is not God, you know. So I was interested in that.

From a production point of view, it meant having a smart crew and a camera operator, Dana Atchley [who died several years ago], who was an artist in his own right and was perfectly suited to the task. It also meant combining a Cinema Verité approach when Jackson was observing, walking, chatting, with all the other requirements of making the piece. So it was a kind of "write it as you go" approach. Jackson would walk down a residential street, say something that we thought was important. And we'd stop for a few minutes and shoot a sequence so we could use it later. In addition to the Verité, I did have a substantial list of shots and sequences that I knew we would need, set pieces from his writings . . . So it was just a matter of mixing our time between gathering string for the big 'essay' and working with our utterly brilliant 'talent' improvising in the field. I was also lucky to work with a very smart editor in San Francisco, Blair Gershkow, who understood Jackson right away.

MENDELSOHN: What was he like to work with during the shoot?

CALO: The first day, John and I drove up from Santa Fe, and the crew was coming from Colorado. We were supposed to meet at Chaco Canyon. And right now you and I would be saying, "God, that sounds like a horrible plan. Meet the crew in Chaco Canyon at 4:00? No, I don't think so; too risky." I wouldn't do that now. So John and I got there, and the crew was late. They had like an axle problem in the Rockies. And on the way I'm thinking, "I haven't planned this very well. It's 4:00 in the afternoon; it just took three hours to get here from nowhere. Where are we sleeping?" And it was like, "Aw, I forgot." You know? And by then he had mentioned the fact that he had just finished working with the "Harvard people," as he put it, "Janet and the Harvard people." He kept using that phrase. And I gathered that Janet and the Harvard people were much more organized than I was [LAUGHTER]. He said, "Janet was always calling ahead" [LAUGHTER]. And I'm sitting there like, "Maybe I should be calling ahead." I hadn't even thought about it. So with all that rolling around in my mind, we get there, go to the visitors' center, and like within, I would say, thirty seconds, he's engaged with the head ranger there in this incredible conversation. And they don't know who he is. It's like they think he's just like this grizzled farmer who's talking about Anasazi [Puebloan] petroglyphs and roads. And it was just great. I kept saying, "Oh my gosh, this is going to work. I just need a camera. Where are those guys?" Finally, they show up, and we just started to roll. I mean, it was like the camera caught up to him. Then someone recognized him, and she was there doing a petroglyph analysis, and there was a campfire, and everyone sat around and talked til midnight. And we slept in this funky cabin. We had no sheets. But no one seemed to care. Especially him. He did not seem to care. He seemed to be really having a good time. And that was the working model. Go to a place, walk around. We kind of came up with this thing where I wasn't in it but we'd walk and he would talk. He got the geometry of the whole thing quite well. And it was really more a matter of collaborating with him. I thought we were good producers, but we weren't; we were just taking what came.

And I think I was like, I was infatuated. In the sense that everything he did seemed really cool to me. And the cameramen felt the same way. We just thought he was like the coolest guy we'd ever met, and we're just going to hang onto his every word, you know?

So the production was very smooth. He never complained, even though I hadn't learned you're supposed to take care of your talent. I never gave it a thought, and he never complained. We were staying in really lousy motels. At one point, we were going to Denver, and he hopefully said, "Could we stay at the Brown Palace?" And I didn't even know what it was. He said, "That's a good hotel."

MENDELSOHN: And that's one of the things I love about your film. It's so relaxed and responsive to the moment.

CALO: Alright. Well, I'll ask you the same question: What was he like to work with? I'm describing like a band of brothers, wandering the countryside with not a care in the world. I mean, you know, he was like a happy camper with us. What was he like with you?

MENDELSOHN: [LAUGHS] He was a courtly camper. You were a bunch of guys, right? We were two women producers, though the camera crew were guys. And this was his first time in front of a camera. We softened him up for you [LAUGHTER]!

When I approached Jackson, he agreed right away, but he never wanted to talk about it. He said he knew nothing about film. I remember sending him a draft of the script, asking for his comments and his ideas, and he wrote back saying something like, "I'm sure it's fine." That was a disappointment to me. I'd hoped it would be a more collaborative process. But he was busy with other projects. He had two books in the works. So Claire and I did all the research and the scouting, and we chose the locations. But I think he learned as we went along. And he watched what we were doing, and he saw that he could do this, he could carry a film. And then, when he worked with you, he was much more relaxed.

And there was the film vs. video thing, But also we had a real script, we were asking him to cover certain things. And that's where, you know, you had this, I forget how you put it yesterday, but it was something about that you liked to just find something that has its own story, you know, right there in the shooting, and capture that. And I actually remember times when he'd start talking about something that really interested him, speculating on something, and it was great, but I'd know we couldn't use it, so I'd sort of rein him in. Which was too bad. I would have loved to be more spontaneous, but we had to stay very true to our script; otherwise, we would have just had a huge muddle. And also, of course, we were shooting film, and we couldn't afford to just let the camera run. Even the length of a 16mm roll of film is a factor. It's what, about twelve minutes? Whereas you could just keep the video rolling.

CALO: And, remember, I wasn't a filmmaker. I was a news producer. So that's two totally different ways of approaching things. In other words, as a news producer you're there to listen, you've got a video camera, you can shoot for hours. So there's a whole different kind of gestalt about what a television documentary is versus a film documentary.

MENDELSOHN: It occurs to me that there may have been something frustrating to him about the premise of our film. We were dwelling on ideas he developed in the 50s and 60s. And by the time we shot the film he was moving on in his thinking. He may have lost interest in the older ideas. And the other thing is, we did this sweeping summation, as if he were all done, and we were giving him the gold watch and sending him off to pasture. But he was still working and having new ideas, and I think, by the time we finished shooting and we did that sunset shot of him walking up the hill, away from camera, with his little dog, Duffy, he was kind of resistant. And now I'm thinking he may have resented that attempt to summarize his career and tie it up in a bow. He still had more to say. And then you wrote to him. And you were interested in what he was thinking at that moment.

CALO: When I was there, he had a job. He was a volunteer janitor at his church, because he had become very religious, too, late in life. He was part of that community, and he was the janitor. And I, of course, wanted to shoot that, because I thought it was emblematic of who he was and how he felt about the vernacular, but he really didn't want to. And I think it was because they didn't know who he was. They just thought he was the old guy who lived down that road. And so I didn't shoot that. And I remember wondering, "Is that something he did in order to feel that way? Or did he feel that way and, therefore, he did it?" Because, you know, he would also get on an airplane and fly off to conferences. I mean he had the same rich intellectual life and people flying in to see him . . .

MENDELSOHN: I have a painful story, kind of the reverse of yours. We filmed our interviews over a few days. And he and I had decided that he'd wear a blue Oxford shirt for the interviews, which was the kind of thing he wore most of the time. And on the last day of filming interviews he comes out in a work shirt, with his name—John—embroidered in red on the pocket. And I think he also had put on his work cap, a baseball cap, also with his name on it.

Before that moment I had never heard him called John. In fact, I remember my first thought was, "Why is he wearing someone else's shirt?" For his whole life, everyone called him Brinck. That's how he introduced himself. But Brinck was his preppy, establishment name, part of an identity he was starting to question right around then. Apparently, he was in the process of changing his preferred name to John. And I had no idea. But we only had two rolls of film left and one or two final topics to cover. So I asked him to change back to the other shirt, because we couldn't go off on that detour; it would have taken several minutes of film time to explain the shirt, and it would have meant taking the film into a much more personal place, and the film just couldn't go off in that direction, we were already dealing with so much of his history, his ideas. But I think he was offering something of himself that I rejected. And he was probably also showing his frustration that we were talking so much about his past work. Anyway, now, of course, I wish I'd just let him go off in that direction and just followed him.

CALO: You were producing your film independently, right?

MENDELSOHN: Yes, but, of course, we depended on a lot of institutional support. The idea for the film evolved at Harvard, but it had no intention of funding it, so I had to look elsewhere. I had been making films about planning and the environment for the Conservation Foundation in Washington, DC. And the president of that foundation, William K. Reilly, was taken with the idea and really sympathetic. So CF took the project under its wing and applied for a production grant from the NEA's Architecture Division, and it provided our major funding. The Film Study Center at Harvard was helpful in other ways. Later, we got grants from the Massachusetts Council for the Humanities and the LEF Foundation. So I was "independent" in that I had to put together funding myself and find people who were sufficiently committed to the project that they were willing to work for very little money. A friend, Claire Marino, came in to help with the script and ended up co-producing the film with me. Our office and cutting room were in her loft living space. We were at one end, and her nine-year-old daughter slept at the other end. For like a year and a half! It was a difficult situation, but we had no choice. And the film was done on a ridiculously small budget, which meant we had to take time out from production to do more fundraising or take other jobs that actually paid something.

Now let's talk about your editing process.

CALO: It was scheduled as kind of a regular doc edit the way we used to do it at KQED, maybe a little longer than usual. It took about six to eight weeks.

MENDELSOHN: And you were editing on tape, right?

CALO: Well, let me think about this . . . We hadn't gone digital yet there, so it was a Beta edit. Basically, like I said before, it was clear what the basic structure was going to be. We had the order of everything. So I think what we did is typical. We made an assembly of all the cool stuff from all the places. Then I went back and wrote stuff. [To] a friend of mine, Eddie Marshall, a great jazz musician, I said, "Hey, I need music." He put together this great band. We went into the studio, and it was all, everything was done in a very quick first take. I said, "OK, when the bird lands on the antenna, the guitar starts, then I need forty more seconds. They were these great players, and they just did their thing. They scored it. It was all done with a lot of faith. I didn't know enough to be worried so it all sounded great to me. I'd say, "That'll work." You know? "That'll work" [LAUGHTER].

MENDELSOHN: Before we started editing, it seemed straightforward; I guess because Jackson made it seem straightforward in his lectures. But when we came to put it together, it did not happen at all easily. It just felt like a shapeless list, with no direction. It took us a long time to find a way to shape it. We had all these fragments that we were trying to put together like a mosaic. But it kept feeling arbitrary. We'd show it to people, and they'd say, "Why are you telling all this? What's your point?" We did at least three screenings, and people weren't getting it at all; it wasn't hanging together. So we'd tear it apart and move things around. For a while, I was terrified that the film would never work.

Finally, we hit on the idea of using chapter breaks, with titles as an organizing device. I remember resisting that, because it seemed too didactic, not organic enough. But, of course, once we put them in, it felt completely self-evident that you'd do it that way. And it echoed Jackson's essay form and his lectures, each with its own title. But that's the way an editing process often works—you have to stumble around for the solution and, once you get it right, it feels obvious and almost inevitable.

The whole editing process was kind of like swimming upstream. We were trying to pull together his ideas, to make them function as a whole. But the man wrote essays! He wanted to dip in and move on; he didn't want to pull everything together into a single statement. He wanted the freedom to invent and to contradict himself. So I think we were going against the grain . . . it was fighting the, you know . . . Just thinking about it now gives me a headache [LAUGHTER]! The guy did not write books. He didn't like to think in ways that hung together.

CALO: I was a staff producer at KQED. In other words, I had the infrastructure, I didn't have to work out of someone's loft, I didn't have to worry. So I think, in terms of the speed, it was much more efficient. And I still teach that now. We have a documentary program here [at UC, Berkeley], but I teach a kind of counter-documentary approach, which says, "Efficiency is valuable." You know, for the life of me, I don't understand why these doc producers spend six months editing endlessly, endlessly, with group screenings and test screenings. So what bullshit is that? Just make your film, do it fast, and be done with it. And then make another one. But only a television person would have that notion.

The film people say, "Oh no, this is special, this is magic." It's all in the consultative process. And they want to know what other people think. I don't care what anyone else thinks [LAUGHTER]. I care what the EP [executive producer] thinks. So this idea that you would have test screenings, I would never have a test screening. I would run from a test screening.

MENDELSOHN: Well, wait a minute. As a TV producer, you are, by definition, making something for an audience. You don't want to know if your audience is going to respond to it?

CALO: I will know if it's working, if I don't get fired [LAUGHTER]. I mean it's totally different.

MENDELSOHN: The other thing is, you were working with an editor. As the director, you could come in fresh and respond to what she'd done. But I was editing it myself, so I didn't have that distance. And a lot of independent filmmakers edit themselves. You're so close to the material. You don't have that executive producer to please, but you need some sort of outside perspective.

Did making the film influence the way you worked on other documentaries?

CALO: It did become my working method in the years after I made the Jackson documentary. It's served me well in both independent shoots as well as highly commercial situations working for network newsmagazines. My approach or strategy for video or film production has always been a hybrid of news and documentary . . . I like the matter-of-factness of news and the breadth of ideas in documentary. But many documentaries are a bit too precious for me . . . too exotic, too self-aware, and too proscriptive. News is much more prosaic and has a humbleness about it that I like. But there's little magic in news. So, for me, it's the combination that works best—a straight-forward account of things that are, in fact, compelling and interesting. I don't like to gin up a film with dense argument to get to a point that I think the audience ought to be given. My preference was and is to think hard about real situations that have the potential of meaning, assemble a team of people who have the right mix of skill *and* attitude, and trust that things will happen in front of the camera that will be memorable and real.

MENDELSOHN: Looking back, what did the project mean to you?

CALO: This was really the first chance I had to like show something that was all mine. So, even though it was just something I did, I've never forgotten it. And I've always thought it was as good a project as you could have, in that it was worth doing and fun to do. And it's the thing I'm most proud of—and the easiest. It just flowed.

MENDELSOHN: It's also the thing I'm most proud of, because it was the hardest thing I've ever done. And then, looking at it, you don't see any of that. You see Jackson's ideas, beautifully visualized. It just looks clear and effortless.

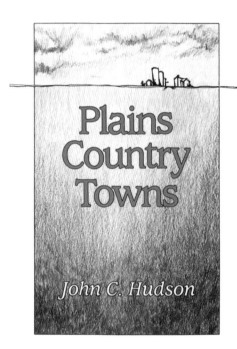

Fig. 7.1 (left). Front cover of John C. Hudson's book, *Plains Country Town* (Minneapolis: University of Minnesota Press, 1985), which won the inaugural John Brinckerhoff Jackson Book Prize awarded by the Association of American Geographers. Used by permission of the University of Minnesota Press.

Fig. 7.2 (right). Front cover of Anita Berrizbeitia's book, *Roberto Burle Marx in Caracas: Parque del Este, 1956–1961* (Philadelphia: University of Pennsylvania Press, 2007), which won the inaugural John Brinckerhoff Jackson Book Prize awarded by the Foundation for Landscape Studies. Used by permission of the University of Pennsylvania Press.

Chapter 7

Passing the Torch:
Landscape Studies in
the Post-Jacksonian Age

TIMOTHY DAVIS

A Disciplined Vision

J. B. Jackson is widely regarded as the founder of cultural landscape studies in North America. His writings, lectures, and teaching introduced the field, shaped its content, and inspired a wide range of scholars, artists, writers, designers, and others to devote their talents to finding meaning and value in the landscapes of everyday life. Prominent figures in disciplines as diverse as architecture, geography, landscape architecture, American studies, and photography have cited Jackson's influence as an inspirational figure and transformative intellect who opened their eyes to new ways of seeing and thinking. Jackson's generosity, passion, and eloquence instilled an almost evangelical zeal among converts to his deceptively simple proposition that even the most seemingly banal landscapes are rich and complex cultural texts, whose meaning and significance can be revealed through close observation, informed analysis, and evocative interpretation.[1]

Jackson articulated his basic premise in the first issue of *Landscape* magazine (Fig. 3.1), which he founded in 1951. "There is really no such thing as a dull landscape," he declared. "A rich and beautiful book is always open before us. We have but to learn to read it."[2] This was a startling assertion at a time when serious writers focused on analyzing the efforts of critically acclaimed designers and denouncing the ways in which the common American landscape fell short of elite ideals. While Jackson was not the first to call attention to the cultural significance of ordinary landscapes, his articulate voice, intellectual rigor, and engaging personae exerted a formidable impact on a wide audience. Summarizing his goals late in his career Jackson observed:

> Over and over again, I have said that the commonplace aspects of the contemporary landscape, the streets and houses and fields and places of work, could teach us a great deal not only about American history and American society, but about ourselves and how we relate to the world. It is a matter of learning how to see.[3]

It is a testament to Jackson's vision and influence that the first part of this statement has become a truism. Few today would contest the proposition that the study of ordinary landscapes is a worthwhile endeavor, or that designers, historians, and other cultural interpreters can learn from the practical and symbolic uses people make of their everyday environments. Postmodernists heightened appreciation for popular architectural elements, the New Urbanism rediscovered the prosaic virtues of traditional neighborhoods, and planners, architects, and developers now extol the virtues of context-sensitivity and "a sense of place." Even art historians have moved beyond elite predilections and formalist strictures to consider broader aspects of the built environment. Artists, authors, popular commentators, and commercial enterprises employ cultural landscape imagery to evoke a wide range of social, historical, and psychological associations. The federal government has provided its imprimatur, listing landscapes on the National Register of Historic Places and creating a program to identify and evaluate cultural landscapes within the National Park System. The terms *landscape* and *cultural landscape* are used so promiscuously, in fact, and with such diverse connotations that it is often hard to determine what they are meant to imply or whether their users understand the meanings and associations they acquired under Jackson's aegis.

The widespread adoption of the "cultural landscape" concept is a laudable development, as is the energizing intellectual diversity that increased popularity has brought to the subject. It does, however, present challenges for those concerned with conveying Jackson's ideas to new audiences while integrating the ever-expanding social and theoretical concerns that make landscape studies such a rich and rewarding field. Pondering the future of the discipline, Jackson expressed concern that contemporary landscape scholars placed too much emphasis on "erudite and theoretical discussions" and too little on the task of introducing students to landscape studies. "What would be an essential bibliography?" he asked, "And how was the student to learn how to see the contemporary world?" Without a concerted effort to present a broad-based interpretive framework, he lamented, landscape studies would become "fragmented among landscape architects, geographers, Americanists, and have no overall character."[4]

This essay is an attempt to provide a wide-ranging yet relatively concise introduction to cultural landscape studies. By summarizing Jackson's contributions, tracing parallel developments in associated fields, and addressing recent themes in landscape scholarship, the goal of this survey is to promote a broad-based approach that combines Jackson's core insights with contemporary intellectual strategies and social concerns. Given the multifaceted nature of the field and the constantly expanding and evolving corpus of thought, these recommendations are not intended to be comprehensive or definitive. The following overview is an attempt to convey a sense of the depth and breadth of related accomplishments—both academic and non-academic—organize them around coherent and manageable themes, and suggest readings that artists, writers, scholars, and designers may find thought-provoking and useful. By presenting a range of possibilities rather than proposing a rigid interpretive model, this essay encourages readers to explore the richness and variety of landscape studies and formulate their own approaches based on personal perspectives and concerns. In keeping with Jackson's injunction, the underlying aim is to combat the tendency toward academic and professional specialization by encouraging the advancement of interdisciplinary approaches to landscape studies.

The Jacksonian Persuasion

At first glance, it would seem that Jackson left few clues about how subsequent scholars might expand upon his legacy. He clearly preferred to lead by example and rarely engaged issues of methodology or pedagogy head-on. His most direct comments on landscape studies education appeared in the preface to *Discovering Vernacular Landscapes* (1984). Observing that a number of universities were beginning to offer courses in landscape history, Jackson welcomed this trend with his characteristic blend of sermonizing and self-deprecation. Suggesting that the primary impact would be to encourage sightseeing in the American heartland, Jackson delivered a typically bold and enigmatic statement, declaring that his ultimate hope was that the increased attention would "produce just the sort of attitude I wish all Americans shared: an intelligent affection for the country as it is, and a vision disciplined enough to distinguish what is wrong in the landscape and should be changed from what is valuable and worthy of protection." Taken together with his assertions that ordinary landscapes "could teach us a great deal not only about American history and American society, but about ourselves and how we relate to the world," this seemingly offhand remark crystallized the core of Jacksonian landscape studies, whether for better or—as some say— for worse.[5]

The easiest target for criticism was Jackson's seemingly mawkish exhortation to embrace the American landscape on an emotional and, perhaps even, spiritual or ideological level. Not only did real academics rarely employ such terms as "affection" and "love," as Jackson was wont to do, but by the 1980s most scholars had long since abandoned the glorification of supposed virtues and shifted their attention to the exposure of purported vices. While Jackson's politics were more conservative than many of his followers, it is important to read these words in the context of his ongoing battle to valorize the American landscape as a subject worthy of study in its own right rather than a debased version of Eurocentric ideals. A simplistic critique also fails to take into account Jackson's crucial qualifier: "Intelligent affection" did not imply naive acceptance or boosterish celebration. Coupled with his call for a "disciplined vision" and the injunction to distinguish what was right from what was wrong, it is clear that Jackson envisioned landscape studies as a rigorously critical moral and intellectual endeavor and not—as some critics have suggested—a passive and relativistic cataloguing of superficial visual phenomena. Jackson wanted people to understand how landscapes embodied cultural concerns, but, even more than that, he wanted them to care about what they saw and consider the ways in which landscapes met or failed to meet the needs of those who used them and depended on them. His eloquence was not a happy accident but a reflection of his desire to engage readers in an empathetic act of moral and social inquiry.

The best way to appreciate the depth, breadth, and vitality of Jackson's approach is to immerse oneself in the first eighteen volumes of *Landscape* magazine, those that he personally edited and published. Viewed in its entirety, this era of *Landscape* bears witness to the intellectual genesis of the field while underscoring the innovative spirit that enlivened the enterprise. By progressing page by page and issue by issue, one can trace the evolution of Jackson's ideas, observing how he developed and refined his perception of landscape studies. While Jackson's own writings were central, it is equally illuminating to note how the contributions he solicited from a wide range of contemporary thinkers to extend the intellectual reach and geographic breadth of the field. The diversity and notoriety of contributors underscored both the sweeping interdisciplinarity Jackson promoted and the degree to which significant scholars, designers, and other experts embraced his vision. Jackson's insatiable curiosity was manifest both in the range of book reviews and in the eclectic array of thought-provoking observations and landscape-related excerpts he sprinkled throughout each issue. Another aspect of Jackson's editorial leadership best experienced by viewing the magazine itself was the prominent use of illustrations and his subtle but sophisticated attention to graphic design. Together with the literary quality of the prose, Jackson's concern with *Landscape*'s visual appeal demonstrated that he was not interested in producing yet another staid academic journal but wanted to reach a broader audience encompassing designers, planners, and, in spirit at least, the educated public.

For those without access to *Landscape* or desiring a more expedient approach, most of Jackson's salient essays have been anthologized in various collections dating from the 1970s to the 1990s, which have the additional benefit of including pieces from the post-*Landscape* period.[6] Since the number and variety of Jackson's published works can be intimidating, some guidance may be helpful in negotiating his oeuvre. Anyone familiar with Jackson's writings will have developed personal favorites, but the following selections represent key aspects of his work and demonstrate his wide-ranging rhetorical style.

By way of introduction, the preface to *Discovering Vernacular Landscapes*, along with the essays "Learning about Landscapes," "The Word Itself," and "Concluding with Landscapes," constitute Jackson's most explicit attempts at articulating his conception of the cultural landscape and reflecting on his interpretive goals.[7] Jackson's penchant for engaging contemporary developments, extrapolating their social significance and historical antecedents, and employing these observations to encourage critics to be more tolerant of evolving conditions and popular predilections is manifest in essays such as "The Four Corners Country," "The Sunbelt City," "Other Directed Houses," "Limited Access," "Truck City," and "To Pity the Plumage and Forget the Dying Bird."[8] Many of these essays displayed Jackson's fascination with the impact of the road and the automobile on American life. "Auto Territoriality" and "The Abstract World of the Hot Rodder" also evinced Jackson's interest in phenomenological and psychological perspectives. A later essay, "The Road Belongs in the Landscape," provided a more historical and comparative overview.[9] Jackson's signature ability to compose evocative and insightful portraits of prototypical landscapes is displayed in vignettes such as "The Stranger's Path," "Two Street Scenes," and "The Almost Perfect Town."[10] His gift for employing fiction to illuminate landscape history is epitomized in "The Westward Moving House," wherein he traced the evolution of ideas about domestic architecture and rural values by imagining the experiences of successive generations of a fictionalized farm family as they moved through time and space from Puritan New England to mid-twentieth-century Texas.[11] More conventional explications of the historical development of landscape features include "The Domestication of the Garage," "Ghosts at the Door" (a pioneering study of the American lawn), "From Monument to Place" (a history of the American cemetery), and "The Past and Future Park."[12] Representative essays charting Jackson's efforts to address cultural landscape history on a broader scale range from early accounts such as "Chihuahua as We Might Have Been" to mid-career musings along the lines of "The Virginia Heritage," "The Nineteenth-Century Rural Landscape," and "The Order of a Landscape," to later ruminations such as "A Pair of Ideal Landscapes" and "A Sense of Place, a Sense of Time."[13] His most sustained historical disquisition, *American Space: The Centennial Years* (1972), remains a valuable resource as a source of basic information and reminder that landscape history can be made engaging and accessible to a broad, non-academic audience.[14] Subsequent scholars have contested some of Jackson's historical interpretations and called attention to his silence on matters of interest to contemporary audiences. While many of these criticisms are well-founded, the enduring value of Jackson's work lies not so much in his specific observations but in the ground-breaking nature of his efforts and the inspiration he provided to a wide range of investigators.

A Matter of Learning How to See

Jackson was the singular product of a time and place in which he seemed at once to be a bold pioneer of populist revolt and a venerable holdover from a vanishing age of classical erudition and noblesse oblige. Given the changes in academic culture and society at large, the idea of perpetuating a "Jacksonian" school of landscape studies has little ethical or intellectual merit. Fortunately, his methods were so protean and diverse as to defy rigid codification or rote repetition. In fact, one of the signature characteristics of the Jacksonian approach was its omnivorous embrace of topics, sources, and interpretive strategies. As Jackson demonstrated, however, creativity and interdisciplinarity were not excuses for superficiality or sloppy communication. To the contrary, the enlarged freedom placed a higher burden on the landscape interpreter to be historically grounded, verbally persuasive, and conversant with theoretical issues and social concerns. What Jackson described with characteristic simplicity as "a matter of learning how to see" was anything but a simple task. In the space of a single essay on some seemingly innocuous landscape feature, he might invoke classical and biblical sources, cite obscure European precedents, make trenchant observations about the appearance and social functions of the topic at hand, and allude to current theoretical texts that ranged through the decades from David Reisman's *The Lonely Crowd* (1950) to Michael Harrington's *The Other America* (1962), to Michel Foucault's *The Order of Things* (1966). Those who critique Jackson's purported lack of theoretical sophistication should note that he read Foucault in the original French long before English translations became a staple of graduate school curricula.[15] Despite the widespread acceptance of landscape studies today, the demands on contemporary landscape interpreters are in many ways even greater than they were in Jackson's time. In order to develop the disciplined and intelligent vision Jackson espoused, they must not only have a thorough understanding of the traditional sources and evolving ideas that led to the formation of landscape studies, but familiarize themselves with the breadth of knowledge that has enriched the field in the ensuing decades.

Several anthologies have attempted the ambitious task of introducing readers to landscape studies and encouraging them to see and interpret the built environment from a variety of perspectives. The first cohesive effort at providing an introduction to the field was D. W. Meinig's *The Interpretation of Ordinary Landscapes* (1979).[16] This collection of essays was intended to familiarize readers with what Meinig characterized as "a lively and expanding realm of interest." While all the contributors save Jackson were cultural geographers, Meinig emphasized that landscape studies is inherently interdisciplinary and suggested that its vitality stems from the ability to transcend "the usual bounds of any one academic guild." Acknowledging that the idea of landscape employed by Jackson and his colleagues was an unfamiliar and ambiguous notion, Meinig took pains to distinguish it from several closely allied concepts. Landscape is not identical to nature, nor is it to be equated with scenery, environment, region, or place. Landscape—or cultural landscape, for additional emphasis—is a more holistic concept, combining all these elements and requiring broad-based analysis to take full measure of its physical character and social complexity. The book's most enduring essays provided basic guidance for approaching the challenge of interpreting ordinary landscapes. By presenting these propositions in vivid, easily accessible prose, essays such as Peirce Lewis's "Axioms for Reading the Landscape" and Meinig's "The Beholding Eye" and "Symbolic Landscapes" became instant classics that retain considerable value as introductory texts. While some precepts might seem simplistic to readers steeped in subsequent social theory, even the more problematic passages afford opportunities for reflection on the origins of landscape studies and the evolution of academic inquiry in general. More speculative contributions by Yi-Fu Tuan, David Sopher, Marwyn Samuels, and David Lowenthal exemplified Meinig's contention that landscape interpretation could transcend disciplinary strictures and flourish as a humane art.[17]

Two anthologies published shortly after Jackson's death underscored the ongoing appeal of landscape studies while illustrating the ways in which the field continued to evolve in response to the theoretical stances and social concerns of late-twentieth-century cultural inquiry. In *Understanding Ordinary Landscapes* (1997), Paul Groth, Jackson's successor at Berkeley, and Todd Bressi, an editor of *Places*, compiled contributions to a symposium on "Vision, Culture, and Landscape," at which Jackson had been a key participant.[18] Groth's opening essay reiterated Jackson's concerns in contemporary academic terminology, characterizing landscape studies as "the history of how people have used everyday space—buildings, rooms, streets, fields, or yards—to establish their identity, articulate their social relations, and derive cultural meaning."[19] While earlier landscape scholars often focused on traditional societies and rural or small-town subjects, Groth observed that the term had become more encompassing, so that not only urban topics, but everything from factory floors to nominally natural areas displaying few overt signs of human intervention fell under the rubric of cultural landscape. Groth also pointed to the growth of interest in issues of race, gender, ethnicity, and class, along with the tendency to view landscapes as sites of cultural contestation rather than as symbols of shared values. Like Jackson, he asserted the primacy of direct observation over archival research and abstract theoretical speculation, while acknowledging that the latter were indispensable for extrapolating unseen cultural forces. The ensuing essays ranged from analyses of specific landscapes to theoretical discussions of the strengths and weaknesses of the cultural landscape approach. Dolores Hayden's "Urban Landscape History: The Sense of Place and the Politics of Space" provided a succinct overview of the topic, deftly summarizing classic interpretive strategies while demonstrating the ways in which recent scholarship had begun to address the spatial manifestations of underlying power structures and engage cultural productions organized around the categories of race, gender, ethnicity, and class.[20]

Everyday America: Cultural Landscape Studies after J. B. Jackson (2003), edited by Groth and Chris Wilson, J. B. Jackson Chair of Cultural Landscape Studies at the University of New Mexico, extended the themes expressed in the preceding anthologies. Drawn from presentations given at the first major conference on cultural landscape studies following Jackson's death, the volume was both retrospective and prospective. Essays by Patricia Nelson Limerick and Jeffery Limerick focused on Jackson's rhetorical style, underscoring the manner in which he encouraged audiences to share both the joy of discovering vernacular landscapes and the burden of making sense of them. Several authors challenged readers to rethink the political and ontological bases of landscape studies, suggesting that the empiricist roots of the field promoted a naive and relativistic moral stance while casting the landscape as the passive and largely stable result of cultural consensus rather than as a continually evolving site of cultural contestation. Essays on African-American landscapes in Kentucky, Latino streetscapes in East Los Angeles, and the segregation of male and female public space in early-twentieth century San Francisco testified to increased attention to cultural diversity. Wilson and Groth concluded that the inherent "polyphony of landscape studies" remained one of its greatest virtues, in that it promoted intellectual cross-fertilization while warding against the field's subordination to the parochial constraints of any one particular discipline.[21]

For many readers, these three anthologies will provide an ample and accessible overview of the historical development and current concerns of cultural landscapes studies—especially when combined with one or more of the classic collections of Jackson's own writing, of which *Landscape in Sight: Looking at America* (1997) is by far the most comprehensive volume.[22] For those interested in more expansive reading or considering developing an academic course in cultural landscape studies, the following suggestions are offered as a guide to relevant resources and as an inducement to further inquiry. The thematic demarcations are somewhat arbitrary, especially in view of the increasingly interdisciplinary nature of scholarly practice, but traditional academic divisions played important roles in the development of landscape studies and they continue to influence its development today.

Human Geography

Human geography—also known as cultural geography, at least to non-specialists—is the academic discipline most closely associated with the origins of landscape studies. Not only did Jackson gain inspiration from French geographers such as Maurice L'Annou and Paul Vidal de la Blache, but geographers were among the first to embrace his agenda, which they augmented with parallel efforts arising from their own personal interests and scholarly traditions. Jackson's emphasis on interpreting landscapes as the concretization of their inhabitants' cultural values bore close relation to the concept of "cultural landscape" developed by the geographer Carl O. Sauer, whose 1925 essay, "The Morphology of Landscape," exerted a profound influence on the field.[23] As chairman of the geography department at the University of California, Sauer presided over what became known as the "Berkeley School" of cultural geography, whose practitioners focused on establishing the ways in which cultural groups imprinted their influence on the landscape. Leading figures of this movement included Meinig and Lewis, as well as Fred Kniffen,

Wilbur Zelinsky, Eugene Cotton Mather, John Fraser Hart, and Terry Jordan. Zelinsky's opus, *The Cultural Geography of the United States* (1973), restated the goals and methods of this approach and provided a sweeping demonstration of its potential.[24] More succinct summaries can be found in Lewis's and Meinig's previously cited essays and in John Fraser Hart's "Reading the Landscape," which appeared in another engaging anthology, *Landscape in America* (1995), edited by George F. Thompson.[25]

By the 1980s, a new generation of geographers steeped in contemporary critical theory and cultural politics began to challenge conventional approaches on both ethical and ontological grounds. Drawing on deconstructivist critiques, postmodern theories, and the British Cultural Studies movement, proponents of the "New Cultural Geography" found fault with reigning notions of both "culture" and "landscape." The primary complaint about the old geography was that it viewed culture as a comprehensive framework that governed human activities rather than as an active process of social contestation among competing interests—as a noun rather than a verb. Geographers working from this mindset were accused of producing exhaustive studies of building patterns and land use while shedding little light on the economic, political, and ideological trans-actions that influenced such creations. Critics also contended that the traditional approach rested on assumptions about universally shared values that no longer seemed tenable in an increasingly pluralistic and contentious society and that it neglected issues of power, resistance, and social inequality that were coming to the fore across a wide range of disciplines. The New Cultural Geography shifted attention to the ways in which these concerns influenced the manner in which people shaped and interpreted their environments. It emphasized that landscapes were not passive reflections of cultural consensus but active agents in promoting ideological constructs and social relationships. The seeming inevitability of familiar landscapes made them powerful forces for rei-fying dominant values and normalizing inequitable social structures.[26]

An influential outgrowth of this emphasis on the ideological functions of landscape was a resurgence of interest in landscape art. Led by the British geographers Denis Cosgrove and Stephen Daniels, scholars from a wide range of disciplines began interrogating traditional land-scape paintings for evidence of the ways in which these seemingly benign compositions encoded messages about class relationships, power structures, and national identity.[27] Similar claims were made about designed landscapes and landscape representations in other media. While exposing the ideological undertones of real or imagined landscapes was a valuable goal, this approach could be taken to extremes where the theoretical ramifications of landscapes belied their func-tion as lived environments whose meaning and significance were derived, at least in part, by the thoughts and actions of their inhabitants. In addition to striking more politicized geographers as an exercise in academic solipsism, the presumption that theoretically informed sophisticates held a monopoly on interpretive authority ran counter to the belief that landscapes embodied multiple, contested, and continually evolving cultural values. A more activist strain of cultural geography was spearheaded by David Harvey and Neil Smith, whose commitments to social justice and emphasis on the spatial ramifications of capitalist economies found expression in works such as Harvey's *Social Justice and the City* (1973) and *Consciousness and the Urban Experience: Studies in the History and Theory of Capitalist Urbanization* (1985) and Smith's groundbreaking 1979 essay, "Toward a Theory of Gentrification: A Back to the City Movement by Capital, not People," and more general assessment, *Uneven Development: Nature, Capital, and the Production of Space* (1984).[28] Just as Cosgrove and his colleagues argued that painting and garden design masked and justified the processes through which economic elites maintained their dominance, Harvey and Smith maintained that conventional explanations of urban development concealed and legitimized the spatial operations of power and capital. Harvey and Smith illustrated their arguments with vignettes drawn from current and historical conflicts, but the strident Neo-Marxism that focused valuable attention on the political economy of landscape formation could strike readers as tendentious, overly deterministic, and stylistically unappealing. Their insistence that geographers could and should engage contemporary social issues may have been rooted in 1960s politics and Marxism's lingering hold on the British academy, but Jackson himself routinely contested establishment attitudes, and the preponderance of landscape scholars have followed suit.

By the 1990s, many geographers sought to combine old and new approaches into expansive interpretive strategies that were theoretically informed and political aware yet grounded in substantive fieldwork and, in the best of cases, expressed in accessible and engaging prose. Don Mitchell's *The Lie of the Land: Migrant Workers and the California Landscape* (1996) exemplified this synthetic and multi-dimensional approach, uniting the interrogation of landscape imagery with socioeconomic analysis, exhaustive historical research, and a healthy dose of moral outrage. Mitchell's methodological chapter summarized the theoretical debates of the previous decades, while his definition of "landscape" provided a concise statement of contemporary concerns: "Landscape is thus best understood as a kind of produced, lived, and represented space constructed out of the struggles, compromises, and temporarily settled relations of competing and cooperating social actors: it is both a thing (or suite of things), as Sauer would have it, and a social process, at once solidly material and ever changing."[29]

Environmental Experience and the Sense of Place

Many of Jackson's most compelling essays owed their efficacy to his ability to evoke the ways in which people experienced the intimate qualities of specific places. Jackson was reticent about his aims and methods in this regard, allowing his poetic insights to speak for themselves.

Several of his contemporaries were more overtly analytical in interpreting how humans made sense of their physical environments. Kevin A. Lynch, the urban planner at M.I.T., sought to understand how people negotiated urban landscapes by examining the mental maps they constructed as embodiments of individual perceptions and broader cultural values. Subsequent critics have questioned Lynch's methodology, but his 1960 classic, *The Image of the City*, spawned innumerable imitations and continues to serve as a thought-provoking and accessible introduction to the question of how people perceive and organize the places in which they live.[30] Yi-Fu Tuan, like Lynch, was an early contributor to *Landscape* who produced a succession of speculative essays and extended ruminations that delved into cultural anthropology, psychology, cosmology, literature, linguistics, and myriad other disciplines to explain not only how people perceived their surroundings, but also how they developed attachments to them.[31] In *The Silent Language* (1959) and *The Hidden Dimension* (1966), Edward T. Hall—yet another early contributor to *Landscape*—developed what he called "the science of *proxemics*" to describe the ways in which people used and experienced space.[32] Hall made a prescient plea for tolerance based on the recognition that ethnic groups differed in their conceptions of appropriate spatial behavior. *The Poetics of Space* (1969), by French philosopher Gaston Bachelard, acquired an almost cult-like following for its reflections on the experiential, psychological, and spiritual qualities of dwellings and their surroundings.[33]

During the 1970s and 1980s, phenomenologist geographers such as David Seamon, Anne Buttimer, and Edward Relph drew on the writings of Edmund Husserl, Maurice Merleau-Ponty, and Martin Heidegger to explicate the ways in which people were immersed in their immediate worlds, emphasizing the importance of feeling rooted in spiritually sustaining places.[34] The phenomenologists' focus on individual experience, their belief in universal human predispositions, and their indifference to broader social structures were unsatisfying to more ideologically oriented landscape interpreters, but the meticulous attention to individual experience served as an important counterbalance to analytical frameworks that cast landscapes as abstract embodiments of sweeping cultural forces. Subsequent scholars have melded the two extremes, demonstrating how various cultural groups have expressed their identities by developing distinctive place-based forms, practices, and associations. Dolores Hayden produced a widely applauded public history project and associated publication, *The Power of Place* (1995), around the assumption that providing disadvantaged communities with opportunities to express their identities and concerns through assertive place-making served both the populations involved and the community at large.[35]

Post-structural cogitations on the social production of space represented another attempt to relate the immediate experience of place to broader social patterns. Theorists such as Allan Pred, Henri Lefebvre, Pierre Bourdieu, and Michel de Certeau emphasized the ways in which individuals appropriated and transformed environments constructed by broader cultural processes, asserting that ordinary people contested dominant power structures through the seemingly prosaic activities of everyday life. By foregrounding cultural theory in their presentations, writers on the social production of space lent academic credence to Jackson's contention that the true measure of a landscape resides in the practices and perceptions of its inhabitants.[36]

Outside the academy, a range of fiction and non-fiction writers have masterfully evoked the experience of place. A few examples of vivid and insightful place-based narratives include Wallace Stegner's *Wolf Willow* (1962), an inventive combination of history, fiction, and memoir based on the author's childhood in southern Saskatchewan during the 1910s; the achingly beautiful preamble to James Agee's *A Death in the Family* (1967); Joan Dideon's unsparing account of mid-twentieth-century Sacramento in "Notes from a Native Daughter"; Leslie Marmon Silko's "Interior and Exterior Landscapes: Pueblo Migration Stories"; and practically anything by John McPhee, most notably *The Pine Barrens* (1968) and *Coming into the Country* (1977).[37] The role of place, memory, and narrative in an American Indian tribe is further explored in the anthropologist Kenneth Basso's *Wisdom Sits in Places: Landscape and Language among the Western Apache* (1996).[38] Historic preservationist Kingston Heath's *The Patina of Place: The Cultural Weathering of a New England Industrial Landscape* (2002) enlisted personal memory, family photos, measured drawings, and more conventional scholarly methods to communicate the experiential quality and historical evolution of New Bedford, Massachusetts.[39] Wright Morris's various photography/text combinations represent another extremely effective way of communicating the telling details and enduring impressions of inhabited landscapes through complementary associations of words and images.[40] James Agee and Walker Evans's *Let Us Now Praise Famous Men* (1941) remains, for many, the apotheosis of this genre.[41]

Vernacular Architecture Studies

The study of vernacular architecture is another wide-ranging interdisciplinary endeavor that has become increasingly aligned with landscape studies. Broadly conceived, the field's origins can be traced to the efforts of an eclectic group of late-nineteenth and early-twentieth-century antiquarians, architects, and photographers who explored the back roads, small towns, and historic districts of the Eastern Seaboard in search of architectural relics of what they saw as a more authentic age, unsullied by the commercialism, modernity, and multiculturalism that was transforming American lives and landscapes. The photographs and writings of individuals such as Frances Benjamin Johnston, Wallace Nutting, and Clifton Johnson may seem overly sentimental—and, in cases where issues of race, class, and gender are involved, they are often offensive to modern sensibilities—but they responded to public desires for a romanticized and sanitized past. Long dismissed as nostalgic reveries, they constitute a valuable, if highly selective index of building traditions, land-use patterns, and contemporary landscape values.[42] A more measured perspective was provided by men such Norman Morrison Isham, Irving Whitall Lyon, and Henry Chapman Mercer, who conducted methodical fieldwork to document colonial buildings around the turn of the twentieth century.[43] Russell Whitehead and other architects continued in this vein during the 1910s and 1920s, producing drawings and descriptions of early American architecture. Many of these studies appeared in a bi-monthly publication titled *The White Pine Series of Architectural Monographs* (1915–1931).[44] The White Pine Series approach strongly influenced the goals and methods of the Historic American Buildings Survey (HABS), a New Deal program aimed at creating a record of American architectural achievement. While HABS maintained a similar emphasis on antebellum architecture, it documented a broader array of structures, from slave cabins and outbuildings to mansions, mills, and gardens. After a brief hiatus during World War II and its aftermath, HABS was revived during the 1950s and continues to conduct broad-ranging architectural history and documentation today.[45]

From a more conventional academic perspective, vernacular architecture studies can be traced to the architectural historian Fiske Kimball and cultural geographer Fred Kniffen. Kimball's 1922 survey, *Domestic Architecture of the America Colonies and Early Republic*, accorded serious consideration to modest dwellings. In a series of studies published from the 1930s into the 1960s, Kniffen traced patterns in folk housing as evidence of the diffusion of cultures through space and time.[46] Kniffen's student, Henry Glassie, expanded this approach beyond buildings and land-use patterns to all manner of hand-made artifacts in his highly readable survey, *Pattern in the Material Folk Culture of the Eastern United States* (1968).[47] The research activities involved with the restoration of Colonial Williamsburg were another important model. Not only did Colonial Williamsburg serve as a training ground and institutional base for subsequent vernacular architecture research, but the emphasis on documenting architectural details, building materials, and methods of construction exerted a lasting influence on the field.[48]

By the 1970s, students of vernacular architecture were expressing the same frustrations as their compatriots in cultural geography. They believed there was too much emphasis on what buildings were, and too little on what they did, how, and why. Scholars of vernacular architecture were strongly influenced by the new social history. By definition, their efforts embraced the call for greater emphasis on the experiences of ordinary people. Like their geographical colleagues, scholars castigated their discipline for being analytically unsophisticated. Advocates of vernacular architecture also had to demonstrate that they were rigorous scholars, not fusty antiquarians or naïve romantics caught up in the counterculture celebration of traditional folkways. A critical breakthrough in combating these accusations and addressing the question of how vernacular buildings materialized the cultural concerns of ordinary people was Glassie's tour de force, *Folk Housing in Middle Virginia* (1975).[49] Combining extensive fieldwork with linguistic theory and structuralist anthropology, Glassie asserted that vernacular builders operated within a complex grammar of formal possibilities that was intrinsically conservative but evolved in response to changing social and material conditions. Glassie's volume might strike modern readers as a cultural artifact in its own right, but it exerted a transformative effect on the field by encouraging researchers to explore new approaches to articulating relationships between built form and culture.

By the 1980s, American vernacular architecture studies had crystallized around the activities of the Vernacular Architecture Forum (VAF), an organization formed by a like-minded array of architectural historians, preservationists, American-studies scholars, folklorists, and representatives of a diverse array of other disciplines. Dell Upton and John Michael Vlach's edited volume, *Common Places: Readings in Vernacular Architecture* (1986), brought together a number of essays from this period and affords an excellent overview of the topical and theoretical interests of the time.[50] Vernacular architecture studies continued to thrive in the decades that followed, expanding both topically and methodologically.[51] Some have argued that the field retained too much of an emphasis on the old, the rural, the domestic, and the white, along with an overly empirical enchantment with the materiality of buildings and associated celebration of fieldwork and graphic documentation as ends in and of themselves.[52] Recent scholarship has demonstrated a wealth of methodological perspectives, however, and engaged a wide range of concerns, from suburban tract homes and drive-in theaters to the ways in which building and landscapes embody issues of race, gender, ethnicity, and class.

From the very start, leading VAF members such as Upton and Vlach employed the cultural landscape perspective and made a point of referring to the field's aims as encompassing both "vernacular architecture and landscapes."[53] Jackson's contributions were repeatedly invoked, and many notable practitioners of landscape studies passed through UC, Berkeley, where Jackson's legacy remained strong under the influence of VAF member Paul Groth. Richard Longstreth, another Jackson student and VAF stalwart, encouraged graduate students at George Washington University to explore a wide range of popular building types and landscape-related topics. Other VAF members in varied academic and professional niches have also contributed important landscape-related scholarship. The best way to witness the vitality of the field, trace its internal debates, and observe the growing diversity and increased representation of cultural landscape studies is to consult the VAF's official publication, which began as an occasional anthology and evolved into a biannual journal. Underscoring the long-time association and increasing confluence between the two endeavors, the organization voted in 2006 to change the publication's title from *Perspectives in Vernacular Architecture* to *Buildings and Landscapes*.

Fig. 7.3. Celebrations, Fairs, and Carnivals [rodeo in Cuba, New Mexico], 1972.
[No slide number.] From the J. B. Jackson Pictorial Materials Collection (Wilson
Collection), Center for Southwest Research and the School of Architecture and
Planning, University of New Mexico, Albuquerque, and is used by permission.

Fig. 7.4. Dwelling; Vernacular Houses, no date. 6-B-14. From the J. B. Jackson Pictorial Materials Collection (Groth Collection), Center for Southwest Research and the School of Architecture and Planning, University of New Mexico, Albuquerque, and used by permission.

American Studies

American studies has long shared interests with landscape studies. Major figures in the mid-twentieth-century conceptualization of the field such as Henry Nash Smith, Leo Marx, and John Kouwenhoven engaged issues of central importance to landscape scholars. Smith's *Virgin Land: The American West as Symbol and Myth* (1950) wove together popular culture and traditional scholarship to explain the region's role in the American imagination. Leo Marx's *The Machine in the Garden* (1964) interpreted literary sources to speculate on Americans' relationships to nature, technology, and modernity. Both became instant classics that strongly influenced subsequent scholarship.[54] While Marx and Smith focused on visual and literary representations, Kouwenhoven placed objects at the forefront of his investigations. In wide-ranging treatises such as *Made in America* (1948) and *The Beer Can by the Highway* (1961), Kouwenhoven speculated on the ways in which buildings, artifacts, and landscape features exemplified American values.[55] The ways in which these authors embraced high and low culture to make sweeping conclusions about American society mirrored Jackson's approach, as did their commitment to communicating in engaging prose, but the emphasis on the interpretation of landscape representations rather than the landscape itself reflected a significant departure from Jackson's goals and methods.[56]

By the 1970s, scholars in American studies were also questioning the assumption that the so-called "Myth and Symbol" approach could adequately explain anything as diverse, contradictory, and constantly changing as American culture. Like their colleagues in other disciplines, they rejected grand narratives in favor of more narrowly focused studies, demonstrating the ways in which cultural processes played out in specific places and situations. Scholars in American studies have produced a wide range of investigations of landscape topics, many grounded in creative combinations of archival research, fieldwork, and speculative analysis. John R. Stilgoe built on Jackson's foundations to produce his sweeping and literary *Common Landscape of America, 1580 to 1845* (1982), then turned to the interpretation of more specific environments in books such as *Metropolitan Corridor* (1983) and *Alongshore* (1994).[57] John Sears scrutinized sightseeing practices and associated landscape values in *Sacred Places: The Tourist in Nineteenth-Century America* (1986).[58] David Nye explored the relationship between technology and the American landscape in studies such as *Electrifying America* (1992) and *American Technological Sublime* (1996).[59] Richard Longstreth answered Jackson's call for more rigorous research on twentieth-century vernacular landscapes with his exhaustive accounts of the evolution of shopping centers, the commercial strip, and, most recently, the department store.[60] Peter Bacon Hales's examinations of the cultural connotations of American landscapes ranged from analyses of nineteenth-century photographs to investigations of atomic test sites, counter-culture communes, and suburban cul de sacs to speculations about the impact of video games and other digital diversions.[61] American studies-based authors such as Kent Ryden, Alicia Barber, and Michael

Aaron Rockland enlisted a variety of methods and sources to explore places and regions, from Idaho mining districts to the New Jersey Turnpike and the strip in Reno, Nevada.[62]

The foregoing is a mere hint of the wealth of landscape analysis produced by scholars in American studies. American studies has also afforded a home for researchers whose goals and methods transcend disciplinary boundaries and served has a springboard for innovative thinkers such as Stephen Pyne and Hal Rothman, who went on to play formative roles in the development of environmental history as a recognized academic discipline.

Art History

Despite the seemingly obvious congruence, art history has long had an ambivalent relationship with the Jacksonian strain of landscape studies; or, perhaps more accurately, Jacksonian landscape studies has had an ambivalent relationship with it. A significant reason for the under-representation of art history in Jacksonian landscape studies was that Jackson essentially defined the field in opposition to prevailing art historical conceptions of the term. Jackson's insistence that actual landscapes, rather than their visual or literary representations, should be the primary focus of interest mediated against the inclusion of art historical perspectives. If the goal was to define landscape as an actual portion of the Earth's surface and interpret it from the perspective of its inhabitants, then the spectator stance and aestheticizing principles of art history had no place in the Jacksonian paradigm. In practice, however, Jackson engaged topics such as the development of parks and landscape architecture that fit within the established purview of art history and routinely invoked sources and associations embedded in the field. Another reason art history played a minor role in Jackson's personal approach might have been that, despite his populist leanings, Jackson was steeped in art historical knowledge; he may well have expected his audience to possess a similarly comprehensive background. While this was perhaps a reasonable assumption at the time, such erudition is not as widespread today.

While some advocates of landscape studies continue to resist the intrusion of image-based analysis, familiarity with art historical perspectives and the traditions of landscape art and garden design would seem to be an incontestable benefit for anyone seeking to make sense of the ways in which people use, shape, and interpret their physical environments. The contention that art historians were so preoccupied with stylistic analysis that they ignored broader cultural concerns was always a bit of a straw man argument and is even less tenable today. Subsequent scholars might contest their methodology and conclusions, but mid-twentieth-century historians of architecture and landscape design such as Christopher Hussey, Wayne Andrews, and Sigfried Giedion routinely related design practices to broader cultural concerns, as did one of Jackson's own favorite writers, the historian and critic Lewis Mumford.[63] Art historians also addressed American landscape painting on broader grounds than formal analysis alone, as epitomized by James Flexner's *That Wilder Image* (1962) and Barbara Novak's *Nature and Culture* (1980), albeit from a celebratory perspective rooted in questionable assumptions of cultural consensus.[64] By the 1980s, many art historians were rebelling against their predecessors' perceived complacency and employing the goals and techniques of the British Cultural Studies movement that informed the work of Cosgrove, Daniels, and their strain of critical cultural geography. Following the lead of John Barrell and Ann Bermingham, art historians such as Albert Boime, Angela Miller, William Treuttner, David Miller, and Alan Wallach interrogated American landscape painting for encoded symbols of national identity and capitalist ideology along with problematic assumptions about race, class, and gender.[65]

J. B. Jackson would have undoubtedly agreed with Peirce Lewis's contention that "landscape has very little to do with the skilled work of landscape architects," but the art historical investigation of designed landscapes has expanded in scope and sophistication since the formative years of the landscape studies movement.[66] During the 1980s and 1990s, broad surveys such as David Schuyler's *The New Urban Landscape: The Redefinition of City Form in Nineteenth-Century America* (1986) were joined by detailed monographs such as Cynthia Zaitsevsky's *Frederick Law Olmsted and the Boston Park System* (1982) and Roy Rosenzweig and Elizabeth Blackmar's social history-oriented *The Park and the People: A History of Central Park* (1992).[67] Research on Olmsted became an industry unto itself with the institution of a multi-volume series of Olmsted's papers and the appearance of multiple studies, biographies, and new editions of classic works.[68] Dumbarton Oaks, Harvard's bastion of refined research on landscape design, even assayed a symposium on "The Vernacular Garden," providing an erudite international perspective on the subject.[69] Reflecting broader cultural interest in gender studies and renewed fascination with Modernism, art historians have turned their attention to the work of women landscape architects and the oeuvres of twentieth-century practitioners such as James Rose, Garret Eckbo, Dan Kiley, and Lawrence Halprin.[70] As long as these efforts respect the populist and interdisciplinary nature of cultural landscape studies and resist the temptation to recolonize the term and its broader aspirations in the service of elite academic inquiry, these developments represent another promising contribution to the perpetuation and expansion of Jackson's vision.

Environmental History

Environmental history is another academic discipline that would seem to have a closer relationship with cultural landscape studies than has historically been the case. Jackson disapproved of strident environmentalism. He considered the belief that nature exists as some sort of idealized entity distinct from and superior to culture to be an intellectually untenable romantic conceit, regardless of whether it was espoused by nineteenth-century philosophers or couched in the rhetoric of ecological awareness. His emphasis on the inhabitant's perspective was at odds with any outlook that elevated the biological requirements of plants and animals to the same footing as human needs and aspirations. In Jackson's view, the human presence is not an unwelcome intrusion but a social, spiritual, and individual achievement—imperfect, perhaps, but a source of wonder and ceaseless curiosity. For Jackson, the ways in which humans seek to make sense of their environments, not the analysis of soil series or the plight of salmon stocks, is the proper focus of landscape studies.

Environmental historians were clearly concerned with explicating human attitudes, but during the field's formative period in the 1960s and 1970s their efforts were unabashedly allied with the goals and principles of environmentalism.[71] Roderick Nash, one of the founders of environmental history, aligned the effort with the new social history. Instead of exposing injustices to disadvantaged social groups, environmental historians would focus on the ways in which the dominant culture had injured and exploited biological victims.[72] Environmental history was often presented as a moral crusade, with Henry David Thoreau, John Muir, Aldo Leopold, and Rachel Carson presented as prophets leading to a more enlightened environmental ethic.[73] By the late 1970s, this biographical and philosophical emphasis began to give way to more broad-based interdisciplinary studies that mustered social history, cultural theory, and scientific observation to trace human impacts on natural resources. William Cronon and Donald Worster chronicled the exploits of New England colonists and Western farmers, ascribing their ecological transgressions to capitalist economic structures that commodified relationships with the land.[74] Richard White contrasted the ways in which indigenous peoples and European settlers interacted with their surroundings in the Pacific Northwest.[75] Stephen Pyne traced the role that fire played in five centuries of American landscape history.[76]

During the 1990s, environmental historians became less strident in their exhortations and more reflective about their assumptions and agendas. They even developed a sense of humor. Most importantly, they came to terms with the fact that nature was not a separate and superior entity but a cultural construct whose meaning and social functions changed dramatically over time. While Jackson and other classically educated landscape interpreters would have been underwhelmed by this revelation, some environmental historians viewed the admission as apostasy. The seminal document in this transformation was Cronon's anthology, *Uncommon Ground: Rethinking the Human Place in Nature* (1996), later editions of which included a revealing account of the controversy.[77]

Environmental historians have gone on to produce a wide range of imaginatively conceived and impressively realized studies of the complex relationships between humans and the environments they construct and inhabit.[78] Scholars of the cultural landscape can learn much from these efforts, especially in regard to their inclusion of insights from the natural sciences, a realm that received minimal consideration in the Jacksonian tradition. Environmentalist sentiments often loom large, but there is greater emphasis on historical contingency and cultural complexity. The racial politics, class bias, and human impacts of hallowed achievements have come under scrutiny in studies such as Mark Spence's *Dispossessing the Wilderness*: *Indian Removal and the Making of the National Parks* (1999) and Karl Jacoby's *Crimes Against Nature: Poachers, Thieves, and the Hidden History of American Conservation* (2001).[79] A number of exemplary works combine urban history with environmental analysis. In *Land of Sunshine: The Environmental History of Los Angeles* (2005), William Deverell and Greg Hise assembled an impressive array of contributors to examine the relationships between the region's environment and human attempts to inhabit, alter, and interpret it; Char Miller edited an analogous volume on San Antonio; Joel Tarr performed a similar task for Pittsburgh.[80] While all three anthologies move from the past to the present and engage contemporary concerns such as environmental justice, the striving for sustainability, and the mixed legacies of well-intentioned interventions, Matthew Klingle's *Emerald City: An Environmental History of Seattle* (2007) goes furthest in addressing the social inequities associated with highly touted reforms.[81] Substitute "scenic beautification" for "environmental improvement" and such critiques echo the populist plea of Jackson's "To Pity the Plumage and Forget the Dying Bird."[82]

Race and Ethnicity

Cultural geographers and scholars of vernacular architecture have long been attuned to the ways in which ethnic groups imprint their identities on the landscape. Throughout most of the twentieth century, this research focused on the spatial distribution and cultural expressions of European ethnic groups such as Swedes, Russians, Germans, and Czechs. Early preoccupations with architectural traditions as indices of migration and adaptation gradually gave way to more complex considerations of the ways in which ethnic groups employed buildings and landscapes to sustain and communicate cultural values. Excellent examples of these sorts of studies can be found in *Common Places* and in Allen Noble's anthology, *To Build in a New Land: Ethnic Landscapes in North America* (1992).[83] More recent investigations in this vein include Arnold R. Alanen's work on Finns in the Upper Midwest and Joseph Sciorra's ethnographic examinations of Italian American yard shrines, sidewalk art, and Christmas displays in New York City's outer boroughs.[84] Other scholars such as Chris Wilson and Steven Hoelscher have looked at the ways in which ethnic identities have been self-consciously embedded in the landscape with varying degrees of authenticity and in service of complex cultural agendas.[85]

Recent scholarship on the cultural landscape has embraced a more comprehensive portrait of America's diverse past and multicultural present. Academics, preservationists, and public historians have paid increased attention to Asian-American landscapes. Gail Dubrow has written about Asian and Pacific Island farmers and agricultural workers in California and the Pacific Northwest, Hilary Jenks has investigated issues of power, memory, and identity in Los Angeles's Little Tokyo, and David Chuenyan Lai has addressed the visual character of the West Coast's Chinatowns.[86] Contemporary Latino cultural landscapes have also become a locus of investigation, as exemplified by Louis Aponte-Paris's work on Puerto Rican casitas in New York City, James Rojas's examinations of East Los Angeles streetscapes, and Eric Avila's analysis of freeway imagery in murals by Chicano artists.[87] Rina Swentzell's insider's perspective sheds important light on conflicts in the ways that the Tewa Pueblo community and Bureau of Indian Affairs administrators conceived and constructed the spaces of everyday life.[88]

The African-American experience and the operation of racial constructs in the built environment have been topics of growing concern. Early research in this area included John Michael Vlach's 1970s studies of the shotgun house, which revealed ways in which people of African descent developed a demonstrably African-American house type that was widely adopted as a model for low-cost dwellings. Dell Upton's 1985 essay, "White and Black Landscapes in Eighteenth-Century Virginia," was another pioneering achievement, combining field research and historic accounts to speculate about the ways in which physical constructs, spatial perceptions, and social behaviors embodied power relations and cultural expectations.[89] In *Back of the Big House: The Architecture of Plantation Slavery* (1993), Vlach mined the Historic American Buildings Survey collection to produce an impressively illustrated overview of slave-related buildings, many of which had disappeared since the pictures were taken in the 1930s.[90] Landscape architect Richard Westmacott documented the persistence of African gardening and landscape design traditions through historical research, field surveys, photographs, and site plans in *African-American Gardens and Yards in the Rural South* (1992).[91] Grey Gundaker and Judith McWillie took a more ethnographic approach in *No Space Hidden: The Spirit of African American Yard Work* (2005).[92]

The wealth of approaches and subject matter related to African-American issues and race-related concerns produced by cultural landscape scholars is represented in anthologies such as Gundaker's *Keep Your Head to the Sky: Interpreting African-American Home Ground* (1998), Paul Shackel's *Memory in Black and White: Race, Commemoration, and the Post-Bellum Landscape* (2003), and Richard Schein's *Landscape and Race in the United States* (2006), which also includes essays on Latino and Asian-American landscapes.[93] *Landscape Journal* devoted a special issue to the theme of "Race, Space, and the Destabilization of Practice" in 2007, which combined theoretical essays with case studies of the role of the built environment in the construction

Fig. 7.5. Land Division; Maps and Miscellaneous. People [Chicano family's picnic in a public park, likely in California], April 1975. 1-M-02. From the J. B. Jackson Pictorial Materials Collection (Wilson Collection), Center for Southwest Research and the School of Architecture and Planning, University of New Mexico, Albuquerque, and is used by permission.

and contestation of racialized practices, identities, and perceptions.[94] *Landscape of Slavery: The Plantation in American Art* (2008) and Vlach's *The Planter's Prospect: Privilege and Slavery in Plantation Paintings* (2001) decode the manner in which racial dynamics informed representations of an iconic yet highly problematic American landscape.[95] Clifton Ellis and Rebecca Ginsburg's edited volume, *Cabin, Quarter, Plantation: Architecture and Landscapes of North American Slavery* (2010) and Louis Nelson's 2011 *Winterthur Portfolio* article, "The Architectures of Black Identity: Buildings, Slavery, and Freedom in the American South," are more in keeping with the Jacksonian tradition of seeking to extract meaning from landscape itself.[96] Michael Crutcher's *Treme: Race and Place in a New Orleans Neighborhood* (2010) combined history, ethnography, and human geography to interpret the social and spatial dynamics of a predominantly African-American neighborhood that experienced repeated incursions, from freeway construction and urban renewal to park development and an HBO miniseries.[97] Lance Freeman's *There Goes the Hood: Gentrification from the Ground Up* (2006) viewed this highly touted phenomenon from the ambivalent perspective of long-term residents desirous of change but threatened by rising property values and community transformation.[98]

Gender and Sexuality

Scholars of the cultural landscape have also followed broader academic and societal trends by paying increased attention to women's history and to the ways in which issues of gender and sexuality have been negotiated in the landscapes of everyday life. Historical studies of the manner in which gender roles were construed and contested in domestic architecture, residential developments, and urban environments range from early efforts such as Dolores Hayden's *Grand Domestic Revolution* (1981) and Cheryl Robertson's "Male and Female Agendas for Domestic Reform: the Middle-Class Bungalow in Gendered Perspective" to later contributions such as Daphne Spain's *How Women Saved the City* (2001) and Jessica Sewell's *Women and the Everyday City* (2011).[99] Historiographical overviews and theoretical perspectives include Sally McMurry's "Women in the American Vernacular Landscape" and Angel Kwolek-Folland's "Gender as a Category of Analysis in Vernacular Architecture Studies."[100] The anthology *Shared Spaces and Divided Places* (2003) examines the manifestation of gender issues across a broad selection of historical and contemporary landscapes, while Diane Harris's essay, "Cultivating Power: The Language of Feminism in Women's Garden Literature, 1870–1920," exemplifies the effort to recover, interpret, and valorize overlooked sources and social practices.[101] The intersections between gender studies, environmental history, and cultural landscape studies are explored in *Seeing Nature through Gender* (2003), an innovative anthology edited by Virginia Scharff covering subjects as diverse as eighteenth-century Virginia, Civilian Conservation Corps camps, and lesbian communes.[102] Rebecca Solnit's *As Eve*

Said to the Serpent: On Landscape, Gender, and Art (2003) affords more personalized reflection on gendered environmental associations and other topics of interest to landscape scholars.[103] The ways in which gays and lesbians have used and experienced cultural landscapes for the purposes of personal pleasure, community identity, and political protest have been explored in books such as *Mapping Desire: The Geographies of Sexuality* (1995), *Stud: The Architecture of Masculinity* (1996), and *Queers in Space Communities/Public/Places/Sites of Resistance* (1997).[104] More recent studies such as Amin Ghaziani's *There Goes the Gayborhood?* (2014) have examined the impact of gentrification and the erosion of social stigmas on storied LGBT enclaves such as New York's West Village and San Francisco's Castro District.[105]

Public historians and historic preservationists have been particularly active in using cultural landscapes to communicate women's history and issues of gender and sexuality. Believing with Jackson that landscape is history made visible, they have sought to promote historical awareness by increasing the visibility of issues, events, and individuals that have been marginalized in mainstream narratives. In *Restoring Women's History through Historic Preservation* (2003), Gail Dubrow and Jennifer Goodman, survey a wide range of related concerns and activities in their edited collection—from efforts to protect and interpret traditionally female spheres such as domestic space, libraries, and nurses residences to the rising interest in preserving sites associated with gay and lesbian heritage, to the role of government agencies and nonprofit organizations in supporting related enterprises.[106] In their collection, *Her Past Around Us* (2003), Polly Welts Kauffman and Catherine T. Corbett provide additional examples, including a consideration of the gardens of house museums associated with notable women and attempts to interpret spaces and stories associated with American Indian women, Irish domestic servants, and female slaves.[107] Both the National Park Service and Parks Canada have embraced the women's history agenda, particularly in the realm of designating significant historic sites. The National Park Service has also created a Women's Rights National Historical Park at Seneca Falls, New York, often cited as the birthplace of the Women's Rights movement. New York City's Stonewall Inn, similarly revered as the physical embodiment of the origins of the Gay Rights movement, was listed on the National Register of Historic Places in 1999 and designated a National Historic Landmark the following year. In May 2014, the U.S. Department of the Interior announced a major initiative to identify, preserve, and interpret sites associated with lesbian, gay, bisexual, and transgender history.

Historic Preservation

Jackson was notoriously ambivalent about historic preservation. He condemned the tendency to valorize elite productions rather than more representative, if prosaic, environments and derided the antiquarian assertion that aging buildings are worthy preservation simply because they are old or associated with famous figures or favored architectural fashions.[108] Like his colleagues David Lowenthal and Kevin Lynch, Jackson was especially dismissive of efforts to freeze living environments in particular time periods or to isolate historic structures from their broader surroundings.[109] At the same time, he believed strongly in the landscape's role as a repository of history and locus of group or individual identity, as long as these bonds were based on meaningful attachments rather than on bourgeois certitudes and superficial stylistic predilections. Fortunately, historic preservation has evolved significantly since Jackson's time, so that many of the approaches he condemned are now widely criticized within the preservation establishment itself. An overview of the ways in which academic historic preservationists have interrogated their profession's assumptions and posited more complex and balanced alternatives can be found in Max Page and Randall Mason's *Giving Preservation a History* (2004), which includes summaries of related publications by Daniel Bluestone, Michael Holleran, James Lindgren, Chris Wilson, and others.[110]

While historic gardens were occasionally preserved as byproducts of efforts to save notable houses as early as the mid-nineteenth-century campaign to save George Washington's Mount Vernon, the goal of perpetuating broader complexes of buildings and spaces was first manifest in public history projects of the 1920s and 1930s. Examples include Colonial Williamsburg, Henry Ford's Greenfield Village in Dearborn, Michigan, and the National Park Service's Cades Cove development in Great Smoky Mountains National Park, where an agricultural community was divested of its inhabitants and reconfigured to serve as a museum of pioneer folkways. These projects exemplified the tendency to create physical and perceptual boundaries between historic and contemporary landscapes while eliminating discordant elements and cultural complexities in order to create sanitized set pieces that reified comforting narratives of social harmony, pioneer hardihood, and agrarian bliss. The historical interpretations and physical interventions associated with these sites were often based more on formal preferences and romantic conjecture than on substantive research and systematic analysis.

The creators of these fanciful tableaux were generally more cognizant of their manipulations than subsequent detractors contend, but landscape preservation made significant strides during the last three decades of the twentieth century, both in the professionalization of its methods and recognition of the complex and multilayered nature of cultural landscapes.[111] The landscape architecture profession played a leading role in this transition. Encouraged by the renewed interest in urban parks fostered by the environmental movement, the American Society for Landscape Architects created a historic preservation committee during the early 1970s. The Alliance for Historic Landscape Preservation was formed in 1978 by a group of preservation-minded landscape architects and related professionals. These initiatives lent support to research and preservation efforts at iconic sites such as Central Park, Prospect Park, the Boston park system, and Mount Auburn Cemetery. The National Park Service (NPS) lent its support to the initiative during the 1980s, recognizing cultural landscapes as a distinct resource type, creating positions for historical landscape architects, developing guidance for managing cultural landscapes within the National Park System and providing instructions for nominating designed landscapes, cemeteries, and rural landscapes to the National Register of Historic Places.[112] During the 1990s, the NPS published a guide to applying the Secretary of the Interior's Standards for the Treatment of Historic Properties to cultural landscapes and developed a protocol for the production of cultural landscape reports that codified evolving practices into a framework that has been widely adopted as a means of combining historical research, site analysis, and treatment recommendations.[113] The NPS also sponsored studies of cultural landscapes within the park system and established a Historic American Landscapes Survey to complement existing programs to document architectural and engineering structures throughout the nation.

While these initiatives employed the term "cultural landscape" and expressed a commitment to the broad-based application of the concept envisioned by Jackson and his followers, the preponderance of activity was initially directed toward professionally executed landscapes. Parks, gardens, and the work of leading landscape architects remained the primary focus of preservation efforts, while stylistic categorization tended to dominate research and interpretation efforts. Important exceptions included the Civil War battlefield protection initiative and NPS efforts to preserve rural landscapes in Arkansas's Buffalo National River, California's Point Reyes National Seashore, and Ebey's Landing National Historical Reserve on Whidbey Island, Washington, along with the rapidly expanding National Heritage Area program, which seeks to promote the stewardship of large-scale environments in ways that recognize their function as evolving everyday landscapes. In 2002, the National Register of Historic Places developed a guide to documenting and evaluating historic suburbs that recognized the significance of this oft-criticized environment.[114] The Historic American Landscapes Survey extended its reach to document a broader range of subjects, including agricultural landscapes, Hawai'ian sacred sites, a tourist camp, and a miniature golf course. The Cultural Landscape Foundation, founded by former NPS landscape architect Charles Birnbaum in 1998, focuses on elite-designed landscapes, but it has made significant contributions to the recognition and preservation of vernacular landscapes.

Since the 1990s, there has also been a growing interest in preserving historic roads and finding ways to balance their practical functions with their significance as cultural landscapes.[115] As suggested in the preceding sections, preservationists at the local, state, and national levels are also working to expand the types of historic landscapes that are being preserved and the nature of the stories they communicate. Two anthologies that showcase these activities are *Preserving Cultural Landscapes in America* (2000), edited by Arnold R. Alanen and Robert Melnick, and *Cultural Landscapes: Balancing Nature and Heritage in Preservation Practice* (2008), edited by Richard

Longstreth. Both publications underscore the value of combining the ambitious social and intellectual aims of such broad-based preservation activities with the technical skills, environmental perspectives, and policy frameworks developed by the historical landscape architecture community. Happily, they also demonstrate that this creative synthesis is already well underway.[116]

Photography

Photographers have long been among the most insightful interpreters of the American cultural landscape. While photography is obviously a selective enterprise that produces highly personalized syntheses of exterior reality and authorial intent, the same can be said of academic research and other forms of landscape interpretation. It can even be argued that the subjective nature of photography enhances its value as both a discursive practice and a resource for cultural landscape research. Landscape scholars can look to the work of historical and contemporary photographers not just for evidence of changes in the landscape itself, but for transformations in the ways in which society interprets both the built environment and the nature and function of visual representation.[117]

William Henry Jackson's authoritative vistas of the American West testified to the nineteenth-century faith in positivist science and may have reflected and facilitated the commodification and exploitation of natural resources. Jacob Riis's images of turn-of-the-twentieth-century slum dwellers exposed both the plight of impoverished immigrants and contemporary cultural anxieties about the transformation of American society.[118] The photographs of Walker Evans, Wright Morris, and the Farm Security Administration underscored both the rapid rate at which the forces of modernization, consumerism, and capitalism were transforming traditional landscapes and the desire for symbols of a more stable and uncomplicated past.[119] During the 1950s, Jackson's fascination with the ambiguous attractions and kinetic fervor of the automobile-oriented environment found parallel expression in Robert Frank's photographic sojourn through the American landscape.[120] Garry Winogrand and Lee Friedlander simultaneously criticized and celebrated an evolving America that seemed chaotic and superficial yet full of life and not entirely devoid of hope.[121] The disenchantment of the 1970s and 1980s was manifest in the work of photographers such as Robert Adams, Lewis Baltz, and Frank Gohlke, who produced bleak and alienating images of the sprawling modern developments condemned by contemporary critics, architects, and planners.[122] Bill Owens's *Suburbia* (1973) slyly subverted the polemics of placelessness, allowing middle-class homeowners to show how they infused supposedly oppressive and undifferentiated subdivisions with meaning and identity.[123] David Plowden took a more ambivalent perspective, combining Jackson's enthusiasm for gritty vernacular environments with nostalgic reverie and environmentalist exposition.[124]

Fig. 7.6. [No title.] Photograph by Miguel Gandert for J. B. Jackson, Albuquerque, New Mexico, 1985. [No slide number.] From the J. B. Jackson Pictorial Materials Collection (Wilson Collection), Center for Southwest Research and the School of Architecture and Planning, University of New Mexico, Albuquerque, and used by permission.

Fig. 7.7. Cities General; Street IV. Photograph by Miguel Gandert for J. B. Jackson, place unknown, October 1985. IV,4-Q(4)-10. From the J. B. Jackson Pictorial Materials Collection (Groth Collection), Center for Southwest Research and the School of Architecture and Planning, University of New Mexico, Albuquerque, and is used by permission.

Stephen Shore's *Uncommon Places* (1982) and Joel Sternfeld's *American Prospects* (1987) expanded the palette of cultural landscape photography with evocative color images of ordinary American landscapes.[125] William Eggleston, another pioneering color photographer, catalogued quotidian America in enigmatic compositions compiled in books such as *William Eggleston's Guide* (1976) and *The Democratic Forest* (1989).[126] Camilo Jose Vergara's *The New American Ghetto* (1995) provided a multi-decade chronicle of the inner-city environments reduced to sociological abstractions by planners and academics.[127] Sternfeld's *On This Site: Landscape in Memorium* (1996) provoked contemplation of the relationships between memory, place, and meaning through photographs of seemingly banal landscapes whose significance was revealed by captions attesting to their roles as settings for historical events such as the assassination of Martin Luther King, Jr. or the beating of Rodney King.[128] Alex McLean and Jim Wark employed aerial photography to produce beautiful and often disconcerting images of the modern American landscape, revealing patterns and juxtapositions difficult to perceive from conventional perspectives. Both McLean and Wark collaborated with various writers to produce works that provided insightful interpretations of evolving American landscapes.[129] Jackson participated in a similar joint venture during the 1980s, adding his insights on the New Mexico landscape to a compilation of the works of a dozen highly diverse photographers.[130]

Photographers working with both film and digital media continue to explore the American landscape, bearing witness to physical changes, personal predilections, and new and ongoing cultural concerns. Laurie Brown's panoramic portrayals of the outskirts of Las Vegas echo the New Topographics's indictments of modern development practices.[131] Andrew Borowiec, in *The New Heartland: Looking for the American Dream* (2016), surveys turn-of-the-twenty-first-century suburban sprawl, combining the lush color compositions of Shore and Sternfeld with the ironic wit of Winogrand, Friedlander, and Owens.[132] While not limited to North America, Edward Burtynsky's *Manufactured Landscapes* (2003), *Oil* (2009), and *Water* (2013) depict industrial impacts on the landscape on a monumental scale.[133] Some of the most telling testimonials to Hurricane Katrina's devastation of New Orleans's working-class neighborhoods can be found in the photographs of Richard Misrach and Robert Polidori.[134] Millennial apprehensions about the fading of the American Dream are evident in the rise of "ruin porn" depicting the decline of Detroit and deterioration of other urban areas, infrastructure, and industrial landscapes.[135] While much of the new landscape work by artists is visually striking and graphically revealing, the visual critiques of mainstream American culture and fin de siècle fascination with images of abandonment, decay, and destruction embody the elitism and aestheticizing "outsider stance" Jackson deplored. Jackson's temperance and innate optimism might seem anachronistic to contemporary audiences, but more varied, nuanced, and informed interpretations of the evolving American landscape by artists would afford illuminating alternatives to the prevailing fashion for predictable polemics and formulaic self-indulgence and despair.

Popular Landscape Interpretation

Perhaps the greatest testament to the broad-based appeal of cultural landscape interpretation is the topic's enduring attraction to popular commentators and their audiences. From the colonial period to the present, writers have interpreted the ways in which Americans have used, shaped, and experienced the landscape as evidence of cultural values and social processes. Both Alexis deTocqueville and Hector St. John de Crèvecoeur relied heavily on landscape practices to convey their perceptions of the American experiment.[136] Frederick Law Olmsted's antebellum observations about the ways in which Southern landscapes embodied the flawed values of slavery continue to serve as examples of insightful and accessible landscape interpretation.[137] Jackson was strongly influenced by social commentators such as Lewis Mumford, Patrick Geddes, and Benton MacKaye, who wrote seriously but engagingly about the cultural implications of the built environment in publications aimed at a general audience.[138] James Agee's closely observed, sympathetic, and evocative 1934 *Fortune* magazine article, "The Great American Roadside," foreshadowed Jackson's treatment of the subject. A 1950 *Harper's Magazine* column entitled "The American Landscape" discussed American roadsides in such quintessentially Jacksonian terms that it is tempting to believe he may have been in direct contact with the author, especially since the short-lived series appeared the same year Jackson founded *Landscape* magazine.[139] John Keats lampooned post-World War II suburbs in *The Crack in the Picture Window* (1956), while Betty Friedan's exposition of the ways in which suburban landscapes oppressed women in *The Feminine Mystique* (1963) played a significant role in the formation of the modern feminist movement.[140]

Jackson strongly supported popularly oriented landscape interpreters, publishing in *Landscape* the work of journalists such as Grady Clay and reviewing book publications intended for a general audience. Eric Sloane's admixture of pen-and-ink sketches, folklore, fact, and whimsy introduced countless readers to the idea of viewing landscapes as repositories of historical information, though they have been largely ignored by "serious" scholars both during their heyday in the 1950s and today. Jackson accorded Sloane's *Return to Taos* (1960) a generous review, applauding his willingness to portray the billboards, gas stations, and other elements of the automobile-oriented landscape with the same skill and enthusiasm he devoted to more conventional icons of America's architectural heritage.[141] Jackson reserved his greatest praise for George Stewart, whose written and pictorial account of a 1950s cross-country trip comprised what many regard as one of the most graceful and lucid interpretations of the American landscape. Praising Stewart's *U.S. 40* (1953), Jackson provided his most effusive declaration of the goals and methods of landscape studies: "The author has a sure-fire formula for writing attractive and informative geography: he writes about what he knows at first hand, and he writes about what he loves: in this case the immense and tawdry and beautiful American countryside. He sees its shortcomings more clearly than most of us do; he does not hesitate to point out the esthetic and economic crimes we have committed across the continent. Nevertheless *U.S. 40* is perhaps the best and most original guidebook yet produced in this country; a geography that in the best sense is human."[142]

Long after he stepped down from editing and publishing *Landscape* and from teaching at Harvard and Berkeley, Jackson continued to endorse informed yet accessible books such as Joel Garreau's *Edge City* (1991), John Herbers's *The New Heartland* (1986), and Richard Louv's *America II* (1985), which combined journalistic reportage and traditional research to interpret contemporary American landscapes, often making significant observations about new developments before they appeared on the radar of academics and design professionals.[143] Subsequent authors have continued this trend, though often without Jackson's optimism and sense of humor. Jane Holtz Kay's *Asphalt Nation* (1997) and James Howard Kunstler's *The Geography of Nowhere* (1993) epitomize the enduring appeal of elitist critiques of popular landscape practices, echoing the polemics of Jackson's adversaries Peter Blake, John Keats, and Bernard DeVoto.[144] Cultural landscape concerns loom large in Mike Davis's Los Angeles chronicles *City of Quartz* (1992) and *Ecology of Fear* (1998).[145] David Brooks's *Bobos in Paradise* (2000) and *On Paradise Drive* (2004) abound with astute and witty observations about the landscape practices and perceptions of modern Americans.[146] While his self-proclaimed "comic sociology" can become belabored and condescending, Brooks's ability to conjure convincing composites through redolent, humor-laden prose recalls Jackson's classic essays. More measured attempts to understand contemporary landscapes and explain them to a mixed audience of academics, design professionals, and general readers range from examinations of specific phenomena such as Robert Lang and Jennifer LeFurgy's *Boomburgs: The Rise of America's Accidental Cities* (2007) to speculations on more comprehensive changes in American lives and landscape such Joel Kotkin's *The New Geography: How the Digital Revolution is Reshaping the American Landscape* (2000) and Alan Ehrenhalt's *The Great Inversion and the Future of the American City* (2012).[147] The efforts of academics to reach beyond the Ivory Tower can be seen in a growing corpus of cross-over literature, ranging from the competing perspectives of Dolores Hayden's *A Field Guide to Sprawl* (2004) and Robert Bruegmann's *Sprawl: A Compact History* (2005) to Hal Rothman's *Neon Metropolis: How Las Vegas Started the Twenty-First Century* (2002), Sharon Zukin's *Naked City: The Death and Life of Authentic Urban Places* (2010), and John R. Stilgoe's exhortation to stop reading and look around in *Outside Lies Magic* (1998).[148] *The New Yorker*, *Harper's*, and *Atlantic Monthly* continue to publish articles that would fit within the rubric of landscape studies, as do *The Wall Street Journal* and even *The Weekly Standard*. Elizabeth Barlow Rogers credits Jackson as inspiration for *Site/Lines*, the biannual journal she has edited and published since 2003 as a forum for landscape interpretation informed by scholarly concerns but unconstrained by academic strictures.[149]

Informative and insightful observations on the changing nature of the American landscape appear in a wide range of media. The National Public Radio shows "Morning Edition" and "All Things Considered" have taken the place of Jackson's beloved *Christian Science Monitor* in providing engaging summaries of widely varied landscape-related topics and occasionally invoking the term "cultural landscape" itself. The rising interest in historic highways and automobile-oriented architecture has created a booming industry of travel guides, postcards, calendars, and coffee-table books extolling charismatic vestiges of roadside America.[150] Most of these productions exhibit a nostalgic bent Jackson would have found lamentable, but they underscore the degree to which the ordinary landscapes of mid-twentieth-century America have evolved from objects of derision to touchstones of cultural values on a par with the New England village, the courthouse square, and Mainstreet U.S.A. The cartoonists Robert Crumb and Bill Griffith have employed their unique gifts to depict evolving environments and changing landscape values. Crumb's cartoon, "A Short History of America" (1979), traced the evolution of a slice of the American landscape from virgin land to the automobile-dominated environment of the 1970s, portraying the transformations wrought by new forms of transportation, commerce, and communication.[151] In Griffith's long-running comic strip, "Zippy," he frequently juxtaposes the lead character with examples of twentieth-century vernacular landscapes. While the meanings are often deliberately obscure, the artist's knowledgeable portrayals of shopping malls, tract homes, and an encyclopedic array of roadside architecture testify to extensive "field work" and a sophisticated engagement with landscape symbolism and the history of the built environment.[152]

Filmmakers have long employed landscape imagery to supply contextual clues and impel their narratives. Examples range from the idealization of the suburban home in *Miracle on 34th Street* (1947) to the demonization of the automobile's influence in *Who Framed Roger Rabbit* (1988), to the contravention of suburban bliss in films such as *Pleasantville* (1998), *The Truman Show* (1998), and David Byrne's ironic excursion through fictional town of Virgil, Texas, in his film, *True Stories* (1986).[153] Televised landscapes pervade the American consciousness to the point where phrases such as "Brady Bunch suburbs" connote a wealth of physical and social associations to audiences that would never think to pick up an academic treatise on the history of residential development.[154]

The Digital Age has had an enormous impact on popular and professional interpretations of the American landscape. The Internet affords a cornucopia of images and information about landscape matters, ranging from the celebration of roadside kitsch to more substantial engagements with historical environments and the evolving landscapes of everyday life. While the content runs the gamut from sophisticated to superficial, digital communications have dramatically expanded opportunities to share insights into the relationships between people and the places they create and inhabit, both physically and imaginatively. From SimCity and the Whitmanesque excess of Facebook and Instagram to readily available historical texts, avant garde interpretations, and reams of raw data to Google Streetview's electronic embodiment of Ralph Waldo Emerson's transparent eyeball, technology affords unprecedented access to information about past and present cultural landscapes. The profusion of sources and propensity for hasty and superficial analysis places even greater onus on scholars, artists, and other interpreters to respect Jackson's vision of landscape studies as an intellectually discipled means of moral and social inquiry.

Passing the Torch

Jackson viewed the tenth anniversary of the foundation of *Landscape* magazine as an opportunity to reflect on the past, present, and future of his efforts (Fig. 3.4). Admitting that the initial focus on rural landscapes of the American Southwest had been too narrow, he stood by his underlying contention: "A rich and beautiful book is always open before us. We have only to learn to read it."[155] He acknowledged that this seemingly modest goal was "more of an undertaking than we had bargained for," but after due consideration he maintained it had been "worth the effort."[156] Judging from the testimonials from an array of notables, ranging from Ansel Adams and Louis Kahn to Ian McHarg and Lewis Mumford, he was not alone in this opinion. Time has only amplified the perception that Jackson's efforts to promote a more complex and profound appreciation of ordinary landscapes constitute a major contribution to our understanding of the ways in which humans find meaning and significance in the world around them.

The challenges of interpreting cultural landscapes have not gotten any easier nor has the field become any less inclined to evolve with the times than it was under Jackson's leadership. The preceding overview represents an attempt to chart the major constellations of thought that comprise the universe of contemporary landscape studies. The fact that each component could be expanded significantly and additional elements might easily be added attests to the vitality of the field and the distance it has come since the days when Jackson lamented the dearth of substantive scholarship on everyday landscapes. Subsequent investigators have not only strengthened the core elements of landscape studies, but expanded its horizons to encompass an ever-broadening array of topical interests and theoretical concerns.

Despite the requisite claims to originality, many of these enrichments were anticipated in Jackson's own writings, though often implicitly and from a more optimistic and politically reticent perspective. While Jackson did not employ currently fashionable academic terminology, he presented the landscape as a site of contestation between elite and vernacular values and staunchly defended those mistreated by the dominant culture. His insistence on asking broader questions about cultural landscapes rather than merely parsing their physical attributes was echoed in internal critiques of associated disciplines. The liberal humanist precepts that motivated Jackson and his collaborators may have lost their appeal, at least in academic circles, but scholars, artists, writers, and designers with diverse interests have followed his injunction to interpret everyday landscapes for insights "not only about American history and American society, but about ourselves and how we relate to the world."[157] Even those whose scholarship or politics are at odds with Jackson's interpretations frequently invoke him as a precedent for their expositions of the ways in which landscapes embody social processes and academic concerns.

While subsequent studies have challenged some of Jackson's theoretical precepts and historical contentions, Jackson was more concerned with raising questions than with providing definitive answers. Like Ralph Waldo Emerson, with whom he has often been compared as an essayist and orator, Jackson may eventually be remembered more for the transformational role he played in debunking hidebound canons and legitimating contemporary cultural expressions than for his extensive literary output. Just as pioneers of American art, literature, and associated fields found encouragement and affirmation in Emerson's calls to forsake Old World formalities and engage their surroundings directly and originally, those seeking to expand traditional notions of cultural geography, architectural scholarship, and related disciplines and art forms have continued to look to Jackson for inspiration and validation.

Jackson might not embrace all the concerns that motivate contemporary practitioners, but he would be happy to know that landscape studies remains a vibrant interdisciplinary effort that continues to attract and incorporate new voices and perspectives. His reflections on the tenth anniversary of *Landscape* magazine underscored his vision of landscape studies as a continually evolving moral, intellectual, and artistic endeavor: "Once born, an idea does not easily die. It is discovered by others, taken over by them, amplified, given form and direction, and finally it is shared by many. . . . *Landscape*, whatever its shortcomings, is as much theirs as it is ours."[158] If future scholars, artists, writers, and designers can combine their ever-broadening array of interests with Jackson's observational powers, intellectual acumen, and communicational skills, then landscape studies will continue to flourish as one of the most engaging and insightful means of exploring the human condition.

J. B. Jackson and the American Landscape, the DVD by Janet Mendelsohn that accompanies the limited hardcover edition of this book (and is available elsewhere), is a fitting way not only to present J. B. Jackson to a new generation of readers, but also a terrific introduction to the concept of the cultural landscape to a new generation of students and teachers. The DVD (Fig. 6.5) includes the two original documentaries made, respectively, by Bob Calo (1989) and Janet Mendelsohn and Claire Marino (1988), about Jackson late in his life; a new segment of interviews in 2006 with six esteemed geographers, historians, writers, and photographers about how they discovered and were influenced by Jackson's ideas, about his impact on their field, and his continuing relevance today; and portfolios of Jackson's drawings, watercolors, and teaching slides that complement Portfolio A and Portfolio C in this book. The DVD's Menu allows one to choose where to start and skip around. Like Jackson's essays, the DVD is a collection of different ways to spend time with the man, with each chapter providing a glimpse of a different aspect of his method, his preoccupations, and his legacy. The DVD is distributed by Documentary Educational Resources (www.der.org), of Watertown, Massachusetts.

I. Contents of the Companion DVD: *J. B. Jackson and the American Landscape* (2015), by Janet Mendelsohn

A. *Figure in a Landscape: A Conversation with J. B. Jackson*, a forty-seven minute film co-directed and co-produced by Janet Mendelsohn and Claire Marino (Santa Monica, CA: Direct Cinema Limited, 1988).

Scene Selections:
Introduction: The American Landscape
The Trailer and the Landscape
Jackson's Education

Jackson's World War II Experience
Pivotal Discoveries
The New England Village
The Grid
The Small Town and the House
The Front Yard
The Road
Autonomous Spaces
The Vernacular Landscape
Credits

B. *J. B. Jackson and the Love of Everyday Places*, a fifty-eight minute video produced by Bob Calo (San Francisco, CA: KQED-TV, 1989).

Scene Selections:
Introduction
Chaco Canyon
Establishment and Vernacular
San Jose, New Mexico
Creation of *Landscape* Magazine
Villanueva, New Mexico
Alamosa, Colorado
The Street
Pueblo, Colorado
Colorado Springs, Colorado
The Highway
Denver, Colorado
Jackson at Home
Credits

C. Portfolios of J. B. Jackson's Artwork and Slides

1. Drawings and Watercolors (courtesy of F. Douglas Adams and Helen Lefkowitz Horowitz)
2. Teaching Slides (courtesy of the J. B. Jackson Pictorial Materials Collection, Center for Southwest Research and the School of Architecture and Planning, University of New Mexico, Albuquerque.)

D. Interviews: J. B. Jackson's Legacy, a thirty-seven minute segment co-produced by Janet
Mendelsohn and Chris Wilson, with Miguel Gandert as the videographer (Albuquerque: Historic
Preservation and Regionalism Program, University of New Mexico, 2007).

Topics:
First Encounters
The Cultural Landscape
The Road
Jackson's Influence
His Impact on Photography
Vernacular vs. Establishment
Imagining Jackson Today

Interviewees:*
Arnold R. Alanen, geographer
Miguel Gandert, photographer
Frank Gohlke, photographer
Lucy R. Lippard, writer and curator
Virginia Scharff, historian
Chris Wilson, cultural historian

*All photographs accompanying Miguel Gandert's comments in the DVD copyright © Miguel
Gandert; for further information, contact: Andrew Smith Gallery, Santa Fe, New Mexico
 (info@andrewsmith.com). All photographs accompanying Frank Gohlke's comments in the
DVD copyright © Frank Gohlke; for further information, contact: Howard Greenberg Gallery,
New York City, New York (info@howardgreenberg.com), and Gallery Luisotti, Santa Monica,
California (info@galleryluisotti.com).

Kansas Counties Billboard, no date.
[No slide number.] From the J. B.
Jackson Pictorial Materials Collection (Wilson Collection), Center for
Southwest Research and the School
of Architecture and Planning, University of New Mexico, Albuquerque,
and used by permission.

Appendix B

Organization of
J. B. Jackson's
Teaching Slides

PAUL GROTH

Below is the organization of J. B. Jackson's teaching slides in a set of binders at the time he turned them over to me as his successor teaching the "American Cultural Landscape" course at the University of California, Berkeley, in 1978. I have added binder numbers below [1, 2, 3, . . . 17] and highlighted Jackson's main titles taken from the spine of the binders, followed by his elaboration of the contents of each as recorded on the binder covers. Within each binder, the order of the thematic names of the individual slide sleeves is Jackson's order. I have also adopted consistent capitalization and these conventions: SMALL CAPS indicate headings on the binder edge and binder cover; *italics* indicate titles on the sleeves of slides; Roman numerals [I, II, III] after a sleeve category indicate additional sleeves with the same heading; [brackets] indicate text added by me; and ~~STRIKETHROUGH TEXT~~ is text crossed out by J. B. Jackson.

1. MAPS, PLANS, AIRVIEWS [76 slides]

LOCAL MAPS, GRID, FLOOR PLANS, CITY MAPS, PLANS, AIRVIEWS, SUBDIVISIONS, PLANS

Local Maps
Maps USA I, II, III, and IV
Floor Plans
Air Views
Subdivisions

2. THE STRIP [123 slides]

THE STRIP, TRAVEL, TRAFFIC, MOTELS, HOTELS, VEHICLES, SHIPS, AIRPORTS, STREETCARS, HARBORS, CANALS, BRIDGES, GAS STATIONS

Garages
Travel
Motels

Hotels—South
Vehicles
Ships
Airports
Harbors
Bridges
Gas Stations

3. FIELDS, LAWNS, PARKS, LANDSCAPING [153 slides]
FIELDS, LAWNS, PARKS, LANDSCAPING, PARKS & COMMONS, PLAYGROUNDS

Fields I, II, and III
Parks & Commons
Playgrounds
Streets I and II
Street Life
Shopping Centers and Ped. [Pedestrian] Malls
Civic Centers
Markets, Vendors
[Unlabeled sheet, mostly street-related images]

4. [Churches, Schools] [164 slides]
CHURCHES, CAMP MEETINGS, CEMETERIES, SCHOOLS, SCHOOL BUSSES, CAMPUSES

Churches I, II, and III
Camp Meetings
Cemeteries
Schools I and II
School Busses
Campus I, II, and III
[No label: Rural images and campus culture]

5. MODERN FARMING II [There is no binder labeled Modern Farming I] [87 slides]
[No cover labels]

Migrant Labor
Tractors
Agribusiness II

Elevators, Feed Mills
Irrigation
[No label: Miscellaneous rural; many images of fields]

6. MILLS, FACTORIES, INDUSTRY IN THE LANDSCAPE, MINING, RR [RAILROAD], RR STATIONS [95 slides]
MILLS, FACTORIES, INDUSTRY IN THE LANDSCAPE, MINING, RR, RR STATIONS, GRIST MILLS, TEXTILE MILLS, MILLS + FACTORIES 19C [NINETEENTH CENTURY], FACTORIES 20C [TWENTIETH CENTURY]

Industry in the Landscape I and II
Mining
Railroads
Grist Mills
Textile Mills
Mills + Factories, 19c [Nineteenth Century]
Factories, 20c I and II [Twentieth Century]

7. [Miscellaneous] [162 slides]
STRIP, ~~MOBILE HOMES~~, COMMERCIAL SIGNS, SMALL TOWN, RURAL CENTERS, ~~GAS STATIONS~~, SPORTS

Strip I, II, and *III*
Commercial Signs I and II
Small Town I and II
Rural Centers
Aleatory Sports
Helix Sports
[No label: Strip and signs]
[No label: Signs]

8. COURTHOUSES, MONUMENTS, CITY BEAUTIFUL, CIVIC CENTERS [78 slides]
~~OFFICE BUILDINGS,~~ COURTHOUSES, MONUMENTS, CITY BEAUTIFUL, CIVIC CENTERS

Courthouses
Monuments I, II, and III
[Unlabeled: Monuments]

9. [Miscellaneous] [92 slides]
[No label on binder edge or cover]

Fairs, Carnivals
Celebrations
Poverty, Skid Row I and II
Blacks I and II
People

10. WESTERN SCENERY [7 slides]

WESTERN SCENERY, AGON SPORTS, ALEATORY SPORTS, HELIX SPORTS, RESORTS, RITUAL SPORTS, RETIREMENT, STREET LIFE, GYMNASTICS, FAIRS + CARNIVALS, PLAYGROUNDS, HUNTING

Western Scenery

11. ROADS, HIGHWAYS [114 slides]

ROADS, HIGHWAYS, TREELINED ROADS, OFFICIAL SIGNS, ROADS HISTORICAL, HIGHWAY ECOSYSTEMS

Road Construction
Country Roads, Paved
Interstate
Tree-lined Roads
Highway Signs, Official
Trucks
Truckstops
Roadlife, Restaurants
[No label: Rural Free Delivery and mailboxes]
[No label: Diners]
[No label: Highway ecology]
[No labels: Miscellaneous roads I and II]

12. [Stores, Offices] [135 slides]
[No labels on binder cover]

Light + Color
Lodges, Clubs, Fraternal, etc.
Banks
Stores I, II and III

Office Buildings
Offices, Blocks
Offices
Warehouses
Parking

13. [1920s–1940s] [69 slides]
1920s–1940s

New Deal IV
Streetcars
Traffic, Streetcars, Urban Transportation
[No label: TVA [Tennessee Valley Authority], streamlining, New Deal, GM [General Motors]
Pavilion of the 1933 World's Fair]

14. CITIES-19TH C. [CENTURY], HISTORICAL CITY VIEWS [67 slides]
CITIES—19TH C. [CENTURY], HISTORICAL CITY VIEWS, HISTORICAL CITY, CITY VIEWS

19th c. [CENTURY] City I
Historical City, City Views I, II, and III

15. [Multi-family Housing] [50 slides]
APARTMENT HOUSES, TENEMENT HOUSES, ROW HOUSES

Apartment Houses
Tenement Houses
Row Houses I and II
Blue-collar Housing

16. [Misc.] [67 slides]
[No label on binder edge or cover]

Aleatory Sports, the Lawn
Lawns
Retirement
Resorts I and II
[No label: Miscellaneous]

17. DOMESTIC ARCHITECTURE I [114 slides]
DOMESTIC ARCHITECTURE I

Porches II
Roofs
Mobile Homes I and II
[No label: House types, chronological]

18. DOMESTIC ARCHITECTURE II [173 slides]
DOMESTIC ARCHITECTURE II

Domestic Architecture I, II, III, IV, V, VI, and VII
[No label: More homes]

[Loose sheets, not in a binder]

Browse Line, Pasture + Forest
Army Posts
[Sheet with no label: Company towns, offices]

Appendix C

The J. B. Jackson Legacy and Archival Collections at the University of New Mexico

CHRIS WILSON

Legacy

After J. B. Jackson retired from teaching at the University of California, Berkeley and Harvard University in the late 1970s, he became an occasional speaker at the University of New Mexico's School of Architecture and Planning, where he also endowed a student scholarship. Following his death, the school organized a conference, "J. B. Jackson and the American Landscape." Attended by more than 300 in the fall of 1998, the conference yielded the book, *Everyday America: Cultural Landscape Studies after J. B. Jackson* (2003), edited by Chris Wilson and Paul Groth.[1]

Early in 1997, with the conference planning underway, it was learned that Jackson had left a large bequest to UNM "for the betterment of education in the School of Architecture and Planning." While some in university leadership considered applying this donation toward the campaign for a new architecture building, Acting Dean James R. Richardson steered it instead to the creation of a J. B. Jackson Endowment. The school quickly directed proceeds from the endowment to student travel, to enhanced course offerings, particularly in the new Masters of Landscape Architecture program; and to the ad hoc establishment of a J. B. Jackson Professor of Cultural Landscape Studies.

In 2001, the school also established an annual J. B. Jackson Lecture to recognize those who have made a significant contribution to cultural landscape studies, while also honoring Jackson's generosity to the school and the continuing example of his work. Jackson Lecturers have included Daniel Arreola, Stanley Crawford, William deBuys, Henry Glassie, Paul Groth, Dolores Hayden, Kenneth Helphand, Helen Lefkowitz Horowitz, Dorothée Imbert, Setha Low, Elizabeth Barlow Rogers, Marc Treib, and Chris Wilson.

In 2004, a portion of the Jackson Endowment, along with fifty-percent matching funds from the state legislature, were used to established a separate endowment dedicated to the J. B. Jackson Chair in Cultural Landscape Studies. Then, in 2007, Dean Roger Schluntz spearheaded the naming of a J. B. Jackson Reading Room in the Fine Arts and Design Library of the new George Pearl Hall.

The UNM School of Architecture and Planning and Center for Southwest Research teamed with the French national landscape architecture school, *Ecole nationale supérieure du paysage de Versailles* (ENSP), to co-sponsor a conference held October 15–17, 2015, in Albuquerque. Entitled "PhotoPaysage / LandscapeRepresentation," the conference explored the role of photography and other forms of representation in changing conceptions of landscape since World War II. Speakers ranged from artist-photographers who have focused on vernacular landscapes to landscape architects employing photography in their design practices, to historians and writers examining the use of photography in the evolution of cultural landscape theory practiced by and in the wake of J. B. Jackson. The conference not only featured the findings of a three-year research initiative at the ENSP, directed by Frédéric Pousin, on the interface of landscape and photography, but also served as the launch for this book, with a number of contributing authors speaking at the conference and Chris Wilson serving as the lead organizer for the conference. In addition to the speakers, three complementary exhibitions surveyed Jackson's teaching slides, the online Jackson Pictorial Archives, and the New Topographic photography movement. Videos of the conference's speaker sessions are available at www.unmphotolandscape.com.

The J. B. Jackson Collections

Jackson also left his books and papers to the University of New Mexico Libraries. The books were integrated into university libraries but remain traceable through an electronic bookplate, searchable as "John Brinckerhoff Jackson Memorial Collection" in the online catalogue, *WorldCat* (http://unm.worldcat.org). Subsequent donations of Jackson-related collections are held at the Center for Southwest Research (CSWR) at the Zimmerman Library, UNM's main library:

1. *J. B. Jackson Papers, 1808–1996.* Thirteen boxes, including an inventory of the materials that came out of Jackson's home office, prepared in 1996 by his literary executor, Helen Lefkowitz Horowitz, and such Jackson materials as drafts of essays, books, and lectures; topical research files; and a 1957 U.S. travel journal. Additional materials, donated in 2002 by Paul Groth and incorporated into this collection, include such materials as class lecture notes for courses at Harvard University and the University of California, Berkeley; various drafts of an unpublished manuscript, "A History of American Landscapes: The First Thousand Years"; and a 1986 Berkeley commencement address. In 2011, Helen Lefkowitz Horowitz also donated a collection of tourist souvenirs, mementos, and hand crafts that had adorned Jackson's mantel at the time of his death, which she had inherited. Photographs donated by Jackson have been placed in the separate Jackson Pictorial Collection.

Promotional post card for the "PhotoPaysage/LandscapeRepresentation" conference held October 15–17, 2015, in Albuquerque, designed by Katya Crawford and used with her permission. Photographs by (left and bottom right, cropped) J. B. Jackson and (second down from top right) Miguel Gandert for Jackson, all three from the J. B. Jackson Pictorial Materials Collection, Center for Southwest Research and School of Architecture and Planning, University of New Mexico, Albuquerque, and used by permission; (top right, cropped) © Saban Delcour and used by permission; and (third down from top right) © Geoffrey Mathieu and Bertrand Stofleth and used by permission.

2. *J. B. Jackson Pictorial Collection, 1940–1990.* Six boxes, including photographic and photo-mechanical prints and twenty-nine sketches and drawings.

3. *D. W. Meinig Correspondence with John Brinckerhoff Jackson, 1963–1995.* One folder, including, in addition to correspondence, two manuscripts of Jackson's public lectures, and a collection of Jackson's home-made Christmas cards.

4. *J. B. Jackson Pictorial Materials, 1940–1996.* Four boxes, including approximately 5,500 teaching slides, which Jackson had given to Paul Groth, Marc Treib and Chris Wilson and which they subsequently donated to UNM. (Additional information on the organization of and topics covered by the collection appear in Chapter 4 and Appendix B. Scans of these slides are available online at the New Mexico Digital Collections (www.econtent.unm.edu/cdm/landingpage/collection/groth).

5. *J. B. Jackson Textual Materials, ca. 1970–1996.* Four boxes of materials donated from Paul Groth and Phoebe Cutler. This is an open collection, which can receive further donations; each donor will be represented as a new series within the collection.

Inventories of the J. B. Jackson Printed Materials, Legacy, and Archival Collections are available online at the CSWR page of the UNM Library's Website (www.library.unm.edu/cswr/index.php) by searching Archival Collections. The Center for Southwest Research (CSWR) at the University of New Mexico (UNM) welcomes the donation of additional materials relating to J. B. Jackson, such as personal and professional correspondence, travel notebooks, teaching slides, field sketches, photographs, recordings, and memorabilia. For further information, contact: Director, Center for Southwest Research and Special Collections, Zimmerman Library, MSC05 3020, University of New Mexico, Albuquerque, New Mexico 87131, U.S.A. (cswrref@unm.edu).

John B. Jackson

In Search of the
Proto-Landscape

JOHN B. JACKSON was born in 1909
in France. He received an A.B. from
Harvard University and an honorary
Doctor of Fine Arts from the University
of New Mexico. He served as a major in
the U.S. Cavalry from 1940 to 1946, and
in 1951 founded *Landscape* magazine,
for which he served as editor and publisher until 1968. He has held numerous
academic appointments while always
maintaining his independence, including regular stints at the University of
California, Berkeley, and at Harvard
University. In 1986 the Association of
American Geographers presented the
first J. B. Jackson Award, given annually
to the American geographer whose
book best contributes to the public's
understanding of human landscapes.
Mr. Jackson's books include *Landscapes:
Selected Writings of J. B. Jackson*, edited
by Ervin H. Zube (Massachusetts, 1970),
*American Space: The Centennial Years,
1865 to 1876* (Norton, 1972), *The Necessity for Ruins and Other Topics* (Massachusetts, 1980), *Discovering the Vernacular Landscape* (Yale, 1984), and *A
Sense of PLACE, a Sense of TIME* (Yale,
1994). He resides near Santa Fe, New
Mexico.

AS I DEFINE the word, a landscape is more than an area of
attractive rural or natural scenery. It is a space or a collection of
spaces made by a group of people who modify the natural environment to survive, to create order, and to produce a just and
lasting society.

Natural environments are not everywhere equally hospi-
table, nor are all groups of people equally skilled in modifying
them. The great diversity of landscapes has long been a matter of
interest and study. Yet, since all of them derive from an intention
to reveal an ordering of space and time, it follows that they all
share certain basic characteristics.

In the past I spent much time studying the older, traditional
landscapes of Europe and Anglo North America. I found they
had many cultural and geographical traits in common. The landscapes of northwestern and central Europe and those of North
America east of the Mississippi River are all situated in much the
same kind of natural environment: one with a temperate climate,
abundant rainfall, good soils, many navigable rivers, and few im-
penetrable mountain ranges. Furthermore, those who live in these
landscapes on both sides of the Atlantic Ocean share a Christian-
classical heritage, a stock of technical skills, a similar class structure, and, from a world perspective, the same historical evolution.
Even the languages they speak are related. These are good reasons
for their various landscapes being made alike.

Recently I undertook to study the landscapes of the prehis-
toric Pueblo Indian communities of New Mexico, where I live.
At the time of the Spanish Conquest in the late sixteenth century
the whole Southwestern region contained a population of not
more than thirty thousand people, living in some one hundred
fifty small, scattered farm villages. It was an isolated society, never
powerful or rich, and it made little or no impact on the surrounding American world. It produced no literature, no fine art, and its
original landscapes have long since vanished. But what survived
in New Mexico were eighteen Pueblo villages; and from studying

The opening page of John B. Jackson, "In Search of the Proto-Landscape," in George F. Thompson, ed., *Landscape in America* (1995). The legendary George Lenox, of Austin, Texas, was the
book's designer. In 2015, Thompson donated to the J. B. Jackson Collections at the University of
New Mexico copies of his correspondence with Jackson regarding the development and publication of this seminal article. Used by permission of George F. Thompson and the Center for the
Study of Place (www.studyofplace.org).[2]

A sketch of Culpepper, Virginia, by J. B. Jackson, from his untitled travel notebook (January 1–February 25, 1957), Box 2, Folder 3, J. B. Jackson Pictorial Collection, MSS#633#BC, Center for Southwest Research and the School of Architecture and Planning, University of New Mexico, Albuquerque. Used by permission.

Notes

Epigraph

John Brinckerhoff Jackson, "The Need to be Versed in Country Things," *Landscape*, Vol. 1, No. 1 (Spring 1951): 1–5, quoted 5.

Introduction (Wilson and Mendelsohn)

1. John Brinckerhoff Jackson, *Discovering the Vernacular Landscape* (New Haven, CT: Yale University Press, 1984), ix–x.

2. John Berger, *Ways of Seeing* (London, UK: Penguin Books, 1972), 8.

3. Jackson, *Saints in Summertime* (New York: W. W. Norton, 1938), and *American Space: The Centennial Years, 1865–1876* (New York: W. W. Norton, 1972).

4. Paul Groth, et al., "John Brinckerhoff Jackson, 1909–1996," *Landscape Journal*, Vol. 16, No. 1 (Spring 1997): 10.

5. Helen Lefkowitz Horowitz, ed., *Landscape in Sight: Looking at America* (New Haven, CT: Yale University Press, 1997).

6. See, for example, William Grimes, "Brinck Jackson, 86, Dies: Was Guru of the Landscape," *The New York Times* (August 31, 1996): 27.

Chapter 1 (Wilson)

Note: An earlier version of this essay first appeared in *DESIGNER/builder: A Journal of the Human Environment*, Vol. 3, No. 1 (November 1996): 25–28. It is reprinted here with revisions and the permission of Jerilou Hammett, the publisher of the magazine (www.designerbuildermag-azine.org), which is based in Santa Fe, New Mexico. For a collection of the best articles to appear in that magazine, see Jerilou Hammett and Maggie Wrigley, eds., *The Architecture of Change: Building a Better World* (Albuquerque: University of New Mexico Press, 2013).

This elegiac reminiscence was written soon after Jackson's death and was based largely on my observations and conversations with Jackson during our friendship from 1980 until his death in 1996, during which time I visited him every four to six weeks at his home in La Cienega. We also met occasionally in Albuquerque and took one week-long field trip together to the northern Mexican state of Chihuahua. See, also, these valuable sources on Jackson's biography: Helen Lefkowitz Horowitz, "J. B. Jackson and the Discovery of the American Landscape," in John Brinkerhoff Jackson, *Landscape In Sight: Looking at America* (New Haven, CT: Yale University Press, 1997), ix–xxxi, and "J. B. Jackson as a Critic of Modern Architecture," in Chris Wilson and Paul Groth eds., *Everyday America: Cultural Landscape Studies after J. B. Jackson* (Berkeley: University of California Press, 2003), 37–47.

1. Mark Twain, *Life on the Mississippi* (Boston, MA: James R. Osgood, 1883).

2. The information from the previous five sentences comes from an earlier draft of Chapter 2 of this book and represents the conversations of F. Douglas Adams with Jackson, which is consolidated here along with other biographical information at the suggestion of George F. Thompson, the publisher.

3. Santa Fe regularly ranks, along with New York City, Los Angeles, and Chicago, as one of America's premier art centers in terms of annual sales. See, also, Chris Wilson, *The Myth of Santa Fe: Creating a Modern Regional Tradition* (Albuquerque: University of New Mexico Press, 1987).

4. The information from the previous sentences comes from F. Douglas Adams. See note 2, above.

5. John Brinckerhoff Jackson, "The Need to be Versed in Country Things," *Landscape*, Vol. 1, No. 1 (Spring 1951): 1–5, quoted 5.

6. John Brinckerhoff Jackson, "Other-Directed Houses," *Landscape*, Vol. 6, No. 2 (Winter 1956–1957): 29–35, quoted 33. See, also, Robert Venturi, Denise Scott Brown, and Steven Izenour, *Learning from Las Vegas: The Forgotten Symbolism of Architectural Form* (Cambridge, MA: The MIT Press, 1972; revised edition 2001).

7. J. B. Jackson, "The Stranger's Path," *Landscape*, Vol. 7, No. 1 (Autumn 1957): 11–15, quote 11; reprinted in Helen Lefkowitz Horowitz, ed., *Landscape in Sight* (New Haven, CT: Yale University Press, 1997), 19–29, quoted 11.

8. Ibid., 14 and 25.

9. Jackson, "The Stranger's Path," 15.

10. Personal conversation with the author, no date.

11. Herbert Mushchamp, "Eloquent Champion of the Vernacular Landscape," *The New York Times* (April 21, 1996): 36.

12. Jackson, *The Essential Landscape: The New Mexico Photographic Survey*, edited by Steven A. Yates (Albuquerque: University of New Mexico Press, 1985), *Landscapes: Selected Writings of J. B. Jackson,* edited by Ervin H. Zube (Amherst: University of Massachusetts Press, 1970), *American Space: The Centennial Years, 1865–1876* (New York: W. W. Norton, 1972), *The Necessity for Ruins and Other Topics* (Amherst: University of Massachusetts Press, 1980), *Discovering the Vernacular Landscape* (New Haven, CT: Yale University Press, 1984), and *A Sense of Place, a Sense of Time* (New Haven, CT: Yale University Press, 1994); Helen Lefkowitz Horowitz, ed., *Landscape in Sight: Looking at America* (New Haven, CT: Yale University Press, 1997).

13. Jackson, *Discovering the Vernacular Landscape*, xii.

Chapter 2 (Adams)

1. For a key account, see Harold Winters, *Battling the Elements: Weather and Terrain in the Conduct of War* (Baltimore, MD: The Johns Hopkins University Press, in association with the Center for American Places, 1998).

2. John Brinckerhoff Jackson, "Landscape as Seen by the Military," in *Discovering the Vernacular Landscape* (New Haven, CT: Yale University Press, 1984), 135–36.

3. As quoted in "Dunster House" (www.dunster.harvard.edu); accessed November 4, 2014.

4. Ibid.

5. Jackson, "Landscape as Seen by the Military," 135.

6. Jackson's essay, "Southeast to Turkey," *Landscape*, Vol. 7, No. 3 (Spring 1958), was written during or just after his visit to Turkey. On that trip, he also spent time in Bulgaria, France, Germany, and Ireland.

7. Jackson, *Discovering the Vernacular Landscape* (New Haven, CT: Yale University Press, 1984), and *A Sense of Place, a Sense of Time* (New Haven, CT: Yale University Press, 1994).

8. Le Corbusier [Charles Édouard Jeanneret], *Vers une Architecture* (Paris, France: G. Cres, 1924).

9. Frank Gohlke, *Measure of Emptiness: Grain Elevators in the American Landscape* (Baltimore, MD: The Johns Hopkins University Press, in association with the Center for American Places, 1992). Gohlke was greatly influenced by Jackson's writings, as Gohlke makes plain in Janet Mendelsohn's interview with him in her DVD, *J. B. Jackson and the American Landscape* (Appendix A).

10. Herbert Mushchamp, "Eloquent Champion of the Vernacular Landscape," *The New York Times* (April 21, 1996): 36.

Chapter 3 (Starrs and Goin)

Note: The authors owe a considerable debt of thanks to Bonnie Loyd, Paul Groth, the late Grady Clay and Judith McCandless, David and Mary Alice Lowenthal, Les Rowntree, and the families of Jim Parsons and Dan Luten.

1. Walter Starkie, *The Road to Santiago: Pilgrims of St. James* (London, UK: Murray, 1957).

2. Peirce Lewis discusses a number of these figures in "Axioms for Reading the Cultural Landscape," in D. W. Meinig, ed., *The Interpretation of Ordinary Landscapes: Geographical Essays* (New York: Oxford University Press, 1979), 11–32. David Lowenthal has long been among the strongest supporters of George Perkins Marsh, and his biography of Marsh (revised) is an utterly remarkable effort. See David Lowenthal, *George Perkins Marsh: Prophet of Conservation* (New York: Columbia University Press, 1958; revised edition Seattle: University of Washington Press, 2000).

3. Jackson's essays on landscape were remarkably far ranging and can be seen in various anthologies of his work: *Landscapes: Selected Writings of J.B. Jackson,* Ervin H. Zube, ed. (Amherst: University of Massachusetts Press, 1970); Jackson, *Changing Rural Landscapes*, Ervin and Margaret Zube, eds. (Amherst: University of Massachusetts Press, 1977); Jackson, *The Necessity for Ruins and Other Topics* (Amherst: University of Massachusetts Press, 1980); Jackson, *Discovering the Vernacular Landscape* (New Haven, CT: Yale University Press, 1984); Jackson, *The Essential Landscape: The New Mexico Photographic Survey*, edited by Steven A. Yates (Albuquerque: University of New Mexico Press, 1985); Jackson, *A Sense of Place, a Sense of Time* (New Haven, CT: Yale University Press, 1994); and Jackson, *Landscape in Sight: Looking at America,* Helen Lefkowitz Horowitz, ed. (New Haven, CT: Yale University Press, 1997). The reach of Jackson's work is presented effectively by Janet Mendelsohn in her companion DVD, *J. B. Jackson and the American Landscape* (Appendix A).

4. Horowitz, *Landscape in Sight*, n. 25, 374. Chris Wilson also addresses this matter in Chapter 1, pages 27–28.

5. Jackson was a voracious reader with a deep library, and a regular stream of journals and magazines, in multiple languages, arrived monthly in his mailbox. He particularly favored European geographers and historians such as Pierre Deffontaines, whose work in the early- to mid-twentieth century emphasized place, landscape, and regional studies, which, in turn, fit broadly into his plans for *Landscape* magazine, with interests in what the French, German, Spanish, and Italian schools might describe using the French *paysage*.

6. Horowitz, *Landscape in Sight*, x.

7. Ibid, xvi.

8. J. B. Jackson, "Notes and Comments," *Landscape*, Vol. 10, No. 1 (Fall 1960); *The Need of Being Versed in Country Things*, the title of Robert Frost's poem (originally published in *Harper's Magazine* in December 1920), served as a maxim for that first issue, which announced that *Landscape* was prepared to remedy the 'need.'"

9. Paul Groth and Todd W. Bressi, "Frameworks for Cultural Landscape Study," in *Understanding Ordinary Landscapes,* edited by Groth and Bressi (New Haven, CT: Yale University Press, 1997), 1–21, quoted 2.

10. J. B. Jackson, "Chihuahua; as We Might Have Been," *Landscape*, Vol. 1, No. 1 (Spring 1951): 16–24, quoted 16.

11. How curious that, more than sixty years later, the U.S.-Mexican border remains porous despite monstrous walls, hovering drones, and an army of body-armor clad border patrol officers dedicated to enforcing that "Euclidean line drawn across the desert." That Jackson should choose the borderlands as a theme was no accident. He spent considerable time in the Southwest, eventually settling in La Ciénega, ten miles south of Santa Fe, New Mexico. He knew the scholarship of such historians of borderlands as Hubert Eugene Bolton and Edward H. Spicer, whose respective books, *Rim of Christendom: A Biography of Eusebio Francisco Kino, Pacific Coast Pioneer* (New York: Macmillan, 1936) and *Cycles of Conquest: The Impact of Spain, Mexico, and the United States on the Indians of the Southwest, 1533–1960* (Tucson: University of Arizona Press, 1962) were fixtures in Jackson's library. The borderlands school continues unabated, plowing deep into history, geography, ecology, and fiction, with work ranging from *The Changing Mile Revisited: An Ecological Study of Vegetation Change with Time in the Lower Mile of an Arid and Semiarid Region* by Raymond M. Turner, Robert H. Webb, Janice E. Bowers, and James Rodney Hastings (Tucson: University of Arizona Press, 2003) to "Forget the Alamo: The Border as Place in John Sayles's *Lone Star,*" by Daniel D. Arreola, in *Journal of Cultural Geography*, Vol. 23, No. 1 (2005): 23–42. See, also, Peter Goin, *Tracing the Line: A Photographic Survey of the Mexican-American Border* (Artist's limited edition, 1987).

12. *Landscape, Human Geography of the Southwest: Human Geography is the study of how man modifies the face of the earth as he works and moves about and provides himself with shelter*, Vol. 1, No. 3 (Winter 1952): 1.

13. *Landscape: Magazine of Human Geography: Human Geography Is the Study of Man the Inhabitant*, Vol. 2, No. 2 (Autumn 1952): 1.

14. *Landscape: Magazine of Human Geography*, Vol. 5, No. 3 (Spring 1956): 1.

15. J. B. Jackson, "The Southwest Revisited," *Landscape*, Vol. 10, No. 1 (Fall 1960): 10.

16. J. B. Jackson, "The Need of Being Versed in Country Things," *Landscape*, Vol. 1, No. 1 (Spring 1951): 1–4, quoted 4.

17. The American Geographical Society sponsored major photographic expeditions during the first half of the twentieth century, as did the National Geographic Society. The theme of "below from above," as aerial photographer Georg Gerster would title one of his books (New York: Abbeyville Press, 1986), clearly had legs. An interesting summary of one photographer's work is sketched by Lauren Collins, "Profiles: Angle of Vision: George Steinmetz's Aerial Alchemy," *The New Yorker* (April 19, 2010): 70–82. For a formal discussion of geography and aerial reconnaissance, see William M. Denevan, "The 1931 Shippee-Johnson Aerial Photography Expedition to Peru," *Geographical Review,* Vol. 83, No. 3 (July 1993): 238–51.

18. See, for example, Antoine de Saint-Exupéry, *Wind, Sand and Stars*, Lewis Galantiere (translator), (New York: Reynal and Hitchcock, 1939), and considerably later, the book by André Humbert, *Le géographe et le Tapis Volant* (Madrid, Spain: Casa de Velázquez, 2012). Aerial photography was not just an exploration technique or one drawn on for military purposes; it was also aesthetic and, with time, became a source of both poetic reflection and an active research tool for geographers. The same can be said of cartography, although that was not a particular *Landscape* specialty, since the cartographic resources were limited. Still, it is notable that, for the Tenth Anniversary issue, the now-legendary Harvard geographer-cartographer Erwin Raisz would send a letter of congratulations noting, "It is, perhaps, not a coincidence that three of our leading cartographers worked in architecture before. I was always puzzled by this until I became a reader of *Landscape.* Here the relationship became clear. It [cartography] is the art of space. *Landscape* serves the people whose first question is *where?* but have some other questions too." From *Landscape*, Vol. 10, No. 1 (Fall 1960): 6.

19. Edgar Anderson, *Landscape Papers*, edited by Bob Callahan (Berkeley, CA: Turtle Island Foundation, 1976), 9.

20. Groth and Bressi, *Understanding Ordinary Landscapes*, 19.

21. The Tenth Anniversary issue of *Landscape,* published in Fall 1960 (at a cost of "One Dollar"), was something momentous. "We are happy," Jackson wrote in the Notes and Comments section, "to have reached such an advanced age, but it is the part of modesty to leave any appraisal of the accomplishment to others. The birthday presents of friends will be found elsewhere in the magazine; here is the place to take stock of what we have been saying during the past years" (Vol. 10, No 1, quoted 1).

22. Paul Groth, one of Jackson's early students, would pick Jackson's enthusiasm for the city scene as the theme of a seminar paper written for a graduate course in geography at Berkeley,

which he titled "The Urban-Landscape Sales Campaign in *Landscape* Magazine, 1951–1968," submitted in Spring 1978. In it, Groth acutely picks up on Jackson's annoyance with architectural Modernism, his preference for Beaux Arts designs, and his admiration for suburbs and dispersed city forms—views that were close to anathema at the time. The theme of Jackson's resistance is extended and deepened in the recent doctoral dissertation by Jeffrey D. Blankenship, in geography and geosciences, entitled "Reading *Landscape:* Mid-Century Modernism and the Landscape Idea," (Amherst: University of Massachusetts, 2011). Jackson's resistance to Modernism is a theme Paul Groth noted in his 1978 paper and Patricia Nelson Limerick would add to in "J.B. Jackson and the Play of the Mind: Inquiry and Assertion as Contact Sports," *Geographical Review*, Vol. 88, No. 4 (October 1998): 483–491. Without a doubt, Jackson relished his role as contrarian (see Propositions Two and Six in Limerick's essay). Jackson's calm embrace of vernacular artifacts such a trailer courts and flea markets would drive some later commentators on the American scene to near-apoplectic distraction. See, for example, James Howard Kunstler, *The Geography of Nowhere: The Rise and Decline of America's Man-Made Landscape* (New York: Simon and Schuster, 1994).

23. J. B. Jackson, "Notes and Comments," Vol. 1, No. 1 (Fall 1960): quoted 1–2.

24. Conventionally, the quotation is attributed to Peirce Lewis, in his "Axioms" essay in Meinig, *The Interpretation of Ordinary Landscapes*. More likely the originator was Aldous Huxley, although it was certainly popularized by Lewis.

25. Horowitz, *Landscape in Sight*, x.

26. Donald W. Meinig's edited volume, *The Interpretation of Ordinary Landscapes*, is a gold mine of *Landscape* magazine-based insights and a trove of observations of the every-day grounded in geographical fieldwork. See D. W. Meinig, "Reading the Landscape: An Appreciation of W. G. Hoskins and J. B. Jackson," in Meinig, *The Interpretation of Ordinary Landscapes*, 235.

27. Parsons was interviewed in Bob Calo, producer, *J. B. Jackson and the Love of Everyday Places* (San Francisco, CA: KQED-TV, 1989), videocassette, which now appears in Mendelsohn's DVD (Appendix A).

28. Patricia Nelson Limerick puts the matter succinctly and casts Jackson's protestations of his inadequate academic credentials in context: "But think about it: This man taught at Harvard and Berkeley for years; he was—certifiably—an acute and penetrating observer of the activities of human beings; and we are supposed to believe him when he says he does not understand much about academics? Unless I have missed something important, when it comes to academics, Harvard and Berkeley are the belly of the beast, and for Jackson to say that he doesn't know about

academics is the equivalent of Jonah saying that he doesn't know much about whales." Limerick, "J. B. Jackson and the Play of the Mind," quoted 484.

29. Jane Holtz Kay, "Design Notebook: A Singular Observer of Everyday Places," *The New York Times* (September 14, 1989): C1.

30. Jackson's notes in 1968 about the changing of the guard are mini-masterpieces, and telling in their generosity. See Jackson, "Announcing a Change of Editors," *Landscape*, Vol. 17, No. 3 (Spring 1968): 1; followed in 1969 by "1951–1969: Postscript," *Landscape*, Vol. 18, No. 1 (Winter 1969): 1. And it was no accident that, in 1968 as the transition was beginning, Jackson added to the *Landscape* canon his essay on "The Vanishing Epitaph: From Monument to Place," Vol. 17, No. 2 (Winter 1967–1968): 22–26. Nineteen sixty-eight was a fertile time and, in many regards, revolutionary in world history, and Jackson was well aware of the tenor of ongoing conversations.

31. Bonnie Loyd later served as a founding editorial consultant to George F. Thompson's acclaimed book series, "Creating the North American Landscape," which was published by the Johns Hopkins University Press for more than twenty years.

32. Bret Wallach, after completing bachelor's, master's, and doctoral degrees in geography at Berkeley in record time, had moved onto a series of short-term jobs at U.S. and Canadian universities, without catching on at any of them, seemingly stalled in a tenure-track millrace without publications. Not that he couldn't write—Wallach (a nephew of film critic Pauline Kael) was stunningly productive, knocking out essays and even book manuscripts of formidable literary quality that he would mail to friends and his mentors, but they were never in the illustrated and footnoted-mode favored by 1970s academia. After rattling around for a time, Wallach ended up at the University of Maine at Fort Kent, a lovely spot but an academic backwater along the Canadian border at the northern terminus of U.S. 1. There he wrote an essay on the local agricultural landscape, focusing on the distinctive potato-growers in upstate Maine, which he sent along to Dan Luten, who had served on Wallach's dissertation committee. Without consulting Wallach, Luten forwarded the essay to Blair Boyd, submitting it, in Wallach's name, to *Landscape*. The first that Wallach heard about it was a letter of acceptance but one asking, politely, if he could, perhaps, add a map and a photograph or two to go along with the text. That began Wallach's career in geographic publishing. Jim Parsons and Dan Luten confirmed details of this account, and, in 2004, so did Blair Boyd; see Wallach, "The Potato Landscape: Aroostook County, Maine." *Landscape*, Vol. 23, No. 1 (No season, 1979): 15–22.

Emboldened by his unplanned success with *Landscape*, Wallach soon after submitted a manuscript, based on his doctoral dissertation, on the West Side oil fields of the San Joaquin Valley (California) to Doug McManis, then editor of *The Geographical Review*. That was published with a concluding editorial note by McManis noting the distinctive literary quality—and an absence of the usual scholarly impedimenta—of Wallach's essay; see "The West Side Oil Fields of California," *Geographical Review*, Vol. 70, No. 1 (January 1980): 50–59. When Paul Starrs took over as editor of the *GR* from McManis in 1996, as that journal's first university-based editor, McManis remarked that he still regarded that note as one of his few recognizable mistakes as an editor. "I should have published it without the note, which could be read as an apology—quite the opposite, it was one of my happiest acquisitions." It was *Landscape* magazine, however, that first recognized the talent.

33. Paul Starrs began conversations with Blair Boyd in early 2004 about *Landscape*, and, taking to heart Boyd's interest in keeping the magazine's legacy alive, Starrs and Peter Goin completed the transaction with Boyd in September 2005, which became effective December 1, 2005, with rights to all artwork and texts transferred. The visits went easily; Boyd was amply familiar with Goin's work, since he had published four of Goin's articles in *Landscape.* Starrs did his doctoral work in geography at Berkeley, maintained a long friendship with Berkeley geographer Jim Parsons (who had published two pieces in *Landscape*—though twenty-seven years apart), and the *Landscape* link came via Jay (James) and Jean Vance and through the estimable presence of Dan Luten, whose contributions to *Landscape*'s pages were frequent.

34. Formed in 2005, the Black Rock Institute is a 501(c)(3) nonprofit organization, incorporated in Nevada, with a mission statement that reads: "The Black Rock Institute in Reno, Nevada, supports research and innovative projects focusing upon the diverse and complex reality of landscapes in western North America. These include variously a sense of place, a lyrical interpretation of the nature of mountains and aridity, the material reality of physical landscapes, and spreading word of their significance."

35. Jackson on daily bread: J. B. Jackson, Voiceover in Calo, *J. B. Jackson and The Love of Everyday Places* (1989); discussed in Paul F. Starrs, "Brinck Jackson in the Realm of the Everyday," *Geographical Review*, Vol. 88, No. 4 (October 1998): 492–506, quoted 504.

36. John R. Stilgoe, *Outside Lies Magic: Regaining History and Awareness in Everyday Places* (New York: Walker and Company, 1998), quoted 179–80.

37. Groth and Bressi, "Frameworks for Cultural Landscape Study," quoted 5.

Chapter 5 (Horowitz)

1. Janet Mendelsohn and Claire Marino, codirectors and producers, *Figure in a Landscape: A Conversation with J. B. Jackson* (Direct Cinema Limited, 1988), videocassette; Bob Calo, producer, *J. B. Jackson and the Love of Everyday Places* (San Francisco, CA: KQED-TV, 1989), videocassette.

2. W. G. Hoskins, presenter, and Peter Jones, producer, *Horizon: The Making of the English Landscape* (London, UK: BBC, 1972).

3. John Brinckerhoff Jackson, *Landscape in Sight: Looking at America*, Helen Lefkowitz Horowitz, ed. (New Haven, CT: Yale University Press, 1997).

4. Jackson, "The Abstract World of the Hot-Rodder," in *Landscape*, Vol. 7, No. 2 (Winter 1957–1958): 22–27.

5. Jackson, *The Necessity for Ruins and Other Topics* (Amherst: University of Massachusetts Press, 1980).

Chapter 6 (Mendelsohn and Calo)

1. Janet Mendelsohn and Claire Marino, codirectors and producers, *Figure in a Landscape: A Conversation with J. B. Jackson* (Santa Monica, CA: Direct Cinema Limited, 1988), videocassette; Bob Calo, producer, *J. B. Jackson and the Love of Everyday Places* (San Francisco, CA: KQED-TV, 1989), videocassette.

2. See Helen Lefkowitz Horowitz's Chapter 5 in this book.

Chapter 7 (Davis)

1. Jackson's biography and influence has been recounted in numerous sources, including: D. W. Meinig, ed., *The Interpretation of Ordinary Landscapes: Geographic Essays* (New York: Oxford University Press, 1979); Paul Groth and Todd Bressi, eds., *Understanding Ordinary Landscapes* (New Haven, CT: Yale University Press, 1997); Chris Wilson and Paul Groth, eds., *Everyday America: Cultural Landscape Studies after J. B. Jackson,* (Berkeley: University of California Press, 2003); Paul Groth, et al., "John Brinckerhoff Jackson, 1909–1996," *Landscape Journal*, Vol. 16, No. 1 (Spring 1997): 1–45; and Helen Horowitz's introduction to her edited collection on John Brinckerhoff Jackson, *Landscape in Sight: Looking at America* (New Haven, CT: Yale University Press, 1997), which constitutes the most comprehensive anthology of his writings to date.

2. Jackson, "The Need of Being Versed in Country Things," *Landscape*, Vol. 1, No. 1 (Spring 1951): 1–5, quoted 5.

3. Jackson, *Discovering the Vernacular Landscape* (New Haven, CT: Yale University Press, 1984), ix–x.

4. Letter, Jackson to the author, March 16, 1990.

5. Jackson, *Discovering the Vernacular Landscape*, ix–x.

6. Ervin Zube, ed., *Landscapes: The Selected Writings of J. B. Jackson* (Amherst: University of Massachusetts Press, 1970); *The Necessity for Ruins and Other Topics* (Amherst: University of Massachusetts Press, 1980); *Discovering the Vernacular Landscape* (New Haven, CT: Yale University Press, 1984); *A Sense of Place, a Sense of Time* (New Haven, CT: Yale University Press, 1994); and *Landscape in Sight*.

7. "Learning About Landscapes," in *The Necessity for Ruins*, 1–18; "Preface," "The Word Itself," and "Concluding with Landscapes," in *Discovering the Vernacular Landscape*, ix–xii, 1–8, and 147–57.

8. "The Four Corners Country," *Landscape*, Vol. 10, No. 3 (Fall 1960): 20–26; "The Sunbelt City," in Jackson, *The Southern Landscape Tradition in Texas* (Fort Worth, TX: The Amon Carter Museum, 1980), 25–36; "Other-Directed Houses," *Landscape*, Vol. 6, No. 2 (Winter 1956–57): 29–35; "Limited Access," *Landscape*, Vol. 14, No. 1 (Autumn 1964): 18–23; "Truck City," in *A Sense of Place, a Sense of Time*, 171–85; and "To Pity the Plumage and Forget the Dying Bird," *Landscape*, Vol. 17, No. 2 (Autumn 1967): 1–4. Most of these essays have been republished in anthologies such as *Landscapes* and *Landscape in Sight*.

9. "Auto Territoriality," *Landscape*, Vol. 17, No. 3 (Spring 1968): 1–2; "The Abstract World of the Hot-Rodder," *Landscape*, Vol. 7, No. 2 (Winter 1957–58): 22–27; "The Road Belongs in the Landscape," in *A Sense of Place, a Sense of Time*, 185–205. I provide a more comprehensive overview of Jackson's writings on road-related topics in "Looking Down the Road: J. B. Jackson and the American Highway Landscape," in Wilson and Groth, *Everyday America*, 62–80.

10. "The Stranger's Path," *Landscape*, Vol. 7, No. 1 (Autumn 1957): 11–15; "Two Street Scenes," *Landscape*, Vol. 3, No. 3 (Spring 1954) , 4–5; and "The Almost Perfect Town," *Landscape*, Vol. 2, No. 1 (Spring 1952): 2–8.

11. "The Westward-Moving House," *Landscape*, Vol. 2, No. 2 (Spring 1953): 8–21.

12. Ghosts at the Door," *Landscape*, Vol. 1, No. 2 (Autumn 1951): 3–9; "The Domestication of the Garage," *Landscape*, Vol. 20, No. 2 (Winter 1976): 10–19; "From Monument to Place," *Landscape*, Vol. 17, No. 2 (Winter 1967–1968): 22–26; "The Past and Future Park," in *A Sense of Place, a Sense of Time*, 105–16.

13. "Chihuahua as We Might Have Been," *Landscape*, Vol. 1, No. 1 (Spring 1951): 16–24; "The Virginia Heritage: Fencing, Farming, and Cattle Raising" and "The Nineteenth-Century Rural Landscape: The Courthouse, the Small College, The Mineral Spring, and the Country Store," in *The Southern Landscape Tradition in Texas*, 1–11 and 13–22; and "The Order of a Landscape," in Meinig, *The Interpretation of Ordinary Landscapes*, 153–63; "A Pair of Ideal Landscapes" in

Discovering the Vernacular Landscape, 9–55; "A Sense of Place, a Sense of Time," in *A Sense of Place, a Sense of Time*, 149–63.

14. Jackson, *American Space: The Centennial Years* (New York: W. W. Norton, 1972).

15. David Reisman, *The Lonely Crowd* (New Haven, CT: Yale University Press, 1950); Michael Harrington, *The Other America* (New York: Macmillan, 1962); and Michel Foucault, *The Order of Things: An Archeology of the Human Sciences* (Paris, France: Éditions Gallimard, 1966).

16. Meinig, *The Interpretation of Ordinary Landscapes*.

17. Meinig raised this proposition in his introduction and expounded on it at greater length in ""Environmental Appreciation: Localities as a Humane Art," in *Western Humanities Review,* Vol. 25, No.1 (Winter 1971): 1–11.

18. Paul Groth and Todd Bressi, eds., *Understanding Ordinary Landscapes* (New Haven, CT: Yale University Press, 1997).

19. Paul Groth, "Frameworks for Cultural Landscape Study," in Groth and Bressi, *Understanding Ordinary Landscapes*, 1–21, quoted 1.

20. Dolores Hayden, "Urban Landscape History: The Sense of Place and the Politics of Space," in Groth and Bressi, *Understanding Ordinary Landscapes*, 111–33.

21. Chris Wilson and Paul Groth, eds., *Everyday America: Cultural Landscape Studies after J. B. Jackson* (Berkeley: University of California Press, 2003).

22. Horowitz, ed., *Landscape in Sight*.

23. Carl O. Sauer, "The Morphology of Landscape," in *University of California Publications in Geography,* Vol. 2, No. 2 (No season, 1925): 19–53. Peirce Lewis has pointed to Sauer's later publication, "The Education of A Geographer," in *Annals of the Association of American Geographers,* Vol. 46, No. 3 (September 1956): 287–99, as a more mature and accessible expression of Saur's precepts. Both essays are reprinted in John Leighly, ed., *Land and Life: A Selection from the Writings of Carl Ortwin Sauer* (Berkeley: University of California Press, 1963), 389–404. The classic compilation of this genre is Philip Wagner and Marvin Mikesell, eds., *Readings in Cultural Geography* (Chicago, IL: University of Chicago Press, 1962).

24. Wilbur Zelinsky, *The Cultural Geography of the United States* (Englewood Cliffs, NJ: Prentice Hall, 1973). Meinig's magnum opus, *The Shaping of America: A Geographical Perspective on 500 Years of History*, 4 vols. (New Haven, CT: Yale University Press, 1986, 1993, 1998, and 2004), affords an encyclopedic demonstration of the Berkeley School's efforts to provide a geographical perspective on American history.

25. John Fraser Hart, "Reading the Landscape," in George F. Thompson, ed., *Landscape in*

America (Austin: University of Texas Press, 1995), 23–42. Thompson's anthology also includes Jackson's essay, "In Search of the Proto-Landscape," 43–50, which was among the last essays he published (see page 237). Lewis summarized pre-Jackson approaches to cultural geography and expanded on his early advice in "The Monument and the Bungalow: The Intellectual Legacy of J. B. Jackson," in Wilson and Groth, *Everyday America*, 85–108.

26. For elaborations on the evolution of academic cultural geography during this period, see Peter Jackson, *Maps of Meaning: An Introduction to Cultural Geography* (London, UK: Unwin Hyman, 1989); James Duncan, "The Superorganic in American Cultural Geography," in *Annals of the Association of American Geographers*, Vol. 70, No. 2 (June 1980): 181–98; Don Mitchell, "There's No Such Thing as Culture: Towards a Reconceptualization of the Idea of Culture in Geography," in *Transactions of the Institute of British Geographers*, New Series, Vol. 20, No. 1 (No season, 1995): 102–16; Deryck Holdsworth, "Landscapes and Archives as Texts," in Groth and Bressi, *Understanding Ordinary Landscapes*, 44–55; George Henderson, "What Else We Talk About When We Talk About Landscape: For a Return to the Social Imagination," in Wilson and Groth, *Everyday America*, 178–88; and the introduction to Don Mitchell's *The Lie of the Land: Migrant Workers and the California Landscape* (Minneapolis: University of Minnesota Press, 1996). Mitchell provides a more elaborate overview in *Cultural Geography: A Critical Introduction* (Oxford, UK: Blackwell Publishing, 2000).

27. Denis Cosgrove, *Social Formation and Symbolic Landscape* (London, UK: Croom Helm, 1984; reprint edition, Madison: University of Wisconsin Press, 1998); Stephen Daniels and Denis Cosgrove, eds., *The Iconography of Landscape: Essays on the Symbolic Representation, Design, and Use of Past Environments* (New York: Cambridge University Press, 1988); and Stephen Daniels, *Fields of Vision: Landscape Imagery and Ideology in England and the United States* (Princeton, NJ: Princeton University Press, 1993).

28. David Harvey, *Social Justice and the City* (Baltimore, MD: The Johns Hopkins University Press, 1973), *Consciousness and the Urban Experience: Studies in the History and Theory of Capitalist Urbanization* (Baltimore, MD: The Johns Hopkins University Press, 1985), and *Spaces of Global Capitalism: Toward a Theory of Uneven Economic Development* (London and New York: Verso, 2006); and Neil Smith, "Toward a Theory of Gentrification A Back to the City Movement by Capital, not People," *Journal of the American Planning Association* Vol. 45, No. 4 (October 1979): 538–48, *Uneven Development: Nature, Capital, and the Production of Space* (New York: Blackwell, 1984), and *The New Urban Frontier: Gentrification and the Revanchist City* (London, UK: Routledge, 1996).

29. Mitchell, *The Lie of the Land*, 30.

30. Kevin Lynch, *The Image of the City* (Cambridge, MA: The MIT Press, 1960).

31. Yi-Fu Tuan, "Place: An Experiential Perspective," in *Geographical Review*, Vol. 65, No. 2 (April 1975): 151–65, *Topophilia: A Study of Environmental Perceptions, Attitudes, and Values* (Englewood Cliffs, NJ: Prentice-Hall, 1974), and *Space and Place: The Perspective of Experience* (Minneapolis: University of Minnesota Press, 1977). Tuan summarizes and expands upon his views in his final book, *The Last Launch: Messages in the Bottle* (Staunton, VA: George F. Thompson Publishing, 2015).

32. Edward T. Hall, *The Silent Language* (Garden City, NY: Doubleday, 1959), and *The Hidden Dimension* (Garden City, NY: Doubleday, 1966).

33. Gaston Bachelard, *The Poetics of Space* (Boston, MA: Beacon Press, 1969).

34. Relatively succinct attempts to explain the phenomenological approach to cultural geography include Anne Buttimer, "Grasping the Dynamism of the Lifeworld," *Annals of the American Association of Geographers*, Vol. 66, No. 2 (June 1976): 277–92, and J. Nicholas Entriken, "Contemporary Humanism in Geography," *Annals of the American Association of Geographers*, Vol. 66, No. 4 (December 1976): 615–32. Two books showcased associated authors and approaches: *The Human Experience of Space and Place*, Anne Buttimer and David Seamon, eds. (New York: St. Martin's Press, 1980), and *Dwelling, Place and Environment: Towards a Phenomenology of Person and World,* David Seamon and Robert Mugerauer, eds. (Boston, MA: Martinus Nijhoff Publishers, 1985; reprint edition, Malabar, FL: Krieger Publishing Company 2000). Phenomenology strongly influenced Edward Relph's *Place and Placelessness* (London, UK: Pion, 1976), *Rational Landscapes and Humanistic Geography* (London, UK: Croom Helm, 1981), and *The Modern Urban Landscape* (Baltimore, MD: The Johns Hopkins University Press, 1987).

35. Dolores Hayden, *The Power of Place: Urban Landscapes as Public History* (Cambridge, MA: The MIT Press, 1995).

36. Allan Pred, "Place as a Historically Contingent Process: Structuration and the Time-Geography of Becoming Places," *Annals of the Association of American Geographers*, Vol. 74, No. 2 (June 1984): 279–297; Pierre Bourdieu, *Outline of a Theory of Practice* (Cambridge, UK: Cambridge University Press, 1977); Henri Lefebvre, *Writings on Cities*, translated and edited by Eleonore Kofman and Elizabeth Lennas (London, UK: Blackwell, 1996); and Michel de Certeau, *The Practice of Everyday Life* (Berkeley: University of California Press, 1984). The author attempted to translate these theoretical cogitations into the vernacular and apply them to the investigation of a quotidian American space in Timothy Davis, "Designed Space vs. Social Space: Intention and Appropriation in an American Urban Park," in David Nye, Jeffrey Meikle, and Miles Orvell, eds., *Public Spaces and the Ideology of Place in American Culture* (Amsterdam, The Netherlands: Rodopi, 2009), 339–65.

37. Wallace Stegner, *Wolf Willow: A History, a Story, and a Memory of the Last Plains Frontier* (New York: Viking Press, 1962); James Agee, "Knoxville: Summer 1915," in *A Death in the Family* (New York: Grosset and Dunlap, 1967), 3–7; Joan Dideon, "Notes from a Native Daughter," in *Slouching Toward Bethlehem* (New York: Farrar, Straus and Giroux, 1968), 173–87; Leslie Marmon Silko, "Interior and Exterior Landscapes: The Pueblo Migration Stories," in Thompson, ed., *Landscape in America*, 155–69; and John McPhee, *The Pine Barrens* (New York: Farrar, Straus and Giroux, 1968) and *Coming into the Country* (New York: Farrar, Straus and Giroux, 1977).

38. Keith Basso, *Wisdom Sits in Places: Landscape and Language among the Western Apache* (Albuquerque: University of New Mexico Press, 1996).

39. Kingston William Heath, *The Patina of Place: The Cultural Weathering of a New England Industrial Landscape* (Knoxville: The University of Tennessee Press, 2002).

40. Wright Morris, *The Inhabitants* (New York: Scribner's Sons, 1946; 2nd edition, New York: De Capo Press, 1971) and *The Home Place* (New York: Scribner's Sons, 1948). Morris's memoirs and works of fiction are also highly evocative of the places in which they are set. See, also, Stephen Longmire, *Picture a Life: The Photo texts of Wright Morris*, Ph.D. dissertation (Chicago, IL: University of Chicago, Department of Comparative Literature, 2010).

41. James Agee and Walker Evans, *Let Us Now Praise Famous Men* (Boston, MA: Houghton Mifflin, 1941), which is available in numerous reprint editions.

42. Bettina Berch chronicled Johnston's extraordinary career in *The Woman Behind the Lens: The Life and Work of Frances Benjamin Johnston, 1864–1952* (Charlottesville: University of Virginia Press, 2000). Wallace Nutting's immensely popular "States Beautiful" series presented highly romanticized images of buildings, roads, and landscapes in dozens of Eastern and Midwestern states; Thomas Denenberg discussed Nutting's career and cultural significance in *Wallace Nutting and the Invention of Old America* (New Haven, CT: Yale University Press, 2003). Less well-known today, Clifton Johnson produced illustrated travelogues such as *Highways and Byways of the South* (New York: McMillan, 1904) and *New England and its Neighbors* (New York: McMillan, 1902); many of Johnson's sketches first appeared in newspapers and popular magazines.

43. Norman Morrison Isham and Albert F. Brown, *Early Rhode Island Houses: An Historical and Architectural Study* (Providence, RI: Preston and Rounds, 1895), and *Early Connecticut Houses* (Providence, RI: Preston and Rounds, 1900). Dell Upton described the contributions of Isham, Lyon, and Mercer and traced subsequent developments in vernacular architecture studies in "Outside the Academy: A Century of Vernacular Architecture Studies, 1890–1990," in Elisa-

beth Blair MacDougall, ed. *The Architectural Historian in America: A Symposium in Celebration of the Fiftieth Anniversary of the Founding of the Society of Architectural Historians*, *Studies in the History of Art* Vol. 35, (Washington, DC: National Gallery of Art, 1990), 199–207.

44. *The White Pine Series of Architectural Monographs*, Vols. 1–17 (1915–1931).

45. The Historic American Buildings Survey's origins and early activities are described in Catherine Lavoie, "Architectural Plans and Visions: The Early HABS Program and Its Documentation of Vernacular Architecture," in *Perspectives in Vernacular Architecture*, Vol. 13, No. 2 (2006/2007): 15–35; and Lisa Pfueller Davidson and Martin J. Perschler, "The Historic American Buildings Survey During the New Deal Era: Documenting a 'Complete Resume of the Builder's Art,'" in *CRM: The Journal of Heritage Stewardship*, Vol. 1, No. 1 (Fall 2003): 55–58.

46. Fiske Kimball, *Domestic Architecture of the American Colonies and Early Republic* (New York: Charles Scribner's Sons, 1922); Fred Kniffen, "Louisiana House Types," *Annals of the Association of American Geographers*, Vol. 26, No. 4 (December 1936): 179–93; and Kniffen, "Folk Housing: A Key to Diffusion," *Annals of the Association of American Geographers*, Vol. 55, No. 4 (December 1965): 549–77, reprinted in Dell Upton and John Michael Vlach, eds., *Common Places: Readings in American Vernacular Architecture* (Athens: University of Georgia Press, 1986), 3–26.

47. Henry Glassie, *Pattern in the Material Folk Culture of the Eastern United States* (Philadelphia: University of Pennsylvania Press, 1968).

48. Travis McDonald provided an insightful account of the history of architectural research at Colonial Williamsburg and its influence on vernacular architecture studies in "The Fundamental Practice of Fieldwork at Colonial Williamsburg," in *Perspectives in Vernacular Architecture*, Vol. 13, No. 2 (2006/2007): 36–53.

49. Henry Glassie, *Folk Housing in Middle Virginia: A Structural Analysis of Historic Artifacts* (Knoxville: University of Tennessee Press, 1975).

50. Upton and Vlach, *Common Places*.

51. The origins, aims, and evolving debates about the nature and purpose of Vernacular Architecture Studies are highlighted in Camille Wells, "Old Claims and New Demands: Vernacular Architecture Studies Today," in Camille Wells, ed., *Perspectives in Vernacular Architecture II* (Columbia: University of Missouri Press, 1986), 1–4; Thomas Carter and Bernard Herman, "Introduction: Toward a New Architectural History," in Thomas Carter and Bernard Herman, eds., *Perspectives in Vernacular Architecture IV* (Columbia: University of Missouri Press, 1991), 1–6; Dell Upton, "Architectural History or Landscape History?" in *Journal of Architectural Education*, Vol. 4, No. 4 (August 1991): 195–99; Annmarie Adams and Sally McMurry,

"Exploring Everyday Landscapes: An Introduction," in Annmarie Adams and Sally McMurry, eds., *Exploring Everyday Landscapes: Perspectives in Vernacular Architecture VII* (Knoxville: University of Tennessee Press, 1997), 17–30; and Warren Hofstra and Camille Wells, "Embracing Our Legacy: Shaping Our Future," in *Perspectives in Vernacular Architecture*, Vol. 13, No. 2 (2006/2007): 2–6.

52. Dell Upton, a leading figure in the VAF, raised concerns about the direction of the field in "The VAF at 25: What Now?" in *Perspectives in Vernacular Architecture*, Vol. 13, No. 2 (2006/2007): 7–13. By the standards articulated in Upton and Vlach's *Common Places* and reaffirmed here, Jackson's murky slides and impressionistic sketches disqualified him from serious consideration as an interpreter of the American landscape. The ongoing emphasis on artifactual analysis and graphic documentation can be seen in the VAF's official introduction to the field: Thomas Carter and Elizabeth Collins Cromley, *An Invitation to Vernacular Architecture: A Guide to the Study of Ordinary Buildings and Landscapes* (Knoxville: University of Tennessee Press, 2005).

53. In their introduction to *Common Places*, the editors employed the couplet "vernacular architecture and landscapes" as well as the broadly encompassing terms "the American vernacular environment" and "common places" (Upton and Vlach, *Common Places*, xiii–xxiii). Also, professors William Tishler and Arnold R. Alanen were, by 1980, pioneering an innovative master's degree in landscape history and cultural resource preservation, with an emphasis on vernacular landscapes and buildings, in the Department of Landscape Architecture at the University of Wisconsin-Madison.

54. Henry Nash Smith, *Virgin Land: The American West as Symbol and Myth* (Cambridge, MA: Harvard University Press, 1950); and Leo Marx, *The Machine in the Garden: Technology and the Pastoral Ideal in America* (New York: Oxford University Press, 1964).

55. John A. Kouwenhoven, *Made in America: The Arts in Modern Civilization* (Garden City, NY: Doubleday, 1948), *The Beer Can by the Highway: Essays on What's "American" about America* (Garden City, NY: Doubleday, 1961 reprinted with an introduction by Ralph Ellison, Baltimore, MD: The Johns Hopkins University Press, 1998), and *Half a Truth is Better than None: Some Unsystematic Conjectures about Art, Disorder, and American Experience* (Chicago, IL: University of Chicago Press, 1982).

56. "Beware of any book on the landscape which has more than 10 pages of bibliography," Jackson cautioned, for "it means the research has been done in a library, and not outside!" Reiterating one of his fundamental tenets, Jackson insisted, "The most valuable books on the subject are those which tell of firsthand, intelligent experience" (Letter, Jackson to the author, June 16, 1989).

57. John R. Stilgoe, *Common Landscape of America, 1580 to 1845* (New Haven, CT: Yale University Press, 1982); *Metropolitan Corridor: Railroads and the American Scene* (New Haven, CT: Yale University Press, 1983); and *Alongshore* (New Haven, CT: Yale University Press, 1994).

58. John Sears, *Sacred Places: American Tourist Attractions in the Nineteenth Century* (New York: Oxford University Press, 1986).

59. David Nye, *Electrifying America: Social Meanings of a New Technology, 1880–1940* (Cambridge, MA: The MIT Press, 1992), and *The American Technological Sublime* (Cambridge, MA: The MIT Press, 1996).

60. Richard Longstreth, *City Center to Regional Mall: Architecture, the Automobile, and Retailing in Los Angeles, 1920–1950* (Cambridge, MA: The MIT Press, 1997); *The Drive-In, The Supermarket, and the Transformation of Commercial Space in Los Angeles, 1914–1941* (Cambridge, MA: The MIT Press, 1999); *The American Department Store Transformed, 1920–1960* (New Haven, CT: Yale University Press, in association with the Center for American Places at Columbia College Chicago, 2010); and "The Neighborhood Shopping Center in Washington, D.C., 1930–1941," *Journal of the Society of Architectural Historians*, Vol. 51, No. 1 (March 1992): 5–34.

61. Peter Bacon Hales, *Silver Cities: Photographing American Urbanization, 1839-1915* (Philadelphia, PA: Temple University Press, 1984); *William Henry Jackson and the Transformation of the American Landscape* (Philadelphia, PA: Temple University Press, 1988); *Atomic Spaces: Living on the Manhattan Project* (Champaign: University of Illinois Press, 1997); and *Outside the Gates of Eden: The Dream of America from Hiroshima to Now* (Chicago: University of Chicago Press, 2014).

62. Kent Ryden, *Mapping the Invisible Landscape: Folklore, Writing and the Sense of Place* (Iowa City: University of Iowa Press, 1993); Alicia Barber, *Reno's Big Gamble: Image and Reputation in the Biggest Little City* (Lawrence: University Press of Kansas, 2008); and Angus Kress Gillespie and Michael Aaron Rockland, *Looking for America on the New Jersey Turnpike* (New Brunswick, NJ: Rutgers University Press, 1989).

63. Christopher Hussey, *The Picturesque: Studies in a Point of View* (New York: George Putnam's Sons, 1927); Oliver Larkin, *Art and Life in America* (New York: Rinehart, 1949; revised edition, New York: Holt Hinehart and Winston, 1960); Wayne Andrews, *Architecture, Ambition and Americans* (New York: Harper, 1955); John Burchard and Albert Bush-Brown, *The Architecture of America: A Social and Cultural History* (Boston, MA: Little, Brown and Company, 1961); and Sigfried Giedion, *Space, Time and Architecture; The Growth of a New Tradition*

(Cambridge, MA: Harvard University Press, 1949), and *Mechanization Takes Command: A Contribution to Anonymous History* (New York: Oxford University Press, 1948).

64. James Flexner, *That Wilder Image: The Painting of America's Native School from Thomas Cole to Winslow Homer* (Boston, MA: Little, Brown and Company, 1962); and Barbara Novak, *Nature and Culture: American Landscape and Painting* (New York: Oxford University Press, 1980).

65. John Barrell, *The Dark Side of Landscape: The Rural Poor in English Painting, 1730–1840* (Cambridge, UK: Cambridge University Press, 1980); Ann Bermingham, *Landscape and Ideology: The English Rustic Tradition* (Berkeley: University of California Press, 1986); Angela Miller, *The Empire of the Eye: Landscape Representation and American Cultural Politics, 1825–1875* (Ithaca, NY: Cornell University Press, 1993); Albert Boime, *The Magisterial Gaze: Manifest Destiny and American Landscape Painting, ca. 1830–1865* (Washington, DC: Smithsonian Institution Press, 1991); David Miller, ed., *American Iconology: New Approaches to Nineteenth-Century Art and Literature* (New Haven, CT: Yale University Press, 1993); Jules David Prown, Nancy K. Anderson, William Cronon, Brian W. Dippie, Martha A. Sandweiss, Susan P. Schoelwer, and Howard R. Lamar, *Discovered Lands, Invented Pasts: Transforming Visions of the American West* (New Haven, CT: Yale University Press, 1992); W. J. T. Mitchell, ed., *Landscape and Power* (Chicago, IL: University of Chicago Press, 1994); and William H. Truettner and Alan Wallach, eds., *Thomas Cole: Landscape into History* (New Haven, CT: Yale University Press, 1994).

66. Lewis, "Axioms for Reading the Landscape," in Meinig, ed., *The Interpretation of Ordinary Landscapes,* 12.

67. David Schuyler, *The New Urban Landscape: The Redefinition of City Form in Nineteenth-Century America* (Baltimore, MD: The Johns Hopkins University Press, 1986); Phoebe Cutler, *The Public Landscape of the New Deal* (New Haven, CT: Yale University Press, 1985); Cynthia Zaitsevsky, *Frederick Law Olmsted and the Boston Park System* (Cambridge, MA: Harvard University Press, 1982); and Roy Rosenzweig and Elizabeth Blackmar, *The Park and the People: A History of Central Park* (Ithaca, NY: Cornell University Press, 1992).

68. *The Papers of Frederick Law Olmsted*, Charles E. Beveridge and various editors, 12 vols. (Baltimore, MD: The Johns Hopkins University Press, since 1977); Charles E. Beveridge and Paul Rocheleau, *Frederick Law Olmsted: Designing the American Landscape* (New York: Rizzoli, 1995); Lee Hall, *Olmsted's America: An "Unpractical Man" and His Vision of Civilization* (Boston, MA: Little, Brown and Company, 1995); Witold Rybczyinski, *A Clearing in the Distance: Frederick Law Olmsted and America in the Nineteenth Century* (New York: Scribner, 1999); and Frederick Law Olmsted, *Walks and Talks of an American Farmer in*

England, introduction by Charles C. McLaughlin (Amherst, MA: Library of American Landscape History, 2002).

69. John Dixon Hunt and Joachim Wolschke-Bulmahn, eds., *The Vernacular Garden* (Washington, DC: Dumbarton Oaks, 1993).

70. Judith B. Tankard, *The Gardens of Ellen Biddle Shipman* (Sagaponack, NY: Sagapress, in association with the Library of American Landscape History, 1996); Catherine Howett, *A World of Her Own Making: Katharine Smith Reynolds and the Landscape of Reynolds* (Amherst: University of Massachusetts Press, in association with the Library of American Landscape History, 2007); Cynthia Zaitzevsky, *Long Island Landscapes and the Women Who Designed Them* (New York: Society for the Preservation of Long Island Antiquities in association with W. W. Norton, 2009); Marc Treib, ed., *Modern Landscape Architecture: A Critical Review* (Cambridge, MA: The MIT Press, 1993); Marc Treib and Dorothée Imbert, *Garrett Eckbo: Modern Landscapes for Living* (Berkeley: University of California Press, 1997); Jane Brown, *The Modern Garden* (New York: Princeton Architectural Press, 2000); and Charles Birnbaum, ed., *Preserving Modern Landscape Architecture II: Making Postwar Landscapes Visible* (Washington, DC: Spacemaker Press, 2004).

71. Overviews of the environmental history movement include Roderick Nash, "American Environmental History: A New Teaching Frontier," *Pacific Historical Review*, Vol. 41, No. 3 (August 1972): 362–72; Richard White, "American Environmental History: The Development of a New Historical Field," *Pacific Historical Review*, Vol. 54, No. 3 (August 1985): 297–335, and "Environmental History: Watching a Historical Field Mature," in *Pacific Historical Review*, Vol. 70, No.1 (February 2001): 103–11; and William Cronon, "The Uses of Environmental History," *Environmental History Review*, Vol. 17, No. 3 (Fall 1993): 1–22.

72. Nash, "American Environmental History: A New Teaching Frontier," 363.

73. Classic examples of this formative period of environmental history include Roderick Nash, *Wilderness and the America Mind* (New Haven, CT: Yale University Press, 1967); Alfred Runte, *National Parks: The American Experience* (Lincoln: University of Nebraska Press, 1979); Robert Righter, *Crucible for Conservation: The Creation of Grand Teton National Park* (Boulder: Colorado Associated University Press, 1982); and biographies such as Susan Flader, *Thinking Like a Mountain: Aldo Leopold and the Evolution of an Ecological Attitude Toward Deer, Wolves, and Forests* (Columbia: University of Missouri Press, 1979); Stephen Fox, *John Muir and His Legacy: The American Conservation Movement* (Boston, MA: Little, Brown and Company, 1981); and Michael Cohen, *The Pathless Way: John Muir and the American Wilderness* (Madison: University of Wisconsin Press, 1984).

74. William Cronon, *Changes in the Land: Indians, Colonists and the Ecology of New England* (New York: Hill and Wang, 1983); and Donald Worster, *Dust Bowl: The Southern Plains in the 1930s* (New York: Oxford University Press, 1979), and *Rivers of Empire: Water, Aridity, and the Growth of the American West* (New York: Pantheon, 1985).

75. Richard White, *Land Use, Environment, and Social Change: The Shaping of Island County, Washington* (Seattle: University of Washington Press, 1980).

76. Stephen Pyne, *Fire in America: A Cultural History of Wildland and Rural Fire* (Princeton, NJ: Princeton University Press, 1982).

77. William Cronon, ed., *Uncommon Ground: Rethinking the Human Place in Nature* (New York: W. W. Norton, 1996).

78. Examples of this more broad-based approach include Alexander Wilson, *The Culture of Nature: North American Landscapes from Disney World to the Exxon Valdez* (Oxford, UK: Blackwell Publishers, 1992); Susan Davis, *Spectacular Nature: Corporate Culture and the Sea-World Experience* (Berkeley: University of California Press, 1997); Ann Vileisis, *Discovering the Unknown Landscape: A History of America's Wetlands.* (Washington, DC: Island Press, 1997); Conevery Bolton Valencius, *The Health of the Country: How American Settlers Understood Themselves and their Land* (New York: Basic Books, 2002); and Brian Donahue, *The Great Meadow: Farmers and the Land in Colonial Concord* (New Haven, CT: Yale University Press, 2004).

79. Mark Spence, *Dispossessing the Wilderness: Indian Removal and the Making of the National Parks* (New York: Oxford University Press, 1999), and Karl Jacoby, *Crimes Against Nature: Poachers, Thieves, and the Hidden History of American Conservation* (Berkeley: University of California Press, 2001).

80. William Deverell and Greg Hise, eds., *Land of Sunshine: The Environmental History of Los Angeles* (Pittsburgh, PA: University of Pittsburgh Press, 2005); Char Miller, ed., *On the Border: The Environmental History of San Antonio* (Pittsburgh, PA: University of Pittsburgh Press, 2001); and Joel Tarr, ed., *Devastation and Renewal: An Environmental History of Pittsburgh* (Pittsburgh, PA: University of Pittsburgh Press, 2003).

81. Matthew Klingle, *Emerald City: An Environmental History of Seattle* (New Haven, CT: Yale University Press, 2007).

82. Jackson, "To Pity the Plumage and Forget the Dying Bird," *Landscape*, Vol. 17, No. 2 (Autumn 1967): 1–4; reproduced in Horowitz, *Landscape in Sight*, 355-65.

83. Upton and Vlach, *Common Places*; and Allen Noble, ed., *To Build in a New Land: Ethnic*

Landscapes in North America (Baltimore, MD: The Johns Hopkins University Press, in association with the Center for American Places, 1992). Both anthologies contain one chapter on African-American landscapes; *To Build in a New Land* also includes essays on American-Indian and Spanish-American landscapes.

84. Arnold R. Alanen, "Back to the Land: Immigrants and Image-Makers in the Lake Superior Region, 1865–1930," in Thompson, ed., *Landscape in America*, 110–40; and Joseph Sciorra, "Yard Shrines and Sidewalk Alters of New York's Italian-Americans," in Carter and Herman, eds., *Perspectives in Vernacular Architecture III*, 185–98.

85. Chris Wilson, *The Myth of Santa Fe: Creating a Modern Regional Tradition* (Albuquerque: University of New Mexico Press, 1997); and Steven Hoelscher, *Heritage on Stage: The Invention of Ethnic Place in America's Little Switzerland* (Madison: University of Wisconsin Press, 1998).

86. Gail Lee Dubrow, "Asian Imprints on the American Landscape," in Arnold R. Alanen and Robert Melnick, eds., *Preserving Cultural Landscapes in America* (Baltimore, MD: The Johns Hopkins University Press, in association with the Center for American Places, 2000), 143–68; Hillary Jenks, "The Politics of Preservation: Power, Memory, and Identity in Los Angeles's Little Tokyo," in Richard Longstreth, ed., *Cultural Landscape: Balancing Nature and Heritage in Preservation Practice* (Minneapolis: University of Minnesota Press, 2008), 35–54; and David Chuenyan Lai, "The Visual Character of Chinatown," in Groth and Bressi, *Understanding Ordinary Landscapes*, 81–83.

87. Louis Aponte-Paris, "Appropriating Place in Puerto Rican Barrios: Preserving Contemporary Urban Landscapes," in Alanen and Melnick, eds., *Preserving Cultural Landscapes in America*, 94–111; James Rojas, "The Enacted Environment: Examining the Streets and Yards of East Los Angeles," in Wilson and Groth, *Everyday America*, 275–292; and Eric Avila, "East Side Stories: Freeways and their Portraits in Chicano Los Angeles," *Landscape Journal*, Vol. 26, No. 1 (January 2007): 83–97.

88. Rina Swentzell, "Conflicting Landscape Values: The Santa Clara Pueblo and Day School," in *Understanding Ordinary Landscapes*, 56–66.

89. John Michael Vlach, "The Shotgun House: An African Architectural Legacy," in *Pioneer America: The Journal of Historic American Material Culture*, Vol. 8, No. 1 (January–July 1976): 47–70; reprinted in *Common Places*, 58–78; and Dell Upton, "White and Black Landscapes in Eighteenth Century Virginia," *Places*, Vol. 2, No. 2 (Fall 1984): 59–72.

90. Vlach, *Back of the Big House: The Architecture of Plantation Slavery* (Chapel Hill: University of North Carolina Press, 1993).

91. Richard Westmacott, "The Gardens of African-Americans in the Rural South," in John Dixon Hunt and Joachim Wolschke-Bulmahn, eds., *The Vernacular Garden*, and *African-American Gardens and Yards in the Rural South* (Knoxville: University of Tennessee Press, 1992).

92. Grey Gundaker and Judith McWillie, *No Space Hidden: The Spirit of African American Yard Work* (Knoxville: University of Tennessee Press, 2005).

93. Grey Gundaker, *Keep Your Head to the Sky: Interpreting African-American Home Ground* (Charlottesville: University of Virginia Press, 1998); Paul Shackel, *Memory in Black and White: Race, Commemoration, and the Post-Bellum Landscape* (Walnut Creek, CA: Altamira Press, 2003); and Richard Schein, *Landscape and Race in the United States* (New York: Routledge: 2006).

94. "Race, Space, and the Destabilization of Practice," *Landscape Journal*, Vol. 26, No. 1 (January 2007): *passim*.

95. Angela Mack and Stephen Hoffius, eds., *Landscape of Slavery: The Plantation in American Art* (Columbia: University of South Carolina Press, 2008); and Vlach, *The Planter's Prospect: Privilege and Slavery in Plantation Paintings* (Chapel Hill: University of North Carolina Press, 2001).

96. Clifton Ellis and Rebecca Ginsburg, eds., *Cabin, Quarter, Plantation: Architecture and Landscapes of North American Slavery* (New Haven: Yale University Press, 2010); and Louis P. Nelson, "The Architectures of Black Identity: Buildings, Slavery, and Freedom in the American South," in *Winterthur Portfolio*, Vol. 45, No. 2/3 (Special Issue: "Objects in Motion: Visual and Material Culture across Colonial North America," Summer/Autumn 2011): 117–94.

97. Michael Crutcher, *Treme: Race and Place in a New Orleans Neighborhood* (Athens: University of Georgia Press, 2010).

98. Lance Freeman, *There Goes the Hood: Views of Gentrification from the Ground Up* (Philadelphia, PA: Temple University Press, 2006).

99. Dolores Hayden, *Grand Domestic Revolution: A History of Feminist Designs for American Homes, Neighborhoods, and Cities* (Cambridge, MA: The MIT Press, 1981); Cheryl Robertson, "Male and Female Agendas for Domestic Reform: the Middle-Class Bungalow in Gendered Perspective," in *Winterthur Portfolio*, Vol. 26, No. 2/3 (Summer–Autumn 1991): 123–41; Daphne Spain, *How Women Saved the City* (Minneapolis: University of Minnesota Press, 2001); and Jessica Sewell, *Women and the Everyday City: Public Live and Public Space in San Francisco, 1890–1915* (Minneapolis: University of Minnesota Press, 2011).

100. Sally McMurry, "Women in the American Vernacular Landscape" *Material Culture*, Vol. 20, No. 1 (Spring 1989): 1–41; Angel Kwolek-Folland, "Gender as a Category of Analysis in Ver-

nacular Architecture Studies," in *Perspectives in Vernacular Architecture,* Vol. 5 (1995): 3–10.

101. Deborah Rotman and Ellen-Rose Savulis, *Shared Spaces and Divided Places: Material Dimensions of Gender Relations and the American Historical Landscape* (Knoxville: University of Tennessee Press, 2003); and Diane Harris, "Cultivating Power: The Language of Feminism in Women's Garden Literature, 1870–1920," *Landscape Journal*, Vol. 13, No. 2 (Fall 1994): 113–23.

102. Virginia Scharff, ed., *Seeing Nature through Gender* (Lawrence: University Press of Kansas, 2003).

103. Rebecca Solnit, *What Eve Said to the Serpent: On Landscape, Gender, and Art* (Athens: University of Georgia Press, 2003).

104. David Bell and Gill Valentine, eds., *Mapping Desire: The Geographies of Sexuality* (London, UK: Routledge, 1995); Joel Sanders, ed., *Stud: The Architectures of Masculinity* (New York: Princeton Architectural Press, 1996); and Gordon Brent Ingram, Anne-Marie Bouthillette, and Yolande Retter, eds., *Queers in Space: Communities/Public/Places/Sites of Resistance* (Seattle, WA: Bay Press, 1997). Don Mitchell provides useful summaries of feminist and gay, lesbian, and transgendered spatial politics in *Cultural Geography: A Critical Introduction*, 171–98.

105. Amin Ghaziani, *There Goes the Gayborhood?* (Princeton, NJ: Princeton University Press, 2014), and Petra L. Doan and Harrison Higgins, "The Demise of Queer Space? Resurgent Gentrification and the Assimilation of LGBT Neighborhoods," *The Journal of Planning Education and Research*," Vol. 30, No. 1 (March 2011): 6–25.

106. Gail Dubrow and Jennifer Goodman, eds., *Restoring Women's History through Historic Preservation* (Baltimore, MD: The Johns Hopkins University Press, in association with the Center for American Places, 2003).

107. Polly Welts Kauffman and Catherine T. Corbett, *Her Past Around Us: Interpreting Sites for Women's History* (Malabar, FL: Kriegar Publishing Company, 2003).

108. See, for example, Jackson, "Sterile Restorations Cannot Replace a Sense of the Stream of Time," Letter to the Editor, *Landscape Magazine*, Vol. 66 (May 1976): 194; reprinted in Horowitz, ed., *Landscape in Sight*, 366–68.

109. Kevin Lynch, *What Time is This Place* (Cambridge, MA: The MIT Press, 1972); David Lowenthal, "Age and Artifact: Dilemmas of Appreciation," in Meinig, ed., *The Interpretation of Ordinary Landscapes*, 103–28; and Lowenthal, *The Past is a Foreign Country* (Cambridge, UK: Cambridge University Press, 1985). Lowenthal pursued these issues in subsequent publications.

110. Max Page and Randall Mason, *Giving Preservation a History: Histories of Preservation*

in the United States (New York: Routledge, 2004).

111. "Focus on Landscape Architecture," in *Preservation Forum: The Journal of the National Trust for Historic Preservation*, Vol. 7, No. 3 (May/June 1993): *passim*; "Introduction" and David Schuyler and Patricia O'Donnell, "The History and Preservation of Urban Parks and Cemeteries," in Alanen and Melnick, eds., *Preserving Cultural Landscapes in America*, 1–21 and 70–93.

112. Robert Melnick, Daniel Spoon, and Emma Jane Saxe, *Cultural Landscapes: Rural Historic Districts in the National Park System* (Washington, DC: U.S. Department of the Interior, National Park Service, Historic Architecture Division, 1984); J. Timothy Keller and Genevieve P. Keller, *National Register Bulletin 18: How to Evaluate Designed Historic Landscapes* (Washington, DC: U.S. Department of the Interior, National Park Service, Interagency Resources Division, 1989); and Linda Flint McLelland, J. Timothy Keller, Genevieve P. Keller, and Robert Melnik, *National Register Bulletin 30: How to Identify, Evaluate, and Register Rural Historic Landscapes* (Washington, DC: U.S. Department of the Interior, National Park Service, Interagency Resources Division, 1990).

113. Charles Birnbaum, ed., with Christine Capella Peters, *The Secretary of the Interior's Standards for the Treatment of Historic Properties with Guidelines for the Treatment of Cultural Landscapes* (Washington, DC: U.S. Department of the Interior, National Park Service, Heritage Preservation Services. Historic Landscape Initiative, 1996); and Robert Page, Cathy Gilbert, and Susan Dolan, *A Guide to Cultural Landscape Reports: Contents, Processes, Techniques* (Washington, DC: U.S. Department of the Interior, National Park Service, Park Historic Structures and Cultural Landscape Program, 1998).

114. David L. Ames and Linda Flint McLelland, *National Register Bulletin: Historic Residential Suburbs: Guidelines for Evaluation and Nomination for the National Register of Historic Places* (Washington, DC: U.S. Department of the Interior, National Park Service, 2002).

115. Publications relating to the historic road preservation movement include Paul Daniel Marriott, *Saving Historic Roads: Design and Policy Guidelines* (Washington, DC: Preservation Press, John Wiley, 1997) and *From Milestones to Mile-Markers: Understanding Historic Roads* (Washington, DC: National Trust for Historic Preservation, 2004); Timothy Davis, Todd A. Croteau, and Christopher Marston, eds., *America's National Park Roads and Parkways: Drawings from the Historic American Engineering Record* (Baltimore, MD: The Johns Hopkins University Press, in association with the Center for American Places, 2004); and Timothy Davis, *Landscape Line 16: Historic Park Roads* (Washington, DC: U.S. Department of the Interior, National Park Service, Park Historic Structures and Cultural Landscape Program, 2004).

116. Alanen and Melnick, eds., *Preserving Cultural Landscapes in America*; and Richard Long-streth, ed., *Cultural Landscapes: Balancing Nature and Heritage in Preservation Practice* (Minneapolis: University of Minnesota Press, 2008).

117. For more on the ways in which cultural landscape photography evolved in step with contemporary cultural concerns, see Peter Bacon Hales, *Silver Cities: The Photography of American Urbanization, 1839–1915* (Philadelphia, PA: Temple University Press, 1984) and *William H. Jackson and the Transformation of the American Landscape* (Philadelphia, PA: Temple University Press, 1984); and Timothy Davis, "Photography and Landscape Studies," *Landscape Journal*, Vol. 8, No. 1 (Spring 1989): 1–12, and "Beyond the Sacred and the Profane: Cultural Landscape Photography in America, 1930–1990," in Wayne Franklin and Michael Steiner, eds., *Mapping American Culture* (Ames: Iowa University Press, 1992), 191–230.

118. Jacob Riis, *How the Other Half Lives: Studies Among the Tenements of New York* (New York: Charles Scribner's Sons, 1890; reprint edition, New York: Dover, 1971).

119. Walker Evans, *American Photographs* (New York: Museum of Modern Art, 1939); Evans, *Walker Evans*, introduction by John Szarkowski (New York: Museum of Modern Art, 1971); and Wright Morris, *The Inhabitants* (New York: Charles Scribner's Sons, 1946; 2nd edition, New York: De Capo Press, 1971).

120. Robert Frank, *The Americans*, introduction by Jack Kerouac (New York: Grove Press, 1959; 3rd revised edition, New York: SCALO Publishers, in association with the National Gallery of Art, Washington, 1998).

121. Garry Winogrand, *Figments from the Real World* (New York: Museum of Modern Art, 1988), provides a biographical summary and representative examples of his work; Lee Friedlander, *The American Monument* (New York: Eakins, 1976) and *Like a One-Eyed Cat: Photographs by Lee Friedlander* (New York: Harry N. Abrams, 1989).

122. Robert Adams, Lewis Baltz, and eight other similarly inclined photographers (Bernd and Hilla Becker, Joe Deal, Frank Gohlke, Nicholas Nixon, John Schott, Stephen Shore, and Henry Wessel, Jr.) were grouped together as "The New Topographics" movement; see *The New Topographics: Photographs of the Man-Altered Landscape* (Rochester, NY: International Museum of Photography, 1975); Greg Foster-Rice and John Rohrback, eds., *Reframing the New Topographics* (Chicago, IL: Center for American Places at Columbia College Chicago, 2010); Lewis Baltz, *The New Industrial Parks Near Irvine, California* (New York; Light Impressions, 1974) and *Park City* (Millerton, NY: Aperture, 1980); Robert Adams, *To Make It Home: Photographs of the American West* (Millerton, NY: Aperture, 1989), which affords an excellent digest of his many publications; and John Rohrbach, with additional essays by Frank Gohlke and Rebecca

Solnit, *Accommodating Nature: The Photographs of Frank Gohlke* (Santa Fe, NM, and Staunton, VA: The Center for American Places, in association with the Amon Carter Museum, 2007). Testaments to the influence of Jackson on contemporary photographers are summarized by Frank Gohlke and Miguel Gandert in Janet Mendelsohn's DVD, *J. B. Jackson and the American Landscape* (2015), which complements this book.

123. Bill Owens, *Suburbia* (San Francisco, CA: Straight Arrow Press, 1973); and Bill Owens, *Suburbia*, introduction by David Halberstam (New York: Fotofolio, 1999).

124. David Plowden, *The Hand of Man on America* (Washington, DC: Smithsonian Institution Press, 1971) and *Commonplace* (New York: Sunrise Books, 1974). Plowden's photographs have been reproduced in several retrospective volumes, including *An American Chronology: The Photographs of David Plowden*, introductory text by David McCullough (New York: Viking Press, 1982); *Imprints: David Plowden, A Retrospective*, preface and text by David Plowden, introduction by Alan Trachtenberg (Boston, MA: Little, Brown and Company, 1997); and *David Plowden: Vanishing Point: Fifty Years of Photography*, forward by Richard Snow, introduction by Steve Edwards (New York: W. W. Norton, 2007).

125. Stephen Shore, *Uncommon Places* (Millerton, NY: Aperture, 1982) and *Uncommon Places: The Complete Works*, essay by Stephan Schmidt-Wulffen and conversation with Lynne Tillman (New York: Aperture, 2004); and Joel Sternfeld, *American Prospects* (New York: Random House, 1987).

126. William Eggleston, *William Eggleston's Guide* (New York: Museum of Modern Art, 1976), *The Democratic Forest* (New York: Doubleday, 1989), and *Los Alamos* (Zurich, Switzerland: Scalo, 2003).

127. Camilo Jose Vergara, *The New American Ghetto* (New Brunswick, NJ: Rutgers University Press, 1995).

128. Joel Sternfeld, *On This Site: Landscape in Memorium* (San Francisco, CA: Chronicle Books, 1996).

129. Alex Maclean, *Designs on the Land: Exploring America From the Air* (London, UK: Thames and Hudson, 2003) and *Over: The American Landscape at the Tipping Point* (New York: Harry N. Abrams, 2008); and Jim Wark, *Flying High in America* (Vericelli, Italy: White Star, 2004).

130. John Brinckerhoff Jackson, *The Essential Landscape: The New Mexico Photographic Survey*, edited by Steven A. Yates (Albuquerque: University of New Mexico Press, 1985).

131. Laurie Brown, *Las Vegas Periphery: Views from the Edge* (Staunton, VA: George F. Thompson Publishing, 2013).

132. Andrew Borowiec, *The New Heartland: Looking for the American Dream* (Staunton, VA: George F. Thompson Publishing, 2016).

133. Edward Burtynsky and Lori Pauli, *Manufactured Landscapes: The Photographs of Edward Burtynsky,* with essays by Mark Haworth-Booth and Kenneth Baker and an interview by Michael Torosian (Ottawa, Canada: National Gallery of Canada, in association with Yale University Press, 2003); Edward Burtynsky and Michael Mitchell, *Oil* (Gottingen, Germany: Steidl, 2009); and Edward Burtynsky and Russell Lord, *Water* (Gottingen, Germany: Steidl, 2013).

134. Robert Misrach, *Destroy This Memory* (New York: Aperture, 2010); and Robert Polidori, *After the Flood* (Gottingen, Germany: Steidl, 2006). See, also, John Woodin, with a conclusion by Craig E. Colten, *City of Memory: New Orleans before and after Katrina* (Chicago, IL: Center for American Places at Columbia College Chicago, 2009), and Jane Fulton Alt, with an introduction by Michael A. Weinstein, *Look and Leave: Photographs and Stories from New Orleans's Lower Ninth Ward* (Chicago, IL: Center for American Places at Columbia College Chicago, 2009).

135. Andrew Moore, photographs, with an essay by Philip Levine, *Detroit Disassembled* (Bologna, Italy: Damiani, in association with the Akron Art Museum, 2010); Yves Marchand and Romaine Meffre, *The Ruins of Detroit* (Gottingen, Germany: Steidl: 2010); Dan Haga, *Urban Atrophy: Mid-Atlantic* (Atglen, PA: Schiffer Publishing, 2011); Daniel Barter and Daniel Marbaix, eds., *States of Decay* (Darlington, UK: Carpet Bombing Culture, 2013); Eric Holubow, *Abandoned: America's Vanishing Landscape* (Atglen, PA: Schiffer Publishing, 2014); and Matthew Christopher, *Abandoned America: The Age of Consequences* (Versailles, France: Jonglez Publishing, 2014).

136. First published in 1835, Alexis de Tocqueville's *Democracy in America* has gone through dozens of editions and reprints; see Alexis de Tocqueville, *Democracy in America*, introduction by Alan Ryan (New York: Alfred A. Knopf, 1994), Crevecouer's 1782 *Letters from an American Farmer* has also been republished repeatedly; see J. Hector St. John de Crèvecoeur, *Letters from an American Farmer,* edited with an introduction and notes by Susan Manning (New York: Oxford University Press, 1997).

137. For a compilation of these accounts, see Frederick Law Olmsted, *The Cotton Kingdom: A Traveller's Observations on Cotton and Slavery in the American Slave States: Based upon Three Former Volumes of Journeys and Investigations by the Same Author*, Arthur M. Schlesinger, Sr., ed. (New York: Modern Library, 1984).

138. Shortly after Mumford's death, Jackson lamented to the author that few academics respected Mumford's contributions and fewer still aspired to emulate his wide-ranging and accessible approach to history and criticism. In a letter complaining about the tendency of contemporary

academics to overburden their writings with historical minutia, Jackson observed, "I find Lewis Mumford, not a dedicated scholar or researcher, wrote the best, most readable stuff we have on the evolving landscape; scholars ignore him, but public opinion has been influenced by his graceful, literate style, his enthusiasm, and brevity" (Letter, Jackson to the author, November 9, 1991).

139. [James Agee], "The Great American Roadside," *Fortune*, Vol. 10, No. 3 (April 1934): 53–63 and 172–77; Mr. Harper, "American Landscape I," *Harper's Magazine*, Vol. 200, No. 1196 (January 1950): 100–01; and Mr. Harper, "American Landscape II," *Harper's Magazine*, Vol. 200, No. 1197 (February 1950): 101–02. (While the identity of "Mr. Harper" is unclear, the essays were probably written by either John A. Kouwenhoven or Bernard DeVoto.)

140. John Keats, *The Crack in the Picture Window* (Boston, MA: Houghton Mifflin, 1956); and Betty Friedan, *The Feminist Mystique* (New York, W. W. Norton, 1963).

141. Jackson, review of Eric Sloane, *Return to Taos* (New York: Wilfred Funk, 1960), in *Landscape*, Vol. 10, No. 2 (Winter 1960/1961): 15. Sloane's other books included *American Barns and Covered Bridges* (New York: W. Funk, 1954), *Our Vanishing Landscape* (New York: W. Funk, 1955), and *American Yesterday* (New York: W. Funk, 1956). Sloane's enduring popularity is evidenced by the fact that his work has appeared in more than seventy volumes, including additional studies, compilations, and reprint editions, published from 1941 to 2008.

142. George Stewart, *U.S. 40: Cross Section of the United States of America* (Boston, MA: Houghton Mifflin, 1953); Jackson, review of E. A. Gutkind, *Our World from the Air* (New York: Doubleday, 1952), and of George Stewart, "*U.S. 40*," *Landscape*, Vol. 3, No. 1 (Summer 1953): 28–29, quoted 29.

143. Joel Garreau, *Edge City: Life on the New Frontier* (New York: Doubleday, 1991); John Herbers, *The New Heartland: America's Flight Beyond the Suburbs and How It Is Changing Our Future* (New York: New York Times Books, 1986); and Richard Louv, *America II: The Book that Captures Americans in the Act of Creating the Future* (New York: Penguin, 1985). Jackson praised Louv's and Herbers's books in letters to the author (January 6, 1988 and February 22, 1989).

144. The historian Bernard DeVoto critiqued many aspects of the evolving American landscape in his long-running *Harper's* column, "The Easy Chair." See, for example, Edward K. Muller, ed., *DeVoto's West: History, Conservation, and the Public Good* (Athens, OH: Swallow Press/ Ohio University Press, in association with the Center for American Places, 2005). Peter Blake's popular polemic, *God's Own Junkyard* (New York: Holt, Rhinehard, and Winston, 1964), epitomized the elitist and Eurocentric critique of the contemporary American landscape that Jackson labored long and hard to contest. Jane Holtz Kay, *Asphalt Nation: How the Automobile Took Over America and How We Can Take it Back* (New York: Crown Publishers, 1997); and James

Howard Kunstler, *The Geography of Nowhere: The Rise and Decline of America's Man-Made Landscape* (New York: Simon and Schuster, 1993).

145. Mike Davis, *City of Quartz: Excavating the Future in Los Angeles* (New York: Vintage: 1992), and *Ecology of Fear: Los Angeles and the Imagination of Disaster* (New York: Metropolitan Books, 1998).

146. David Brooks, *Bobos in Paradise: The New Upper Class and How They Got There* (New York: Simon and Schuster, 2000) and *On Paradise Drive: How We Live Now (and Always Have) in the Future Tense* (New York: Simon and Schuster, 2004).

147. Robert Lang and Jennifer LeFurgy, *Boomburgs: The Rise of America's Accidental Cities* (Washington, DC: The Brookings Institution, 2007); Joel Kotkin, *The New Geography: How the Digital Revolution is Reshaping the American Landscape* (New York: Random House, 2000); and Alan Ehrenhalt, *The Great Inversion and the Future of the American City* (New York: Alfred A. Knopf, 2012).

148. Dolores Hayden, with aerial photographs by Jim Wark, *A Field Guide to Sprawl* (New York: W. W. Norton, 2004), and *Building Suburbia: Greenfields and Urban Growth, 1820–2000* (New York: Pantheon, 2003); Robert Bruegmann offered a competing narrative in *Sprawl: A Compact History* (Chicago, IL: University of Chicago Press, 2005); Hal Rothman, *Neon Metropolis: How Los Vegas Started the Twenty-First Century* (New York: Routledge, 2002); Sharon Zukin, *Naked City: The Death and Life of Authentic Urban Places* (New York: Oxford University Press, 2010); and John R. Stilgoe, *Outside Lies Magic: Regaining History and Awareness in Everyday Places* (New York: Walker and Co., 1998).

149. Elizabeth Barlow Rogers expressed this sentiment in numerous conversations with the author. The journal *Siteline* is associated with her nonprofit organization, Foundation for Landscape Studies, which, since 2007, has awarded an annual John Brinckerhoff Jackson Book Prize (Fig. 7.2).

150. This phenomenon came to the fore during the early 1980s and grew exponentially as aging baby boomers, foreign tourists, and younger Americans embraced the quintessential roadside landscape as the architectural embodiment of a lost Golden Age of automobile-oriented twentieth-century American culture. Examples include John Balder, *Diners* (New York: Harry N. Abrams, 1980) and *Gas, Food, and Lodging: A Postcard Odyssey through the Great American Roadside* (New York: Abbeville Press, 1982); John Margolies, *The End of the Road: Vanishing Highway Architecture in America* (New York: Penguin, 1981), *Pump and Circumstance: Glory Days of the American Gas Station* (Boston, MA: Little, Brown and Company, 1993), and *Home Way From Home: Motels in America* (Boston, MA: Little, Brown and Company, 1995); Michael

Wallis, *Route 66: The Mother Road* (New York: St. Martins, 1990); Tom Snyder, *The Route 66 Traveler's Guide and Roadside Companion* (New York: St. Martins, 1990); Arthur Krim, with Denis Wood, ed., *Route 66: Iconography of the American Highway* (Santa Fe, NM: Center for American Places, 2005; updated commemorative edition, Staunton, VA: George F. Thompson Publishing, 2014), which won the John Brinckerhoff Jackson Prize of the Association of American Geographers; Michael Witzel, *The American Drive-In* (Osceola, WI: Motorbooks International, 1994) and *Route 66 Remembered* (Osceola, WI: Motorbooks International, 1996); Tim Hollis, *Florida's Miracle Strip: From Redneck Riviera to Emerald Coast* (Jackson: University Press of Mississippi, 2004); Peter Genovese, *Roadside Florida: The Definitive Guide to the Kingdom of Kitsch* (Mechanicsburg, PA: Stackpole Books, 2006); and Brian Butko and Sarah Butko, *Roadside Attractions: Cool Cafes, Souvenir Stands, Route 66 Relics, and Other Road Trip Fun* (Mechanicsburg, PA: Stackpole Press, 2007).

151. Crumb's "A Short History of America" was originally published in 1979 in *Snoid Comics* and *Co-Evolutionary Quarterly*. It was rearranged and colored by Peter Poplaski in 1981 and published as a poster by Kitchen Sink Press, of Princeton, WI (1970–1992), and Northampton, MA (1993–1999).

152. Zippy archives, http://zippythepinhead.com; accessed October 25, 2013.

153. *Miracle on 34th Street*, directed by George Seaton (20th Century Fox, 1947); *Who Framed Roger Rabbit*, directed by Robert Zemeckis (Buena Vista Pictures, 1988); *Pleasantville*, directed by Gary Ross (New Line Cinema: 1998); *The Truman Show*, directed by Peter Weir (Paramount Pictures: 1998); and *True Stories*, directed by David Byrne (Warner Brothers: 1986).

154. *The Brady Bunch* was an American sitcom of 117 episodes, created and produced by Sherwood Schwartz, which originally aired on ABC from September 26, 1969 to March 8, 1974.

155. Jackson, "Notes and Comments," *Landscape: The Tenth Anniversary Issue*, Vol. 10, No. 1 (Fall 1960): 1–2, quoted 1.

156. Ibid.

157. Jackson, *Discovering the Vernacular Landscape*, ix–x.

158. Jackson, "Notes and Comments," in *Landscape: The Tenth Anniversary Issue*, Vol. 10, No. 1 (Fall 1960): 1–2, quoted 2.

Appendix C

1. Chris Wilson and Paul Groth, eds., *Everyday America: Cultural Landscape Studies after J. B. Jackson* (Berkeley: Univeristy of California Press, 2003).

2. "In Search of the Proto-Landscape" was among the last essays that J. B. Jackson published. It appeared in George F. Thompson, ed., *Landscape in America* (Austin: University of Texas Press, 1995), 43–50, which was designated a Notable Book of 1995 by *Harper's* Magazine. Of note, J. B. Jackson was an original board member of the Center for American Places, which was founded by Thompson, with Charles E. Little on September 5, 1990, and later renamed the Center for the Study of Place on February 17, 2007.

Acknowledgments

The inclusion of three color portfolios and the overall quality of this publication would have been impossible without three generous grants. Our gratitude for these gifts goes to the Hubbard Foundation, administered by Sasaki Associates; the Foundation for Landscape Studies and its director, Elizabeth Barlow Rogers; and the Albuquerque Community Foundation. Ray A. Graham III, President of the Elizabeth Firestone Graham Foundation, was also extremely supportive of the project during its many years of development.

Miguel Gandert served as our thinking partner and the videographer for the development of the new interviews for the DVD, *J. B. Jackson and the American Landscape*. The University of New Mexico and UNM's Department of Communications and Journalism, where Gandert is a Distinguished Professor, donated the use of video equipment. The George Pearl Historic Preservation and Regionalism Endowment in UNM's School of Architecture and Planning added a grant to help cover video production expenses. Thanks to Gandert, Arnold R. Alanen, Frank Gohlke, Lucy R. Lippard, and Virginia Scharff, for sharing their insights in those interviews.

Our chief collaborator on the conception and development of the book and DVD has been George F. Thompson. We will never forget his long-term encouragement and development of this project or the inestimable contributions he has made to landscape studies as a writer, editor, and publisher through his Center for American Places (renamed the Center for the Study of Place in 2007) and now through George F. Thompson Publishing. David Skolkin, the book's designer and art director, and Mikki Soroczak, George's editorial and research assistant, likewise made significant contributions to the book.

The editors—as well as scholars of the legacy of J. B. Jackson—owe a debt of thanks to a variety of people who have worked to conserve that legacy. Michael Kelly, Director of UNM's Center for Southwest Research, and Audra Bellmore, architectural archivist, have worked over many years not only to process the Jackson collections, but also to add new materials and to secure resources to digitalize his teaching slides and make them available on line. Kelly, Bellmore, and Mark Childs, Associate Dean of the School of Architecture and Planning, facilitated copyright permission from the Jackson estate, in particular covering his teaching slides. Paul Groth and Helen Lefkowitz Horowitz have each not only donated primary materials to the Jackson collections at UNM, but also worked more broadly since Jackson's death to interpret and safeguard his legacy. Thanks to F. Douglas Adams, for conserving the largest collection of Jackson drawings, for permission to reproduce a large selection here, and for his help securing a publication subvention grant. Peter Goin and Paul F. Starrs, through their nonprofit Black Rock Institute, likewise, are working to safeguard the legacy of *Landscape* magazine and have allowed the reproduction of a sampling of front covers, a contents page, and Jackson drawings from the magazine. Timothy Davis has made a distinctive contribution as a leading historiographer of landscape studies.

From Janet Mendelsohn: I owe a particular debt of thanks to Susan Fanshel, for her assistance in the preparation of the companion DVD. Bob Calo not only provided permission to include his video about Jackson on the DVD, but also shared rare stories and insights in our joint interview (Chapter 6). My husband, Marc Levitt, and our daughter, Mirra Levitt, supported me with encouragement and good advice throughout, and for that I will always be grateful.

From Chris Wilson: Kingsley Hammett and Jerilou Hammett, editor and publisher, respectively, of *Designer/builder*, the Santa Fe-based magazine, encouraged me to write and publish the elegy that now appears, in revised form, as Chapter 1. Jackson served as an early mentor to them, and their magazine carried on the legacy of *Landscape*, although with a more overtly political perspective. Thanks, also, to Eric Bernard, Director of UNM's Landscape Architecture Program, for his support of the preparation of the final manuscript; to Patricia Walter, for administrative support; and to Emily Hunt, for research assistance. My love and final thanks go to my wife, Virginia Scharff, environmental historian and cultural landscape fellow traveler, for her unstinting support, encouragement, and insights.

Index

About the Editors

Janet Mendelsohn taught film and still photography at Harvard University before becoming a documentary filmmaker, with a focus on the environment. Her projects include films for the Conservation Foundation on changes in land and water use, documentaries for the PBS science series *NOVA,* as well as independent films about the arts, including *Figure in a Landscape: Conversations with J. B. Jackson*, with Claire Marino (1988), and *J. B. Jackson and the American Landscape* (2015). She lives in Watertown, Massachusetts.

Chris Wilson is the J. B. Jackson Chair of Cultural Landscape Studies at the University of New Mexico, where he developed its Historic Preservation and Regionalism Program. He is the author of many books, including *La Tierra Amarilla: Its History, Architecture and Cultural Landscape* (Museum of New Mexico Press, 1991), with David Kammer, which won the Antoinette Forrester Downing Award from the Society of Architectural Historians; *The Myth of Santa Fe: Creating a Modern Regional Tradition* (University of New Mexico Press, 1997), which received the Abbott Lowell Cummings Award from the Vernacular Architecture Forum; and *Facing Southwest: The Life and Houses of John Gaw Meem* (W. W. Norton, 2001), which sings the virtues of a leading 1930s modern regionalist. He and Paul Groth edited the field survey, *Everyday America: Cultural Landscape Studies after J. B. Jackson* (University of California Press, 2003), and Wilson was the lead author and editor for the landmark study, *The Plazas of New Mexico* Trinity University Press, 2011).

About the Contributors

F. Douglas Adams, AIA, has been the president of ETALstudio, Inc., for more than forty years. ETALstudio, Inc. has won national and regional design awards, and his award-winning designs for schools, commercial buildings, and residences have appeared in publications throughout the United States, Japan, and Italy. Many of his firms' educational and commercial projects combine new additions with historic buildings, configured in a modern design aesthetics to include essential features of energy conservation, lighting, and accessibility. He was as a teaching assistant for John B. Jackson at Harvard University, taught for fourteen years at the Rhode Island School of Design, and has been a visiting critic, instructor, or lecturer at the University of Texas, Austin, University of New Mexico, New Jersey Institute of Technology, Harvard, and Boston Architectural College. He also received a National Endowment for the Humanities Fellowship at Brown University, where he researched the industrial and theater designer Norman Bel Geddes. Adams has also served on many civic boards in the Town of Lincoln, Massachusetts, including service as Head of the Planning Board, on the Historic District Commission, and as a trustee of the Middlesex School.

Bob Calo is a television producer and director based in Oakland, California. He began his career at KQED in San Francisco, where he produced daily news and documentaries. Currently, he is a senior lecturer in the Graduate School of Journalism at the University of California, Berkeley. After making *J. B. Jackson and the Love of Everyday Places* (San Francisco, CA: KQED, 1988), he worked for more than a decade as a news producer in New York City at both ABC News and NBC News, where he actively sought to weave cultural geography into his reporting. His freelance projects include "Sound Tracks" (2012), a PBS documentary series about music and culture for which he was the senior producer. As a fellow at the Shorenstein Center for the Press, Politics, and Public Policy at Harvard University's Kennedy School of Government, he wrote "Disengaged: Elite Media in a Vernacular Nation" (2011). In addition to teaching, he continues to work on video and television projects.

Timothy Davis received his bachelor's degree in Visual and Environmental Studies from Harvard College and a Ph.D. in American studies from the University of Texas, Austin. He has been a historian for the U.S. National Park Service since 1977. His writings have appeared in numerous professional journals, including *Landscape Journal, Perspectives in Vernacular Architecture,* and *Studies in the History of Gardens & Designed Landscapes,* as well as in *Everyday America: Cultural Landscape Studies after J. B. Jackson* (University of California Press, 2003). He served as the principal editor of *America's National Park Roads and Parkways: Drawings from the Historic American Engineering Record* (The Johns Hopkins University Press, in association with the Center for American Places, 2004), and he is the author of *National Park Roads: A Legacy in the American Landscape* (University of Virginia Press in 2016). He has also taught courses on landscape history, theory, and preservation at the University of Texas, Austin, and in the Decorative Arts, Design History, and Material Culture program at the Bard Graduate Center in New York City.

Miguel Gandert, an award-winning documentary and fine-art photographer and the videographer for the new interviews in the companion DVD, is a native of Española, New Mexico. He is the Distinguished Professor of Communication and Journalism and Director of the Interdisciplinary Film and Digital Media program at the University of New Mexico in Albuquerque. Gandert's photographs have been exhibited in galleries and museums throughout the world and are in numerous public collections. His photographic series, *Nuevo México Profundo: Rituals of an Indo-Hispano Homeland* (Museum of New Mexico Press, 2000), was the subject of a book and one-person exhibition for the National Hispanic Culture Center of New Mexico. He is also the co-author, with Enrique R. Lamadrid, of *Hermanitaos Comanchitos: Indo-Hispano Rituals of Captivity and Redemption* (University of New Mexico Press, 2003) and the photographer for Chris Wilson and Stefanes Polyzoides, eds., *The Plazas of New Mexico* (Trinity University Press, 2011).

Peter Goin is a Foundation Professor of Art in photography and time-based media at the University of Nevada, Reno. He is the author of books exploring paradigms of the American landscape, including *Tracing the Line: A Photographic Survey of the Mexican-American Border* (Artist Limited Edition, 1987); *Nuclear Landscapes* (The Johns Hopkins University Press, in association with the Center for American Places, 1991); *Stopping Time: A Rephotographic Survey of Lake Tahoe* (University of New Mexico Press, 1992); and *Humanature* (University of Texas Press, in association with the Center for American Places, 1996). Co-authored book projects include *Changing Mines in America* (Santa Fe, NM: Center for American Places, 2004) and, with Paul F. Starrs, *Black Rock* (Reno: University of Nevada Press, 2005) and *A Field Guide to*

California Agriculture (University of California Press, 2010), which won the John Brinckerhoff Jackson Book Prize of the Association of American Geographers. Goin's photographs have been exhibited in more than fifty museums nationally and internationally, and he is the recipient of two National Endowment for the Arts Fellowships. In 1999, he was awarded Nevada Governor's Millennium Award for Excellence in the Arts.

Paul Groth is Professor Emeritus of U.S. Cultural Landscape History at the University of California, Berkeley, where he taught in the departments of geography, architecture, and American studies. As a geography graduate student at Berkeley, Groth studied with J. B. Jackson and, upon Jackson's retirement from teaching in 1978, took over teaching Jackson's two survey courses in the history of American cultural landscapes. Groth is the author of *Living Downtown: The History of Residential Hotels in the United States* (University of California Press, 1994), which won the John Brinckerhoff Jackson Book Prize from the Association of American Geographers. Groth is also the co-editor of two collections of new essays: *Understanding Ordinary Landscapes*, with Todd Bressi (Yale University Press, 1997) and *Everyday America: Cultural Landscape Studies after J. B. Jackson*, with Chris Wilson (University of California Press, 2003). In numerous other publications he has explored interpretations of urban street grids, parking lots, vernacular parks, ordinary storefronts, and workers' cottage districts.

Helen Lefkowitz Horowitz is the Sydenham Clark Parsons Professor of History and American Studies, Emerita, at Smith College. She served as editor of *Landscape in Sight: J. B. Jackson's America* (Yale University Press, 1997) and was Jackson's choice as his literary executor. Her book, *Rereading Sex: Battles over Sexual Knowledge and Suppression in Nineteenth-Century America* (Alfred A. Knopf, 2002), was one of three finalists for the Pulitzer Prize in History. In addition, she is the author of *Culture and the City: Cultural Philanthropy in Chicago from the 1880s to 1917* (University Press of Kentucky, 1976), *Alma Mater: Design and Experience in the Women's Colleges from their Nineteenth-Century Beginnings to the 1930s* (Alfred A. Knopf, 1984; University of Massachusetts Press, 1993), *Campus Life: Undergraduate Cultures from the End of the Eighteenth Century to the Present* (Alfred A. Knopf, 1987; University of Chicago Press, 1987), *The Power and Passion of M. Carey Thomas* (Alfred A. Knopf, 1994; University of Illinois Press, 1999)*, and *Wild Unrest: Charlotte Perkins Gilman and the Making of "The Yellow Wall-Paper"* (Oxford University Press, 2011); and *A Taste for Provence* (University of Chicago Press, 2016).

Paul F. Starrs is Regents & Foundation Professor of Geography at the University of Nevada, Reno, where he writes and teaches about cultural and historical geography of the American

West and Mediterranean Europe. Author of *Let the Cowboy Ride: Cattle Ranching in the American West*, an early title in the "Creating North American Landscape" series created by George F. Thompson (The Johns Hopkins University Press, in association with the Center for American Places, 1997), he recently coordinated the editing (and authored three chapters of) *Mediterranean Oak Woodland Working Landscapes: Dehesas of Spain and Ranchlands of California* (Berlin, Germany: Springer-Verlag, 2013), with fifty-four contributors from seven countries. He is the co-author, with Peter Goin, of several award-winning books, including *Black Rock* (University of Nevada Press, 2005), and *A Field Guide to California Agriculture* (University of California Press, 2010), which received the John Brinckerhoff Jackson Book Prize from the Association of American Geographers.

About the Book

Drawn to Landscape: The Pioneering Work of J. B. Jackson was brought to publication in a limited hardbound edition of 450 copies that includes Janet Mendelsohn's DVD, *J. B. Jackson and the American Landscape*, and a softcover edition of 1,000 copies. The text was set in Times New Roman; the paper is Kinmari Matte, 157 gsm weight; and the book was professionally printed and bound by P. Chan & Edward, Inc., in China.

Project Director and Publisher: George F. Thompson
Sequencing: Chris Wilson and George F. Thompson
Editorial and Research Assistant: Mikki Soroczak
Manuscript Editor and Proofreader: Purna Makaram
Book Design and Production: David Skolkin

Special Acknowledgments: The publisher extends heartfelt thanks to Stephen Westheimer, of Santa Fe, New Mexico, for introducing Janet Mendelsohn and George F. Thompson, the publisher, many years ago, which got the project started; to Virginia Scharff, Associate Provost for Faculty Development at the University of New Mexico in Albuquerque, who came up with the book's title; to the many unsung heroes and contributors to the book and DVD; to Mark Saunders, Director of the University of Virginia Press, for believing in this book and for serving as its distributor; and to geographer Eugene Cotton Mather (1919–1999), a great friend of Brinck Jackson and a mentor to thousands of students who learned to read the landscape and pioneer their own paths in geography and landscape studies. To talk and share drinks with Cotton and Brinck at Brinck's home in La Cienega provided memories that will last a lifetime.

George F. Thompson Publishing, L.L.C.
217 Oak Ridge Circle
Staunton, VA 24401-3511, U.S.A
www.gftbooks.com

23 22 21 20 19 18 17 16 15   1 2 3 4 5

The Library of Congress Preassigned Control Number for both the limited hardcover edition and
the softcover edition is 2015939372.

ISBN: 978–1–938086–35–9 (Limited hardcover edition)
ISBN: 978–1–938086–36–6 (Softcover edition)